THE COMPLETE
FRESHWATER FISHERMAN

Up-to-Date Proven Techniques for Catching the Most Popular Gamefish in North American Waters

EDITED BY
DICK STERNBERG

DICK STERNBERG blends his years of angling experience and scientific training into a text loaded with important facts about fish and helpful tips for the modern angler. A professional fisheries biologist for 16 years, Dick has fished from the mountain streams of Alaska to the Everglades of Florida. His articles have appeared in numerous regional and national outdoor magazines.

Published in 1993 by

North American Outdoor Group, Inc.
12301 Whitewater Drive
Minnetonka, Minnesota 55343

Published by arrangement with Cy DeCosse Incorporated

Library of Congress Catalog Card Number: 87-14544

ISBN 0-88365-799-6

Printed in the United States of America.

CREDITS:
Editorial Director: Dick Sternberg
Design and Production: Cy DeCosse Creative Department, Inc.

Photos on pages 26 and 27 are reprinted courtesy of Berkley and Company, Inc.

Contents

Introduction

The burgeoning popularity of freshwater fishing has demanded an increased level of sophistication among today's anglers. Fishing pressure has reduced gamefish populations in many waters, and has made the remaining fish warier and more difficult to catch. And this trend is certain to continue in years to come.

For consistent success, today's fishermen must know enough about different types of waters to select the ones where fish are most likely to be biting. They must have enough knowledge to choose the proper equipment for the job, including rods, reels, line, terminal tackle, boats, motors and electronics. And they must understand enough about gamefish behavior to plot their fishing strategy and vary it to suit different types of water, different times of year and different weather conditions.

The Compleat Freshwater Fisherman is a complete reference volume that provides state-of-the-art information on how to catch every major kind of freshwater gamefish. The text combines the knowledge of hundreds of America's top fishermen and biologists, and is supplemented by extensive research — more extensive than ever done for any fishing publication. And to make this detailed information easier to understand and digest, the book contains nearly 800 color photographs.

Section One, "The Fishes' World," discusses every type of fresh water where gamefish are likely to be found, from shallow farm ponds to deep, canyon reservoirs and from tiny brooks to mile-wide rivers.

You'll learn the different types of habitat found in each of these waters, and how to link different habitat types with different species of gamefish.

Section Two, "Equipment," not only gives you the information you need to select major equipment items, like boats and motors, but also provides detailed recommendations for important but often overlooked items like hooks, sinkers, bobbers, leaders and connectors. You'll get a complete course on fish finders, as well as detailed information on adjusting them and interpreting their signals.

Section Three, "How to Catch Freshwater Gamefish," outlines strategies for catching every important species. You'll learn what they eat, where they're found and how they behave under different environmental conditions. Then we'll show you the most productive live-bait and artificial-lure techniques, each described with step-by-step photos.

Section Four, "Cleaning Techniques," shows you what to do with your fish after you've caught them. Besides all the basic cleaning techniques, like filleting and steaking, we've included many tips to improve the eating quality of your catch.

After a few minutes reading this book, you'll see that it's very different from other fishing books you've read. It contains no stories or tall tales, only distilled fishing information. And the information is not "trendy," but solid and basic. *The Compleat Freshwater Fisherman* will be your most valuable angling tool for years to come.

The Fishes' World

Natural Lakes

Every lake is unique, the end-product of a host of factors that combine to shape its character, including its fish population. Among these factors are geographic location, size and shape of the basin, and water fertility. Scientists separate lakes into three broad categories based on water fertility.

INFERTILE LAKES. The lands surrounding infertile or *oligotrophic* lakes release few nutrients into the water. Most oligotrophic lakes are located on the Canadian Shield, a vast, rock-bound area that covers eastern Canada and dips into the northern states from Minnesota to Maine. Some oligotrophic lakes occur at high elevations where the climate is cold. Coldwater species, such as trout, predominate. Because their fish are slow to grow and mature, these lakes can withstand little fishing pressure.

MODERATELY FERTILE LAKES. Classified as *mesotrophic*, lakes of intermediate fertility are located primarily in the northern United States and southern Canada. However, they can be found almost anywhere on the continent. Coolwater spe-

MOUNTAIN lakes, because of their altitude and rock-lined basins, are usually cold and produce few fish. This oligotrophic lake is home for cutthroat trout.

CANADIAN SHIELD lakes often have deep, rocky basins. Water in their depths is cold, though the shallows may be warm. Lake trout dominate in this oligotrophic lake.

SHALLOW, SHIELD lakes have warmer water, more vegetation and larger fish populations than deep Shield lakes. This mesotrophic lake contains walleyes and smallmouths.

cies dominate, though most support warmwater fish and a few have coldwater species.

FERTILE LAKES. *Eutrophic* or fertile lakes are surrounded by nutrient-rich soils which add large amounts of nitrogen, phosphorus and other fertilizing elements. They are typically found in agricultural areas in the southern two-thirds of the United States, although there are many in the North. Eutrophic lakes are best suited for warmwater fish.

Every lake is oligotrophic when first formed. As time passes, aquatic plants and animals die and their remains fall to the bottom to form a layer of organic ooze. As this layer thickens, the lake becomes shallower and is more easily warmed by the sun. Plant growth increases and the water becomes more fertile. At this stage, the lake is mesotrophic. Eventually, more ooze builds up on the bottom. The lake becomes shallower and warmer, so it reaches the eutrophic state. Finally, the water becomes too shallow for fish. This process, which may take thousands of years, is called *aging*. Below are six lakes which, from left to right, range from infertile to very fertile.

SHALLOW, SANDY lakes usually have warm water, moderate weed growth and a varied and abundant fish population. Walleyes, bass and panfish live in this mesotrophic lake.

CATTAIL-FRINGED lakes have muddy bottoms and heavy algae blooms. The depths usually lack oxygen. This eutrophic lake has largemouths, northern pike and bullheads.

MARSH lakes have plants growing throughout. In the North, they have few gamefish, but in the South, fish are plentiful. This eutrophic lake is noted for trophy largemouth bass.

Ponds

Natural and man-made ponds support about one-fourth of all freshwater fishing. Farm ponds alone total about 2½ million in the United States. They are created mainly to provide water for livestock or to control erosion. But hundreds of thousands have also been stocked with gamefish, providing new angling opportunities where fishable waters were once in short supply.

Ponds are popular with fishermen because they can usually be managed to yield more fish per acre of water than natural lakes. About 20 species of fish are stocked or occur incidentally in ponds. They vary from native brook trout that settle in a newly-formed beaver pond to channel catfish stocked and raised in a man-made pond.

The same factors that determine which types of fish inhabit a lake also decide which species can live in a pond. Most important are size, depth and location of the pond. However, water source has a greater impact on ponds than it does on lakes. For example, a spring flowing into a large lake has little effect on the lake's temperature. But a similar spring feeding a pond would chill the water enough to support trout. Unless springs are present or the basin is deep enough to stay cold in summer, a pond can support only warmwater or a few coolwater species.

FARM PONDS are usually man-made, formed by damming small streams or bulldozing shallow basins that fill with runoff. To support fish, ponds in the North should be at least 15 feet deep over half of the water area. Those in the South can be shallower. Largemouth bass and bluegills are the most popular farm pond species, although catfish are rapidly gaining popularity in the South. Some small, stagnant ponds harbor only bullheads.

BOG PONDS are typical of forested regions in the North. They are surrounded by spruce, cedar or tamarack trees. Sphagnum moss and other plants eventually form a spongy mat that covers much of the surface. Their waters are usually stained dark by acids from decaying vegetation. Northern pike, yellow perch and bullheads are typical species. In the aging process of lakes, bogs are the last stage that supports fish life.

MINE PITS or quarries often fill with ground water and runoff after mining operations cease. Ponds that are deep, infertile and cold are well-suited for trout. Some strip-mine pits have excellent largemouth fishing.

BEAVER PONDS can support such species as northern pike, largemouth bass, sunfish and crappies. Ponds linked to coldwater streams often hold trout. However, trout will move out if the pond gets too warm.

Reservoirs

Reservoirs are man-made lakes that form behind dams on rivers. They have characteristics of both lakes and streams. Like lakes, deeper reservoirs develop temperature layers and lose oxygen in their depths. Like rivers, some have current and hold typical river species such as catfish and white bass.

CANYON RESERVOIRS. Sometimes 500 feet or deeper, these steep-sided reservoirs have clear, infertile waters. Many have long, deep arms that are flooded valleys of feeder streams.

COVE RESERVOIRS. Most cove reservoirs are 50 to 200 feet deep. The arms are shorter and narrower than those of canyon reservoirs. Many arms are shallow and sprinkled with flooded timber. These reservoirs are moderately fertile and fairly clear, with a wide variety of fish habitat.

MARSHLAND RESERVOIRS. Called flowages in northern states, marshland reservoirs have extensive areas of flooded timber. Most are less than 50 feet deep and have large expanses of water 20 feet deep or less. Those in the South have fertile waters, ranging from fairly clear to turbid. Northern flowages usually have moderately fertile water.

CANYON RESERVOIRS support fewer fish than other man-made lakes because their fast-sloping bottoms produce little food. Most have bass and other warmwater fish, though some are better suited for trout.

STEEP ROCK WALLS are typical of canyon reservoirs. In dry years, water drawn off for irrigation may lower the water level 150 feet. As the water drops, fish change location, making angling difficult.

NASA INFRARED PHOTOGRAPH

COVE RESERVOIRS have a variety of habitat and may support largemouth and smallmouth bass, crappies, walleyes, catfish, white bass and striped bass. Some deep cove reservoirs have trout.

NARROW ARMS often provide the best fishing in cove reservoirs. Flooded timber and brush in the upper ends of arms support bass and panfish. Lower, deeper portions of the arms may produce catfish and walleyes.

NASA INFRARED PHOTOGRAPH

MARSHLAND RESERVOIRS in the South are havens for largemouth bass, including many over 10 pounds. Northern flowages usually have walleyes, muskies, northern pike and some bass and panfish.

FLOODED TIMBER is common in many marshland reservoirs. Although they seldom have well-defined arms or coves, they may have shallow bays with thick vegetation and flooded brush.

Rivers & Streams

Beyond every bend in a stream lies a new fishing challenge, for no pool, riffle or rapids is just like the previous one. One moment the stream flows slowly over nearly level ground and the next, becomes a churning rapids as it plummets over steep terrain.

The slope or *gradient* of the streambed is one of many factors that determine which fish species live in a particular river or stream. Others include water chemistry, clarity, bottom type and depth. The overriding factor, however, is water temperature.

Spring-fed creeks, mountain streams and Arctic rivers never exceed 70°F. These coldwater streams usually host trout, steelhead, salmon, grayling or whitefish. Warmwater streams exceed 70°F for at least part of the year. They contain such species as largemouth and smallmouth bass, white bass, walleyes, catfish and carp.

To improve their fishing success, anglers should become more familiar with the various types of rivers and streams. Especially helpful is knowing how to *read* moving water and to recognize the haunts of river fish.

Below are four rivers and streams typical of flowing waters in North America.

SMALL TROUT STREAMS occur throughout much of the continent. Usually spring-fed, their waters are divided into recognizable pools, riffles and runs (page 18). This stream supports native brook trout.

LARGE TROUT STREAMS are common to mountainous areas of the West. Their current is fast and pools, riffles and runs are less distinct than in smaller streams. Rainbows, browns and cutthroats thrive in this stream.

SMALL WARMWATER STREAMS are most numerous in eastern and midwestern states and in southern Canada. Most have well-defined pools, riffles and runs. Smallmouth bass predominate in this stream.

LARGE WARMWATER RIVERS lace the eastern two-thirds of the United States. Many are dammed, so their waters appear as a series of long pools. Walleyes, largemouth bass, panfish and catfish live in this river.

Big Rivers

Large, warmwater rivers offer a wider choice of fishing opportunities than any other freshwater environment. A fisherman can catch a limit of scrappy white bass in the morning, battle a trophy northern pike at midday, cast for walleyes at dusk and that same evening, still-fish for flathead catfish.

Big rivers can support so many species of fish because their habitat is so diverse. Six or more distinct habitat types (below) may occur on rivers that have been dammed. A few fish species spend their lives in just one or two areas, though most move freely throughout the river system, especially when water levels change.

MAIN CHANNEL. Swift current and a bottom of fine sand or silt are typical main channel features. There is little vegetation or other cover for fish.

CHANNEL BORDERS. The channel border separates the main channel from shore. It may have man-made current deflectors or *wingdams* of rocks and sticks that force the current toward midstream to keep sediment from settling in the channel.

SIDE CHANNELS. Often called *cuts*, side channels connect the main channel with backwater lakes and sloughs. Their sand or silt bottoms are often choked with timber. The current is slow to moderate.

BACKWATER SLOUGHS. At normal water levels, backwater sloughs have no current. They have muck bottoms, dense growth of vegetation and very shallow water.

BACKWATER LAKES. Deeper than sloughs, backwater lakes have weeds only along their shorelines. Like sloughs, they have muck bottoms and little or no current.

TAILWATERS. Also called *tailraces*, tailwaters are stretches of turbulent water just below dams. They have rock, gravel or sand bottoms. Numerous *eddies*, places where current flows opposite of the main stream, are found along the channel margin.

MAIN CHANNEL waters seldom support large numbers of gamefish. Their current is too swift for most fish and they lack food and cover.

CHANNEL BORDERS often attract walleyes, white bass, smallmouths and catfish. Wingdams, downed trees and riprap shores draw the most fish.

SIDE CHANNELS are ideal for catfish. The current is slow and downed trees provide cover. Crappies and bluegills also hide among the limbs.

BACKWATER SLOUGHS hold northern pike, largemouth bass, bluegills and crappies. During high water, sloughs attract most river fish.

BACKWATER LAKES appeal to many species but are best for crappies and northern pike. Like sloughs, they draw fish when water is high.

TAILWATERS collect large numbers of fish in spring when dams block spawning migrations of walleyes, saugers and white bass.

BIG RIVERS feature a vast array of fish habitat. This high-altitude, infrared photograph shows (1) tailwaters below a lock and dam, (2) main channel, (3) main channel border, (4) side channel, (5) a maze of backwater sloughs and (6) a chain of backwater lakes. Other features of interest include (7) a large tributary stream and (8) heated discharge water from a power plant, both potential fishing spots.

Small Rivers and Streams

Over one million miles of small rivers and streams crisscross the North American continent. Because many streams are lightly fished, they have excellent gamefish populations and offer anglers a chance to escape the crowd.

Most streams and small rivers have three distinct habitat types.

RIFFLES. Moderate to fast current and a turbulent surface are typical features of riffles. They have bottoms of gravel, rocks or boulders and are less than 2 feet deep. Extremely fast, whitewater riffles are called *rapids*.

RUNS. Runs are similar to riffles, but are deeper and less turbulent.

POOLS. Slow current and a surface that appears smooth on a calm day identify pools. They have bottoms of silt, sand or small gravel. Shallow pools are often called *flats*.

In slow-moving streams, pools are generally wide, while runs are narrow. In fast-flowing streams, riffles, runs and pools may be difficult to identify because they are nearly the same width. Nevertheless, fish recognize the different habitat types and so can the angler with a well-trained eye.

Species such as largemouth bass, crappies, catfish and walleyes spend most of their time in deep pools. Smallmouth bass and trout also inhabit pools but may be found in runs if the current is not too swift. Riffles are usually too shallow to provide enough cover for large fish, although they are important morning and evening feeding areas for many river species. Small gamefish and minnows stay in riffles throughout the day.

The photograph at right shows the typical riffle, run and pool sequence in a small stream. Numbers on the photo correspond to numbers on the diagram below which profiles the same section of stream.

RIFFLES, RUNS AND POOLS are formed by the awesome excavating force of moving water. Fast water in a riffle (1) digs a deeper channel or run (2). As the run deepens, the current slows, forming a pool (3). The slower current causes sediment to settle at the pool's tail or downstream end. As sediment builds up, the water

becomes shallower, channeling streamflow into a smaller area. Once again, the current speeds up, forming a new riffle. In most streams, this pattern is repeated about once for every seven stream widths. In other words, a new riffle, run and pool sequence would be repeated about every 140 feet in a stream 20 feet wide.

Equipment

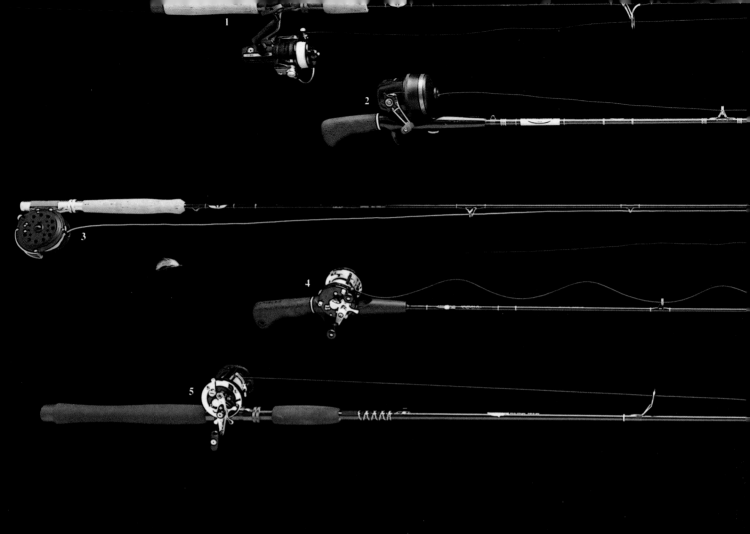

RODS AND REELS include: (1) Spinning rod with open-face reel, (2) spin-cast rod with closed-face reel, (3) fly rod with

Rods & Reels

Many fishermen use only one rod and reel for a variety of angling purposes. Certainly, a 6- to 6½-foot, medium-action spinning outfit is acceptable when bobber-fishing for crappies, casting spoons for

northern pike or trolling for walleyes. Some situations, however, demand a specific rod and reel combination. For example, casting a tiny, weightless fly requires fly-fishing tackle. Or, casting a foot-long muskie plug is possible only with a stout rod and heavy-duty reel.

Anglers who regularly switch from one type of fishing to another carry as many as four rods, each rigged and ready for different kinds of fish. Not every fisherman needs that much tackle, but at least one backup rig is a good idea.

Following are five basic rod and reel combinations:

SPINNING. Spinning tackle is popular because it is versatile, backlash-free, and designed for extra casting distance. The open-face reel allows line to whip off a fixed spool. The rod has large guides, so

single-action fly reel, (4) bait-casting rod with free-spool casting reel, (5) trolling rod with star-drag reel.

coils of line can flow through with little friction. One drawback to the open-face reel is that beginning anglers may have trouble with line snarling behind the spool.

SPIN-CASTING. Spin-casting equipment offers many of the same advantages of spinning tackle. The closed-face design of the reel reduces tangling and its push button line release makes casting easier. However, the reel's closed face increases line friction, which reduces casting distance. Spin-casting reels clamp to the top of the rod handle, while spinning reels attach underneath the rod.

FLY-CASTING. Fly reels are not as important as other types of reels. Their primary function is to store line. Fly rods are usually quite long. The shorter rods are 7½ feet, while many exceed 9 feet in length. Most fly rods are designed to flex from tip to butt. This whipping action helps the angler pick up and cast long lengths of line.

BAIT-CASTING. Bait-casting tackle excels for casting accuracy. Modern reel design has all but eliminated backlashes, once a constant headache for many fishermen. Bait-casting rods, especially those used to cast heavy lures or crankbaits, are stiffer than spinning rods.

TROLLING. Rods and reels used for big-water trolling are similar to bait-casting outfits, but are much heavier. Trolling reels are rugged, store a lot of line and have smooth drags. Because they are not designed for casting, they are less expensive than fine-tuned bait-casting reels. Trolling reels do not have the line-twist problems of spinning reels.

Choosing the Right Rod for the Job

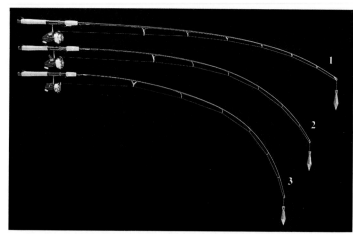

ACTION is demonstrated by lifting equal weights with different rods. A fast-action rod (1) bends near the tip. A medium-action rod (2) starts to bend near the middle. A slow-action rod (3) bends over its entire length.

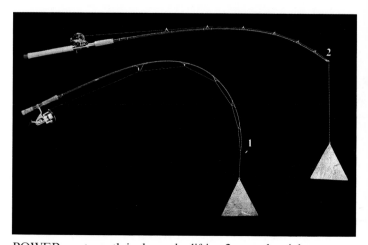

POWER or strength is shown by lifting 2-pound weights with (1) an ultralight spinning rod and (2) a heavy-duty casting rod. The spinning rod doubles over from the weight, while the casting rod flexes much less.

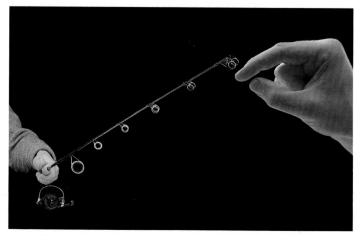

SENSITIVITY can be tested by gently tapping the rod tip with a finger. With a sensitive rod, the vibrations are easily felt at the handle. A sensitive rod makes it easier to feel bottom and to detect bites.

Fishermen must choose from a wide array of rods, many designed for specific purposes. Before making a selection, it is important for anglers to understand basic rod qualities.

Action refers to where a rod bends. It is determined by the degree of taper in the rod shaft. *Power* or strength is the amount of force needed to bend the rod. It is determined by the thickness of the shaft walls. Many fishermen, and even some rod manufacturers, confuse the terms action and power. When buying a rod, remember that when a salesman talks about light-, medium- or heavy-action rods, he is referring to power instead of action.

Sensitivity is the ability of the rod to telegraph vibrations from the line through the tip and on to the hand. It is determined by the material and by the rod's action. A fast-action rod is generally more sensitive than a slow-action rod of the same material.

Rod materials differ in many ways. Fiberglass is durable, economical and well-suited to most angling situations. Graphite is stronger and more sensitive, but is more expensive than fiberglass. Boron is slightly stronger and more sensitive than graphite, but is even more expensive. Bamboo requires more care and lacks the power of space-age materials. It is mainly used for custom-made fly rods.

Length, by itself, should not be a major consideration when choosing a rod. However, length is important in certain situations. A short rod works best for casting in tight quarters, while a long rod is essential for long-distance casting. The current trend is toward shorter, thinner rods that are equally as powerful as the longer, thicker rods of years past.

FAST-ACTION rods are good for working a surface popper, jigging, setting the hook or other uses which require a responsive tip.

SLOW-ACTION rods are often used with downriggers. As a fish strikes and the line releases, the rod pops out of its deep bend, taking up slack line.

FIGHTING FISH is easier with a slow rod. The added flex acts like a shock absorber, keeping the line tight while the fish thrashes.

ULTRALIGHT rods bend with only a light weight, making it possible to cast tiny lures. They make small fish feel big to the angler.

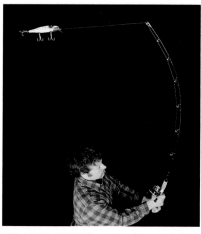

HEAVY-DUTY rods are needed to cast big lures such as muskie plugs. They also have the power to drive the hooks into a muskie's bony jaw.

OBSTACLES such as timber and thick weedbeds make it necessary to use a rod with enough power to stop a fish's run and keep it away from snags.

MATERIALS shown have equal power. Boron (right) is thinnest and most sensitive, followed by graphite (center) and fiberglass (left).

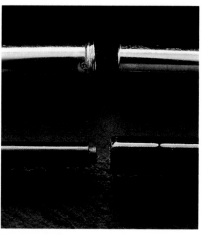

FERRULES, especially metal ones (top), reduce sensitivity. Fiberglass or graphite ferrules are better; one-piece rods are best of all.

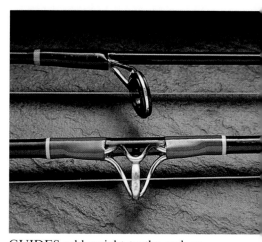

GUIDES add weight to the rod, reducing sensitivity. Single-foot guides (top) are light and retain sensitivity better than conventional guides.

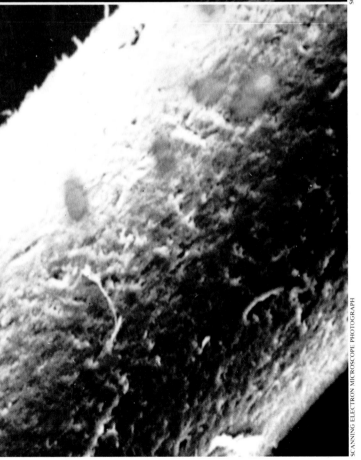

USED LINE (bottom) shows signs of wear compared to new 10-pound, nylon monofilament. Abrasion, chemicals in the air and many other factors deteriorate line. These lines are enlarged 400 times actual size.

Lines

The age of synthetics has given fishermen a wider selection of lines than ever before. Today, there is a line for virtually every angling situation.

MONOFILAMENT LINES. Used by spinning, spin-casting and many bait-casting fishermen, mono line is easy to cast, inexpensive, nearly invisible in water and very strong for its diameter. Monofilament differs greatly in quality. Premium mono is durable and its diameter is consistent. Cheap mono weakens quickly with use and often has thin spots.

Many types of monofilament line are available. Highly-visible or even fluorescent mono is favored by many plastic worm and jig fishermen who need to see the subtle line twitch that indicates a strike. Abrasion-resistant mono is preferred by those who fish in rocky lakes or streams. Thin, flexible monofilament is used by live-bait fishermen who want to present the bait naturally.

BRAIDED LINES. Whether nylon or dacron, braided lines stretch very little, so they are good for sinking a hook into hard-mouthed fish such as northern pike. Braided lines are normally used on bait-casting reels.

FLY LINES. Fly fishermen choose from four basic lines. *Level,* though not widely used, is the same diameter over its entire length. It is an all-purpose line. *Double taper* line has a level middle section or belly, but gradually tapers at each end. It presents flies delicately and is economical to use. When one end wears out, simply reverse it and use the other end. *Weight forward* line has a short, thick belly just behind the tapered front end. The back portion is level line. The extra weight up front enables the fisherman to make longer casts or punch into a strong wind. *Shooting head* is similar to weight forward line, except the back portion is monofilament. It can be cast farther than any other line. Most fly lines are designed to float, but sinking or sinking-tip models are available. All shooting head lines are made to sink.

Numbers designate the weight of fly lines. No. 2 is the lightest and No. 11 the heaviest. For best casting performance, the line must be matched to the rod.

SPECIAL PURPOSE LINES. Monel wire lines are designed for extremely deep trolling. Lead-core lines are more flexible and easier to work with, but do not sink quite as deep. Some speed trollers use color-coded mono lines that help determine how deep their lures are running.

Knots

A fishing line is only as strong as the knots in it. All knots weaken line. The best have little effect on line strength, while the worst cut strength in half.

The knots on pages 28 and 29 work well for the purposes described, though many other knots can be used. Two favorites, the clinch and improved clinch are not recommended, because few fishermen tie them consistently well. As a result, these knots often have sharp bends which fracture under stress. Choose knots that are easy to tie correctly, because even the strongest knot is weak if not properly tied.

Knots weaken with use. Good fishermen tie new knots before a trip and test their knots frequently.

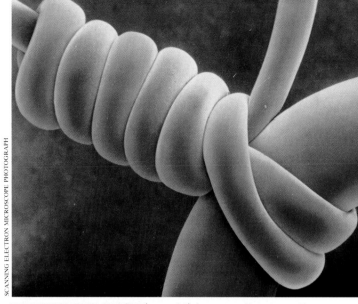

THE TRILENE KNOT (page 28) is unusually strong. It is rated at 90 percent of the line strength, compared to about 75 percent for other knots. This knot was tied with 10-pound mono and enlarged 40 times.

TIE knots carefully. A slight scratch from a clippers is barely visible to the human eye. But reproduced 40 times actual size, the nick in this improved clinch knot appears as a large rupture in the line's skin.

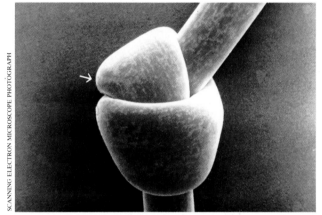

AVOID overhand knots. When stress is applied, sharp edges (arrow) cause the skin to fracture, greatly reducing its strength. Shown is an overhand or wind knot in 10-pound mono at 50 times actual size.

Tips for Tying Knots

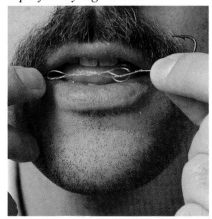

MOISTEN the knot with saliva before snugging it up. This reduces friction and helps to form a knot that is smooth and tight.

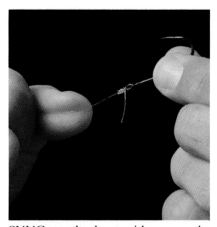

SNUG up the knot with a smooth, strong pull. Do not be timid about testing it. Better that it breaks while being tied, than after hooking a big fish.

CLIP the tag end of the line carefully. It pays to leave a little extra line, because all knots slip slightly just before they break.

Basic Knots Every Fisherman Should Know

Knowing how to tie these six knots will prepare the fisherman for virtually every angling situation. For demonstration purposes, these knots were tied with extra-heavy line.

Hook to Line: Trilene Knot, Strength 90%

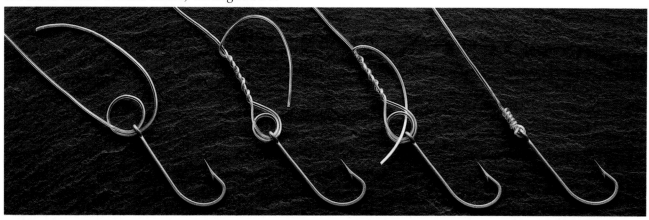

PASS the line through the eye of the hook twice from the same side. Leave a small loop next to the eye. Wrap the free end of the line around the standing line five times. Then, insert the free end through the double loop next to the eye. Snug up with a firm steady pull on the line and the hook.

Hook to Line: Palomar Knot, Strength 85%

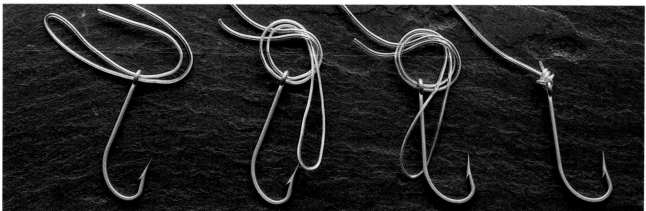

FOLD the line against itself to form a double strand. Next push the end through the eye of the hook. Tie an overhand knot in the double strand, leaving a loop big enough to pass the hook through. Snug up the knot by pulling on the hook with one hand and the double strand with the other.

To Form a Loop: Double Surgeon's Loop, Strength 70%

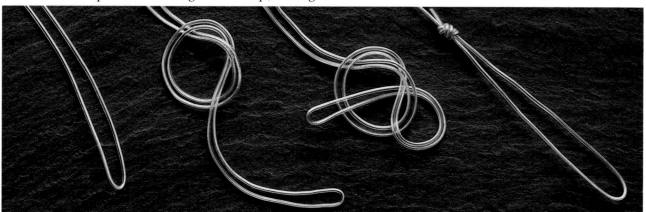

FOLD the line against itself to form a double strand. Next, tie an overhand knot in the double strand. Pass the end of the double strand through the opening in the overhand knot again, then tighten firmly. Loops are often tied at the end of a leader, so they can be attached quickly to a snap or to another loop.

Line to Spool: Improved Arbor Knot, Strength 60%

LOOP the line around the spool, then tie an overhand knot around the standing line to form a loose slip knot. Tie an overhand knot in the free end. Next, pass the free end through the overhand knot again (arrow). Snug up the knot in the free end, then pull firmly on the standing line to tighten the knot around the spool.

Lure to Loop: King Sling, Strength 75%

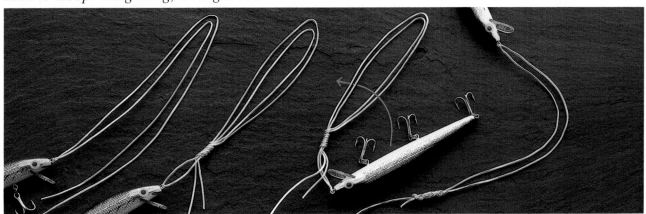

PASS the line through the eye of the lure to form a double strand. Form a large loop in the double strand and twist it three times. Drop the lure through the loop (arrow) and snug up the knot with a steady pull. The loop allows the lure to swing freely as it is pulled through the water, providing the best possible action.

Line to Line: Blood Knot, Strength 65%

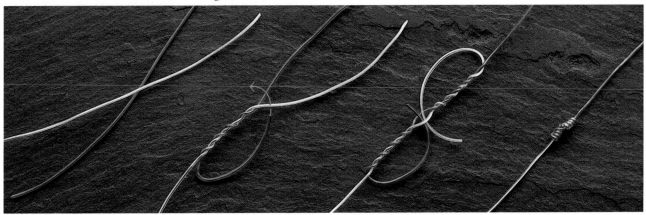

OVERLAP the lines so they point in opposite directions. Twist one line four times around the other, then bring the free end back and insert it between the two lines (arrow). Twist the other line the same way and bring it back through the same opening that holds the other line. Tighten the knot with a jerk.

Hooks

A hook is the least expensive item in a tackle box but probably the most important. Experienced anglers consider many factors when selecting a hook.

Hook size is determined by the size of the fish's mouth and the bait. To catch fish, the hook must be large enough so the point protrudes slightly from the bait. Fish may ignore the bait if the point or shank is too visible. Use a hook no longer than needed for the bait and method of hooking.

Wire thickness depends on the size of the bait and bottom conditions. A light-wire hook works best for small baits such as insects; a heavy-wire hook would damage them. A light-wire hook may straighten enough to pull free when snagged but it could also straighten while you fight a large fish. Most anglers use heavy-wire hooks for large, hard-fighting fish.

The finish of a hook can be important but is largely a matter of personal preference. Most bait hooks have a bronze finish, which is inexpensive but rusts quickly. Nickel, cadmium, Perma Plate® and stainless steel hooks are corrosion-resistant. Some fishermen believe that silver or gold-colored hooks attract more fish. Green hooks are least visible under water. Hooks also come in blued and black finishes.

Other considerations when choosing a hook include length and shape of the point, position of the eye, and hardness. Hooks come in a variety of styles. Choose the style best suited to your type of fishing.

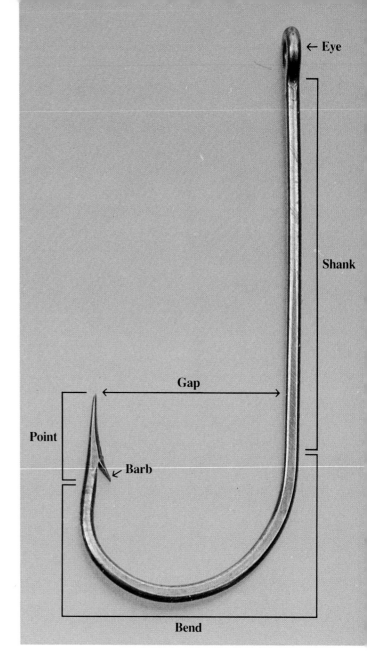

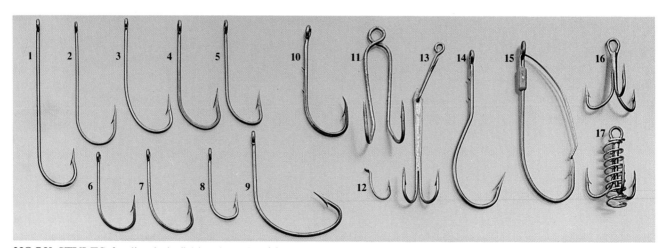

HOOK STYLES for live-bait fishing include: (1) Carlisle, (2) Aberdeen, (3) Sproat, (4) O'Shaughnessy, (5) Limerick, (6) National Round, Round Bend or Viking, (7) Faultless, Claw or Beak, (8) Kirby, (9) Wide Gap, Wide Bend or Kahle®, (10) sliced-shank Baitholder hook, (11) Super Hook®, (12) egg hook, (13) double-needle hook, (14) plastic-worm hook, (15) weedless hook, (16) treble hook, (17) Soft Bait Treble.

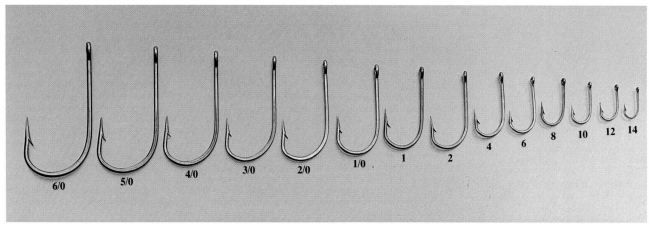

SIZE is designated by a number which reflects the *gap*, or distance between the point and the inside of the shank. Manufacturers produce a full range of sizes for each style. Larger hooks, from 1/0 to 6/0, increase in size as the number increases. But smaller hooks, from #1 to #14, decrease in size as the number increases. Hooks come in larger and smaller sizes, but these are the most commonly used. Shown are actual size VMC National Rounds.

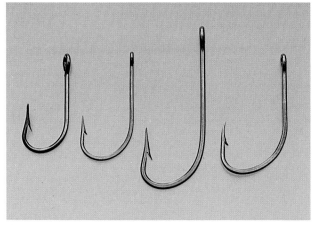

GAP varies from one hook style to another. Shown are four styles of 3/0 hooks from the same manufacturer. Each has a different gap size. To further complicate the matter, different manufacturers may produce the same hook style and size with different gaps.

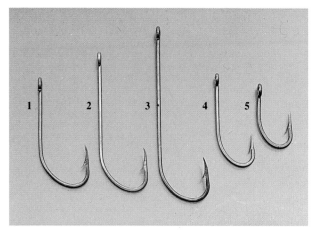

SHANKS are available in different lengths in the same style. A Claw hook is produced in a (1) standard length, but is also made in (2) long and (3) extra-long shanks. An O'Shaughnessy hook is produced in (4) standard length and (5) short shank.

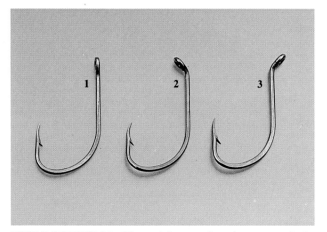

EYE POSITION is (1) straight, or *ringed*, on most bait hooks. Some fishermen claim that a (2) *turned-down* eye is better for hooking because it directs the point into the fish. (3) A *turned-up* eye is often used for snelling.

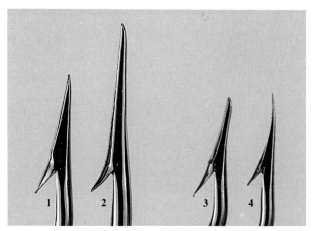

POINT LENGTH AND SHAPE determines how well a hook penetrates and holds. (1) A short point sinks easily; (2) a long point holds better. (3) A spear point is stronger; (4) a hollow point is thinner and penetrates better.

Bobbers

Called a bobber, float or cork, this simple device serves several important functions. It provides extra weight for casting light baits, suspends the bait where fish are feeding and signals a bite.

When selecting a bobber, take into account the size of the bait, the depth of fish, and how well the float can be seen by you and the fish.

A 1-inch round plastic bobber will easily float a small fathead minnow, but a 10-inch sucker will pull the bobber under and swim away with it. Experienced anglers carry a variety of sizes, and choose the smallest bobber that will still hold up the bait.

Fishermen use two types of bobbers: *fixed* and *sliding*. Fixed bobbers work well when fish are no deeper than a rod length. When fishing deeper water, casting is difficult because of the long length of line between the bobber and bait. To suspend a bait in deep water, thread on a slip-bobber or sliding float. Because the float slides, it can be reeled almost to the rod tip. Once cast, the bobber floats on the surface while the line slips through until stopped by a knot that holds the bait at the desired depth.

Fish in clear, shallow water can easily see a floating object. Many anglers use transparent plastic bubbles for casting tiny baits to stream trout. When fishing deep, murky or choppy water, use a bobber that is highly visible. Bright-colored floats that stand high above the surface are easier to see than low-profile floats.

BALANCE your bobber carefully. Add enough split-shot so the bobber floats just high enough to be seen. An improperly balanced bobber (right) is harder to pull under and may cause the fish to drop the bait.

SELECT a float that is easy to see. A fluorescent cylinder float (left) stands out on a rippled surface much better than a round, white clip-bobber (arrow). Use a lighted bobber when fishing at night.

KEEP your slip-bobber close to the boat (left) when fishing in deep water. Anchor near the fishing spot and lower the line over the side. This way, you can set the hook with a direct pull. Avoid casting the slip-bobber too

far from the boat (right). When the bait sinks into deep water, the float creates a right angle in the line between you and the bait. Then, it is nearly impossible to set the hook because you do not have a straight-line pull.

SLIDING BOBBERS include: (1) cylinder float, (2) slot bobber with wire line-stays, (3) tube bobber, (4) slot bobber with plastic tab line-stays, (5) lighted bobber powered by a lithium battery, (6) Carbonyte® float.

FIXED BOBBERS include: (7) quill float, (8) spring-lock bobber, (9) and (10) casting bubbles, (11) sponge bobber for ice fishing, (12) clip-bobber, (13) Carolina Float®, (14) weighted casting float, (15) peg bobber.

Sinkers

SLIDING SINKERS include: (1) walking sinker, (2) Snap-Loc™ sinker which clips on the line for changing weights easily, (3) cone sinker for retrieving baits through weeds, (4) egg sinker.

Some sinkers attach to the line; others slide on the line. Attached or fixed sinkers are pinched, twisted or tied onto the line. When a fish runs, it must tow the sinker along. Sometimes gamefish will not tolerate this added resistance and will drop the bait. Use the lightest fixed sinker that will still carry your bait to the desired depth.

A sliding or slip-sinker lets the fish swim off without feeling any drag. The sinker rests on bottom while the line slides through it. Slip-sinkers will not work when trolling in mid-water or when bobber-fishing. If the sinker cannot rest on bottom, the line will not slip. A slip-sinker rig is more difficult to tie and requires more hardware than a fixed sinker rig.

When selecting a sinker, consider the depth of water, type of bottom and speed at which the bait is pulled through the water. Fishermen generally switch to heavier sinkers as the depth or speed of the bait increases. When trolling, water resistance pushes the line upward, raising the sinker off bottom. The faster you troll, the more weight you need to keep your bait at the same depth. When drifting, a strong wind pushes the boat faster, making a heavier sinker necessary.

If fishing a river, the speed of the current is important. Switch to heavier sinkers as the current speed increases. To keep baits from rolling downstream, use a flat-sided sinker such as a pyramid. When drifting a bait with the current, use a rounded sinker.

If a lake or stream bottom is covered with rocks or other debris, use a bottom-walker or other type of snag-resistant sinker. Some sinkers are designed to pull free of the line when snagged, leaving the remainder of the rig intact.

Tips for Using Sinkers

SELECT a slip-sinker (right) heavy enough to troll on bottom with a short line. Fish cannot detect the weight because the line slips through. With a light sinker, the line trails too far behind, making it hard to detect a bite.

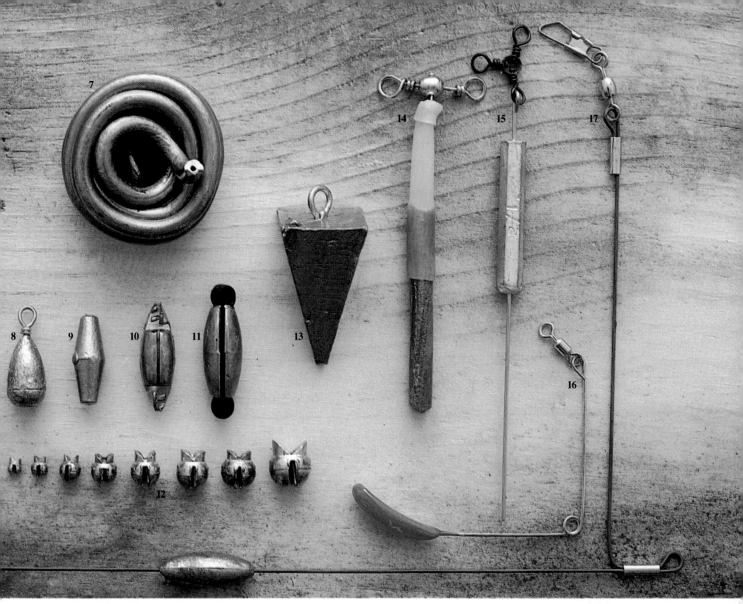

FIXED SINKERS include: (5) keel and (6) torpedo Bead Chain® sinkers to prevent line twist, (7) lead wire which is cut to length and pinched on, (8) bell or dipsey, (9) drift sinker which is pinched on a dropper, (10) pinch-on sinker, (11) Rubbercor®, (12) split-shot in various sizes, (13) pyramid, (14) surgical tubing sinker with lead insert. Bottom-walker types include: (15) Needle Weight™, (16) Bait-Walker™, (17) Bottom Walker™.

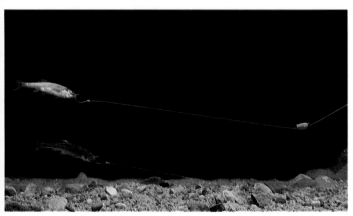

CHOOSE a heavier sinker when using heavier line. Despite identical sinkers, water resistance keeps the 12-pound line (top) from sinking as fast as the 4-pound line, especially when trolled or fished in current.

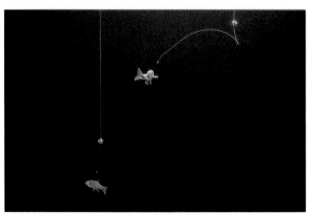

ATTACH the sinker far enough from the bait so it does not interfere with the swimming action. The minnow at left is severely restricted, but the one at right can swim freely, attracting more fish.

Leaders, Swivels & Connectors

A leader, swivel or connector that inhibits the action of your lure or appears unnatural to the fish will greatly reduce the number of strikes you get.

When fishing with monofilament, you can usually attach your lure directly to the line. Most other line is too stiff or too visible for direct attachment, so you will need a mono leader. Always use the lightest leader suitable for the type of fish and the conditions. You would need a heavier leader for fishing in timber or brush, for instance, than you would when fishing over a clean bottom.

Many fishermen attach their lures with heavy wire leaders regardless of what kind of fish they expect to catch. But wire leaders are unnecessary and undesirable for most types of freshwater fish.

Fly fishermen should use tapered monofilament leaders. With most flies, a level leader does not have enough momentum to unroll completely on the cast. Tapered leaders may be either knotted or knotless. Knotted leaders consist of several sections of monofilament, decreasing in diameter from butt to tip. Fishermen tailor their own to suit the conditions. Knotless leaders are more expensive, but have no knots to pick up algae. The weight of the *tippet,* or front section of the leader, depends mainly

on the size of the fly you are casting. On most spools of tippet material, the weight is designated not only by the breaking strength, in pounds, but also by an X-number. As a general rule, divide the fly size by three to determine which tippet weight to use. For example, a size 18 fly would require a 6X tippet.

Most artificial lures do not require a swivel. A swivel makes the lure appear larger, may change its balance and action, and could increase the chances of tangling on the cast. Without a swivel, however, many lures would twist your line. High quality, ball-bearing swivels generally reduce line twist more than cheap brass swivels.

Some types of artificial lures, such as spoons and vibrating blades, work better when attached with a snap or split ring. Tying your line directly to these lures decreases the amount of action and may cut your line.

A round-nosed snap is a better choice than a V-nosed snap because it allows the lure to swing more freely. Snaps made from a length of continuous wire are generally stronger than the safety-pin type. Select the smallest snap, split ring or swivel suitable for the situation.

Tips on Using Leaders, Swivels and Connectors

MAKE a 6-inch *striker* from 20-pound wire line. Thread wire through a clip, twist three times, then make five tight wraps. Attach swivel on other end.

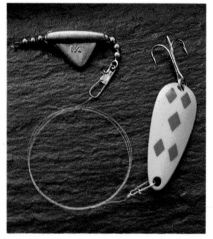

SPLICE in a keel swivel 1 to 2 feet ahead of a lure that could severely twist your line. Keel swivels work especially well for trolling.

SOLDER a split ring to greatly increase its strength. Soldering also reduces the chances of the line slipping into the groove and fraying.

USE a wire leader only when fishing for northern pike, pickerel or muskies. No other freshwater gamefish have teeth sharp enough to cut through nylon monofilament.

Many experts prefer single-strand wire to multi-strand wire because it is smaller in diameter for its strength and easier to straighten should it become curled.

Common Mistakes in Attaching Lures

ATTACHING a surface lure with heavy hardware causes the nose to sink. When you twitch the lure, it will not sputter, pop or gurgle.

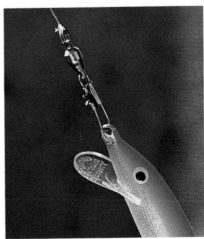

USING a snap-swivel when only a snap is needed may diminish a lure's action. Buy plain snaps or use only the snap from a snap-swivel.

TYING the line in the groove of a split ring rather than on the double wire weakens the connection. And the ring's sharp ends may fray your line.

BASS BOATS are the standard on big southern reservoirs, which may be a hundred miles long. To cover this distance, anglers use outboards up to 150 horsepower, attaining speeds over 60 mph. Bass boats are gaining popularity in the North, but the low-profile hull is not well-suited to the rough water on large northern lakes.

Boats & Motors

Depending on the type of water you fish, the best craft may be a high-powered bass boat, an aluminum or fiberglass semi-V, a jon boat, or a canoe. Anglers who fish a variety of waters often have two or three boats.

BASS BOATS. These boats provide the ultimate in fishing comfort and convenience. Because of their fiberglass construction and tri-hull design, they are very stable, so you can safely stand up while casting. If you prefer to sit, the sides are low enough that you do not have to hold your rod up when retrieving.

Most bass boats have an elevated front casting deck, a carpeted floor to muffle sound, an aerated live well, rod- and gear-storage compartments, a bow-mounted trolling motor, and a flasher set up for high-speed sounding.

SEMI-V BOATS. The term *semi-V* indicates that the boat has a V-shaped bow, but a relatively flat bottom at the stern. The V-shaped bow serves to part the waves, and the flat bottom makes the boat stable. There are two basic types of semi-Vs: aluminum and fiberglass.

Aluminum semi-Vs are light, so the bow rides up on the waves instead of cutting through them, resulting in a rough ride. Fiberglass semi-Vs are heavier, so they ride more smoothly and are less affected by wind. They are also quieter than aluminum, but are less durable and more expensive.

Most freshwater fishermen prefer a semi-V boat with tiller steering. A tiller handle gives you much better boat control than a steering wheel, especially for backtrolling. Other desirable equipment includes a flasher and a transom-mounted electric

ALUMINUM SEMI-Vs are the favorite on northern lakes. Most fishermen use 14- to 16-footers equipped with 10- to 50-horsepower outboards. The V-shaped bow of these boats makes them quite seaworthy, and their light weight makes it possible to get them in and out of the water at even the poorest boat landings.

trolling motor. Some of the more expensive semi-Vs come equipped with bass-boat features like live wells, carpeted floors, air-pedestal seats and elevated casting decks.

JON BOATS. The stability and light weight of a jon boat make it ideal for river fishing. Many rivers lack developed boat landings, but a pair of fishermen can easily carry a 14-foot jon boat to the water. A 6-horsepower outboard provides all the power you will normally need. With a 16-foot jon boat, most anglers use a 10- to 15-horsepower outboard.

Some fishermen rig their jon boats with a bow-mounted trolling motor, flasher and live well. But others would rather go light. They rely solely on their outboard, check the depth visually or with a push pole, and keep their fish in a cooler.

CANOES. Anglers who regularly fish difficult-to-reach waters prefer aluminum canoes. They are inexpensive, durable, and light enough for one person to carry on his shoulders when portaging around dangerous rapids or from one lake to another. Be-

cause of the light weight, they are easy to paddle long distances.

Like fiberglass semi-Vs, fiberglass canoes are heavier than aluminum ones, so the wind does not blow them around as easily. The extra weight also makes them less tippy. When a fiberglass canoe scrapes on rocks, it makes a lot less noise than an aluminum canoe and is not as likely to spook fish.

Most canoe fishermen travel light; the only extra equipment is a portable flasher, paddles, and an anchor rope. For an anchor, they tie on a rock.

Where motors are permitted, use a square-stern canoe (opposite page) or one with a bracket for mounting a motor alongside the stern. A side-mount bracket will usually take a 2- to 4-horsepower outboard. If you prefer, you can attach a transom-mount electric motor to the stern or to the side-mount bracket. With an ordinary canoe, you can simply attach the electric motor to the gunwale. Even a small electric motor will push a canoe at a surprising speed.

FIBERGLASS SEMI-Vs are becoming popular on big lakes because the hull is flared at the bow to deflect waves to the side. Without the flared bow, spray flies up and the wind blows it back into the boat. Fiberglass semi-Vs used for fishing range from 15 to 17 feet and are normally rigged with 35- to 55-horsepower motors.

JON BOATS are the ultimate craft for river fishing. Because they draw only a few inches of water, they will float over shallow, rocky stretches. And should they scrape bottom, the aluminum hull will not be damaged. A jon boat's flat-bottom design gives it excellent side-to-side stability.

CANOES are the only craft practical for long-distance portaging or fishing in wilderness areas where access is difficult and motors are often banned. Canoes also work well for fishing rivers with rocky riffles or whitewater stretches.

SQUARE-STERN CANOES are wide and deep; they carry a lot of gear and take motors up to 10 horsepower.

Adjusting Depth Finders

To get the most from your depth finder, you must know how to adjust it. Otherwise, even the best unit will be of little use in detecting fish or indicating the bottom type.

All depth finders have some type of power adjustment. On some units, power is called *gain;* on others, *sensitivity.* All units also have some type of suppression system. There may be a variable external adjustment, an on-off adjustment called *clean echo,* or a built-in system with no adjustment possible. The higher you turn a variable suppressor, the more interference you eliminate, but the harder it becomes to distinguish individual fish from bottom or from other fish. As a rule, keep the suppressor turned off until you need it. And when you use it, turn it no higher than necessary.

Most graphs, LCRs and videos have a whiteline or grayline adjustment. Use it whenever you are having trouble discriminating fish from bottom.

The paper-speed adjustment on a graph or sweep speed on an LCR or video should be set relatively fast when fishing in shallow water, slower in deep water. A fast speed is also necessary when running a contour in search of fish.

The following examples show you how to make the most important adjustments on flashers and graphs. The same principles apply to adjusting LCRs and videos.

How to Adjust a Flasher (Examples Based on Illustration Above)

POWER. With the power too low (left), the bottom signal will be weak and the fish will not show up. Turn the power up until you get a *double echo* (middle). The bottom signal will be much wider and you will see the fish. With the power too high (right), multiple echoes and interference make it hard to interpret the reading.

SUPPRESSION. Whenever there is too much interference (left), turn up the suppressor until the moving lines scattered around the face of the flasher just disappear (middle). If you turn the suppressor too high (right), the signal from the fish nearest bottom is impossible to distinguish from the bottom signal.

How to Adjust a Graph Recorder (Examples Based on Illustration at Left)

POWER. If the power is too low (left), the bottom reading will be thin and light, there will be little if any *scatter* near the surface, and the fish will not show up. Turn up the power until the bottom signal becomes thick and dark, and you see a moderate amount of surface scatter and some suspended particles in the depths (middle). With the power at this level, the graph should print the fish. If the power is too high (right), surface scatter will be very heavy, and marks from suspended particles and small baitfish will obscure the fish marks.

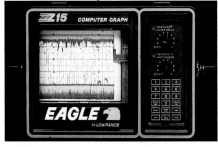  

SUPPRESSION. Interference on a graph appears as vertical lines or scattered specks (left). If there is too much interference, turn up the suppressor until most of the lines and specks, with the exception of the surface scatter, disappear (middle). Both fish should be visible and clearly separated from the bottom. If the suppressor is set too high (right), the fish nearest bottom blends in with the bottom signal, even with the whiteline on.

  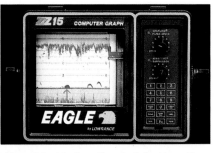

WHITELINE. With the whiteline or grayline adjustment turned off (left), the lowest fish appears as a bump on the bottom. To determine if the bump is a fish or just a rock or other object on bottom, turn up the whiteline until you see a light-colored band just below the dark bottom line. If the bottom line is visible below the bump (middle), the bump is a fish. If there is no line below the bump (arrow at right), the bump may not be a fish.

PAPER SPEED. If the fish appear as narrow, vertical marks (left), the paper speed is too slow. Increase the paper speed until the fish look like upside-down *V*s (middle). If the paper speed is too fast, the fish appear as long crescents (right). There is nothing wrong with long marks, but you will waste a great deal of paper.

How to Interpret Flasher and Graph Readings

Hard Bottom

Bottom signal is thick and bright, and there is a double echo.

Bottom reading is thick and dark; rocks show up as small humps.

Soft Bottom

Bottom signal is thin and dim, even if you turn up the power.

Bottom reading is thin and light; you may see rising gas bubbles.

Weeds

Fine lines appear on the flasher at the depths the weeds are growing.

Vertical columns extend from bottom to the maximum height of the weeds.

Drop-off

Bottom signal is very thick; shallowest reading is top of drop-off.

Depth changes as boat moves, giving a sloped bottom reading.

Baitfish or Plankton

Both baitfish and plankton appear as a scattering of fine lines.

Plankton   Baitfish

Schools of baitfish show some small *V*s; plankton show only tiny specks.

Fish Near Bottom

Appears as a thin line barely separated from the bottom signal.

Appears as an inverted *V* with space between the mark and the bottom.

Small vs. Large Fish

The signals look similar, but the one from the large fish is thicker.

The marks are nearly the same width, but the large fish is much thicker.

Maps

Only a small fraction of the water in any lake contains gamefish. A good *hydrographic*, or contour map, used with a depth finder, can save hours of random searching.

Hydrographic maps indicate water depth by contour lines. Maps usually show a contour line at every 5- or 10-foot depth change. Lines that are close together reveal abrupt bottom changes; lines far apart mean a gradually-sloping bottom.

Maps show the location of good fish-holding structure such as sunken islands, creek channels and submerged points. Maps of reservoirs sometimes pinpoint man-made features that have been flooded, including roads and houses. Most maps show various shoreline features, while some identify bottom types and the locations of weedbeds, flooded timber and brush.

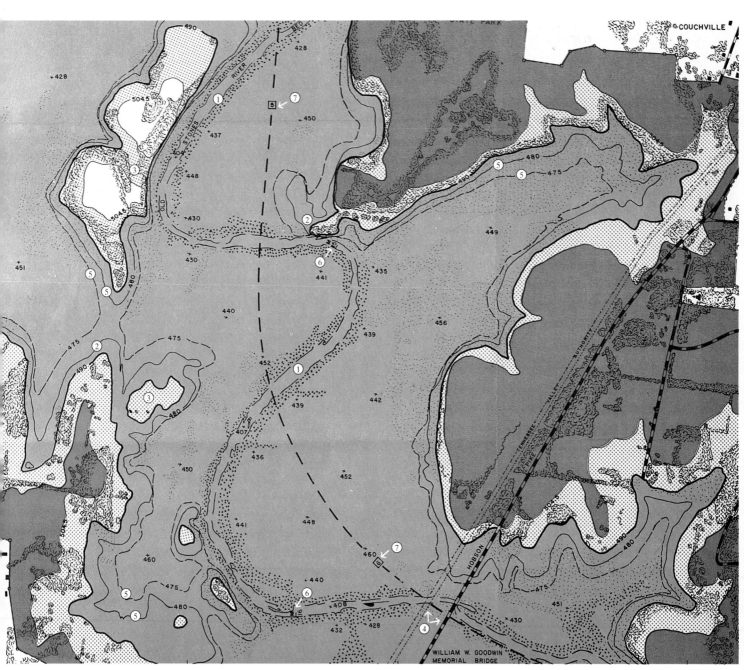

RESERVOIR MAPS show (1) the main river channel, (2) points, (3) islands, (4) road and powerline crossings, (5) contour lines. Mileage from the dam is shown along (6) the river channel and (7) the shortest navigable route. Red indicates a state park, dots are flooded trees and *X*'s show elevations at selected locations.

After studying your contour map, look for a landmark such as a point to help you find the right vicinity. Then use your depth finder to locate the exact spot. If you catch fish, mark the spot on your map. Before leaving, check the shoreline for reference points, then list them on your map. The spot will be easier to find next time.

Contour maps of natural lakes seldom show every detail on bottom. Mapmakers often miss humps and reefs. These small structures may lie between survey lines used by crews when charting lake depths.

It pays to do some extra scouting and pencil in any features that the map does not show. Few fishermen discover these areas, so they sometimes offer prime fishing.

Hydrographic maps are available for most natural lakes and reservoirs. To purchase these maps, contact your state fish and wildlife agency, the U.S. Army Corps of Engineers, the Tennessee Valley Authority, or private map publishers. Power companies sometimes supply maps of cooling lakes which are open to fishing.

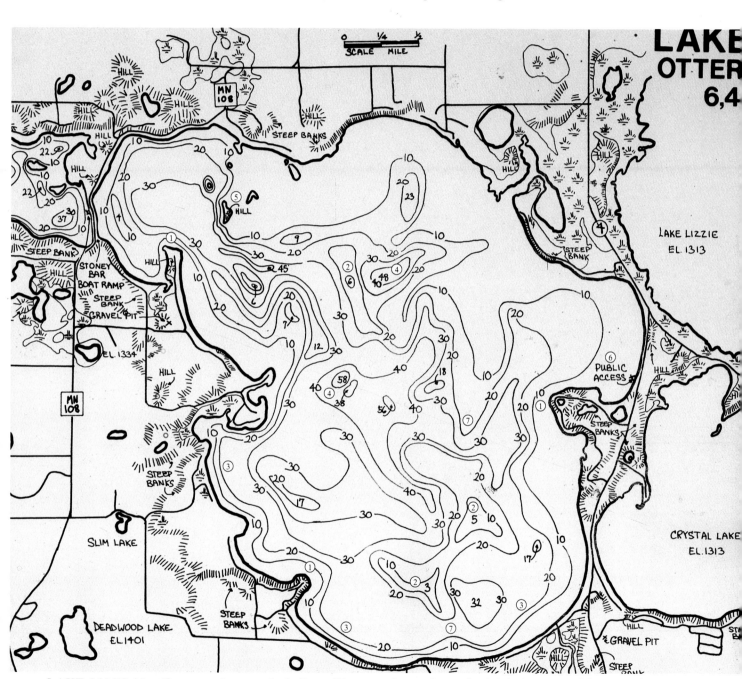

LAKE MAPS identify many features including: (1) points, (2) sunken islands where the shallowest depth is in the center, (3) distinct breaklines, (4) deep holes where the maximum depth is in the center, (5) islands, (6) public boat ramps, (7) submerged points. Hills and steep banks on this map could be used as reference points.

How to Catch Freshwater Gamefish

Largemouth Bass

Jaw Extends Beyond Eye

Black Lateral Band

Largemouth Bass Basics

Renowned for its explosive strikes and spectacular leaps, the largemouth bass is a favorite among millions of freshwater fishermen.

Largemouths were originally found only east of the Mississippi River and south of the Great Lakes. But they have been stocked throughout the United States and in southern Canada and most of Mexico. Bass have also been introduced in Europe, Asia, Africa and South America.

The largemouth bass is the largest member of a group of closely-related fishes called *black bass.* Others include the smallmouth, spotted, redeye, Suwannee and Guadalupe. The largemouth is distinguished from all of these species by a jaw that extends beyond the eye. All black bass belong to the sunfish family.

Biologists have identified two subspecies of largemouth bass: the *Florida largemouth* and the *northern largemouth.* Originally, Florida bass lived only in Florida waters. Stocking efforts have expanded their range to include much of the South, particularly Texas and California.

Although they look alike, the Florida largemouth

Largemouth Bass Range

grows considerably larger than the northern subspecies. A trophy Florida bass weighs from 10 to 12 pounds, compared to 6 to 8 pounds for a northern largemouth bass.

Some biologists believe that the world record largemouth bass was a cross between the northern and Florida subspecies. The 22-pound, 4-ounce largemouth was caught in June, 1932, at Montgomery Lake in Georgia. This lake is one of many waters in Georgia and Alabama where largemouth crosses have been found.

Largemouths vary in color, depending on the type of water. Bass from murky waters are pale; those from clear waters darker. Largemouths range from deep green to pale olive across the back, with bellies that are a shade of white or yellow. All bass have a black lateral band that runs from the head to tail. The band becomes more distinct when a fish is exposed to sunlight, but may disappear when a largemouth is in deep or murky water.

SENSES. The *lateral line,* a series of sensitive nerve endings on each side of the fish, can pick up underwater vibrations as subtle as a swimming baitfish. In one experiment, researchers placed small cups over the eyes of bass, then dropped minnows into a tank with the largemouths. Eventually the bass ate each minnow, using their lateral lines to locate the baitfish.

Largemouth bass hear with internal ears located within the skull. They may be attracted by the ticking or popping of some artificial lures. But when they hear loud, unfamiliar sounds, they usually swim to deeper water or cover.

Bass can see in all directions, except directly below or behind. In clear water, they can see 30 feet or more. But in most bass waters, visibility is limited to 5 to 10 feet. Largemouths can also see objects that are above water.

Bass can detect colors, but most experts are reluctant to say that bass prefer a certain color of lure or bait over another. The best colors vary, depending

BASS GROWTH is faster in southern waters than in northern waters, primarily because the growing season is longer. For example, in four years, the average Louisiana largemouth (top) reaches about 18 inches; an Illinois bass (middle) is about 13 inches, while a Wisconsin bass (bottom) averages about 11 inches.

on light conditions, water clarity and water color. Most believe that a lure's action is more important than its color.

The eye of a largemouth absorbs more light than does the human eye, enabling the fish to see its food in dim light or darkness. Bass will feed at any time of the day or night, but are less inclined to leave cover and search for food under bright conditions. Like most fish, they prefer shade. They find better ambush camouflage in shady spots or under low-light conditions.

Largemouths smell through nostrils, or *nares,* on the snout. The nares are short passageways through which water is drawn and expelled without entering the throat. Like most fish, bass can detect minute amounts of scent in the water. However, bass rely on scent less than catfish, salmon or trout.

Bass use their sense of touch to determine whether to reject or swallow an object. They will usually hold on to a soft-bodied, artificial worm longer than a metal lure.

Sense of taste is not as important to largemouth bass as it is to some fish species, because bass have few taste cells in their mouths.

FEEDING. Newly-hatched largemouths feed heavily on tiny crustaceans and other zooplankton until the bass reach 2 inches in length. Young largemouths eat insects and small fish, including smaller bass. Adult largemouths prey mostly on fish, but crayfish, frogs and insects are important foods in some waters.

Wherever they live, bass rank high in the aquatic food chain. A bass 10 inches or longer has few enemies and will eat almost anything it can swallow. Because of its large mouth and flexible stomach, a bass can eat prey nearly half its own length.

Largemouths *inhale* small foods. The bass opens its mouth quickly to suck in water and the food. It then forces the water out the gills while it either swallows or rejects the object. Bass can expel food as quickly as they inhale it, so anglers must set the hook immediately when using small lures or baits.

Bass usually grab large prey, then turn the food to swallow it headfirst. This explains why anglers who use large golden shiners, frogs or salamanders wait a minute or two before setting the hook.

As the water warms, the metabolism of bass increases and they feed more often. Largemouths

BASS FOODS reflect a varied diet. Adult largemouths feed heavily on crayfish where they are available. In most waters, they feed mainly on fish, including gizzard and threadfin shad, golden shiners, young sunfish and small rough fish. Bass also eat frogs, large insects, shrimp, salamanders, and even small mammals and ducklings.

seldom eat at water temperatures below 50°F. From 50° to 68°F, feeding increases and from 68° to 80°F, they feed heavily. However, at temperatures above 80°F, feeding declines.

No one is certain what causes bass to strike artificial lures or bait. Experts point to hunger as the main reason. However, many of these same experts believe that reflex, aggressiveness, curiosity and competitiveness may play a part.

Reflex, or a sudden instinctive reaction, may explain why a bass with a full stomach strikes an artificial lure the instant it hits the water. The fish has little time to judge what it is grabbing, yet some cue triggers it to strike.

Male bass display aggressiveness when they attack lures or chase other fish that invade their nest sites. Although this behavior is common during nesting season, bass are not as aggressive at other times of the year.

Curiosity may be the reason that bass rush up to inspect new objects or sounds. However, it is doubtful they take food solely out of curiosity. Competitiveness probably explains why fishermen occasionally catch two bass on the same lure at the same time. Often several bass race to devour a single food item, particularly in waters where food is in short supply.

GROWTH. The best trophy bass waters are those where the fish grow rapidly as a result of proper temperatures and abundant food. Largemouths seldom reach large sizes in waters where they have become too abundant.

The amount bass grow in a year depends on the length of their *growing season*, or the number of days suitable for growth. The growing season in the South may last twice as long as it does in the North. Largemouths gain weight most quickly in water from 75° to 80°F. They do not grow in water colder than 50°F.

Although bass in the South grow and mature faster, they rarely live as long as largemouths in colder, northern lakes. In southern waters, bass occasionally reach 10 years of age; in northern waters, bass may live as long as 15 years.

Female bass live longer than males, so they are more apt to reach a trophy size. In one study, 30 percent of the females were 5 years or older, while only 9 percent of the male bass were 5 years or more.

55

Largemouth Bass Spawning Behavior

In spring, when inshore waters reach about 60°F, largemouth bass swim onto spawning grounds in shallow bays, backwaters, channels and other areas protected from prevailing winds. Spawning grounds usually have firm bottoms of sand, gravel, mud or rock. Bass seldom nest on a thick layer of silt. Some spawning areas are in open water; others have sparse weeds, boulders or logs.

Male bass may spend several days selecting their nest sites. The beds are usually in 1 to 4 feet of water, but may be deeper in clear water. Most largemouths nest in pockets in bulrushes, water lilies or other weeds. Bass in open areas often select a site on the sunny side of a submerged log or large rock. The males seldom nest where they can see another nesting male. For this reason, beds are generally at least 30 feet apart, but may be closer if weeds, boulders, sunken logs or stumps prevent the males from seeing each other.

Largemouths spawn when the water reaches 63° to 68°F and temperatures remain within this range for several days. Cold fronts may cause water temperatures to drop, which interrupts and delays spawning.

A female bass lays from 2000 to 7000 eggs per pound of body weight. She may deposit all of her eggs in one nest or drop them at several different sites before leaving the spawning grounds. After spawning, the female recuperates in deep water, where she does not eat for two to three weeks.

Alone on the nest, the male hovers above the eggs, slowly fanning them to keep off silt and debris. He does not eat while guarding the eggs, but will attack other fish that swim near the nest. The male will not attack slow-moving objects, such as a crayfish or even a plastic worm. Instead, he gently picks up the object and drops it outside the nest.

Sunfish often prey on bass eggs or newly-hatched *fry*. In waters with large sunfish populations, the panfish can seriously hamper bass reproduction. A school of sunfish surrounds a nest, and while the male chases some away, others invade the nest and devour the eggs or fry.

Bass eggs hatch in only two days at 72°F, but take five days at 67°F. Cold weather following spawning will delay hatching. If the shallows drop to 50°F, the fry will not emerge for 13 days. At lower temperatures, the eggs fail to develop. A severe cold front sometimes causes males to abandon the nest, resulting in a complete loss of eggs or fry. From 2000 to 12,000 eggs hatch from the typical nest. Of these, only five to ten are likely to survive to reach 10 inches in length.

Basic Features of Spawning Sites

FIRM BOTTOMS make the best nest sites. Bass can easily sweep away light silt. The sticky eggs adhere to bottom and the roots of plants. The male fans the nest constantly to circulate oxygen-rich water over the eggs.

COVER such as weeds, stumps, logs and rocks provides extra protection for the eggs and fry. Bass that build their nests next to these objects have less area to guard against sunfish and other predators.

How Largemouth Bass Spawn

PREPARING the nest, the male largemouth shakes its head and tail to sweep away bottom debris. The typical nest is a saucer-shaped depression about 2 to 3 feet in diameter, or twice the length of the male.

SPAWNING occurs as the male and female move over the nest with their vents close together. The male bumps and nips the female, stimulating her to deposit the eggs. Then the male covers the eggs with his sperm, or *milt*.

NEST-GUARDING is left to the male bass. After hatching, the tiny fry lie in the nest for eight to ten days. Once they are able to swim, the fry remain in a compact school, hovering beneath weeds or other overhead cover. As the fry grow larger, they spread over a wider area, but the male still protects them. The male abandons the fry when they reach about 1 inch in length. After that, he may eat any fry he encounters.

Largemouth Bass Habitat Preferences

Largemouth bass have certain habitat requirements that are important to their survival.

TEMPERATURE. Many studies of bass behavior have concluded that largemouths prefer temperatures of 77° to 86°F. But fishermen know that bass often bite better in water at lower temperatures, even when water in their preferred temperature range is available. This is explained by the fact that bass will abandon an area with ideal temperature to escape bright sunlight or to find food or cover. Bass cannot survive at temperatures above 98°F.

OXYGEN. Bass require more oxygen than most other gamefish. All lakes have sufficient oxygen in the shallows. But in *fertile* lakes, those with a high level of nutrients, the depths may lack oxygen. Fertile lakes produce large amounts of plankton. These tiny plants and animals eventually die and sink to bottom where they decompose. The decomposition process consumes huge amounts of oxygen, making the depths unsuitable for fish. Heavy algae blooms are a symptom of high water fertility.

In the North, fertile lakes may *winter-kill*. Thick ice and snow cover block out sunlight, so plants can no longer produce oxygen. Decomposition continues, drawing all oxygen from even the shallowest water. Bass are one of the first to die in winterkill lakes.

In deep, clear waters such as canyon reservoirs and strip pits, water fertility is usually low. The water contains ample oxygen from top to bottom, so bass can move wherever they want.

FEATURES. A feature is any difference in the underwater world, including cover, structure and less obvious differences like current or shadows. Features are more important to bass than to most other gamefish.

Largemouths require cover from the moment they hatch. Bass fry crowd into dense weedbeds to escape predatory fish. Later in their lives, bass use weeds, rocks, flooded timber and brush, sunken logs and other objects for shade, shelter and ambush points.

Structure is the geologic makeup of the bottom. It may be a reef, point or any other place where the depth changes. It can also be a rock patch or any other place where the bottom material changes from one type to another. Largemouths use structure as a reference point to guide their daily movements. They also locate near structure simply because it is unique from the rest of the area. In a controlled location experiment, researchers discovered that bass will relate to anything different in their surroundings (see photos below).

How Bass Relate to Features in a Controlled Location Experiment

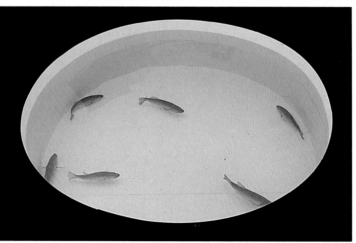

A PLAIN WHITE TANK lacks features. Lighting is evenly distributed and sounds carefully controlled. These 2-pound bass swim about aimlessly.

A BOARD over one edge of the tank provides acceptable cover for the bass. The fish station themselves in the shade under the board.

OVERHEAD COVER in shallow water provides shade and cooler temperatures, allowing bass to remain all summer. Weedy edges provide points of ambush where bass can dart out to capture smaller fish.

ROCKS piled in one area of the tank attract the bass immediately. They form a closely-packed school above and along the edge of the rock pile.

A BLACK STRIPE painted on the wall provides something to which bass can relate. They hover near the stripe, even though it offers no cover.

Selecting Lures & Baits for Largemouth Bass

Many fishermen choose their lures by trial and error. They keep changing until they find one that catches bass. But choosing a lure is not a random choice for expert bass fishermen. They select a lure only after considering the following factors.

DEPTH. This is the prime concern in lure selection. For example, bass in deep water will seldom chase a lure retrieved just under the surface. Try to estimate the most probable depth based on the season, time of day, weather, water clarity and past experience on the body of water.

In water shallower than 10 feet, bass anglers use surface lures, spinnerbaits, spinners or shallow-running crankbaits. Lightly-weighted plastic worms will also work. In deeper water, use deep-running or sinking crankbaits, jigging lures, heavily-weighted plastic worms or spinnerbaits helicoptered to bottom (page 69). Live bait can be used in both shallow and deep water.

COVER. When fishing in thick weeds or brush, use a weedless spoon, Texas-rigged plastic worm, spinnerbait, brushguard jig, or any lure with a device to prevent snagging. When fishing with live bait, use a cone sinker and a weedless hook.

ACTIVITY LEVEL. The activity level of bass determines the size and action of the lure and the speed of the retrieve. Water temperature affects bass activity more than any other factor. However, weather conditions, especially cold fronts, can also play a role.

Bass in their optimum feeding range of 68° to 80°F are more likely to strike a larger, faster-moving lure or bait than bass in warmer or colder water. An 8-inch plastic worm may be a good choice at 75°F,

but a 4-inch worm would probably work better at 83°F. In 55-degree water, bass will respond better to a smaller lure retrieved slowly. But lures like buzz baits would not work properly if retrieved slowly.

Live bait works well in cold water because it can be crawled along bottom or suspended from a bobber. Lures such as jigging spoons and small jigs are also good coldwater choices. Constantly lifting and dropping the lure through a tight school of bass will eventually pay off with a strike.

WATER CLARITY AND LIGHT LEVELS. Bass fishermen have different theories for selecting lure color. However, most agree that water clarity affects their choice of colors.

Many anglers insist that light-colored lures are better for fishing in clear water. But that does not explain the success of black or purple plastic worms in clear waters. Fluorescent lures in yellow, chartreuse or orange seem to work best in murky water. Dark colors usually outproduce light colors on overcast days or at night.

When fishing at night or in a murky lake, use a noisy lure or bait. Good choices include a popper or chugger, a spinnerbait with large blades, a buzz bait with a blade that ticks the shaft (page 76), or a crankbait with beads that rattle. Some anglers hook on a lively frog that will kick across the surface.

Beginning fishermen are often overwhelmed by the huge selection of bass lures at their local tackle shop. Many buy a large tackle box and fill each tray with a different lure. They never stick with one lure long enough to learn to use it properly.

Some beginners go to the opposite extreme. They catch a few fish on a particular lure, then refuse to change. The lure may work well at times, but too often it catches nothing.

Top bass fishermen contend that you cannot catch fish unless you have confidence in your *presentation,* meaning your choice of lure and how you retrieve it. When buying lures, select a few of each basic type, then learn how and when to use them. Catching fish is the quickest way to gain confidence in a lure.

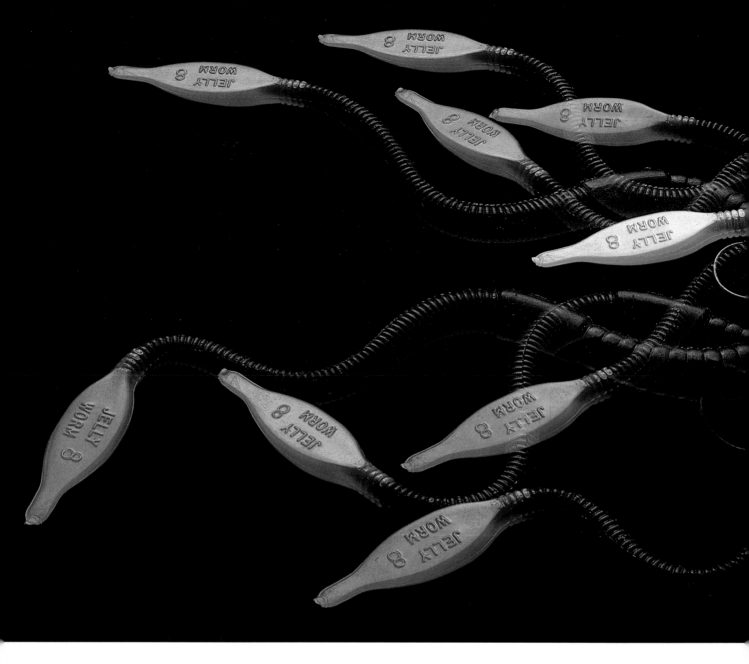

Fishing for Largemouth Bass with Plastic Worms

When asked to choose their favorite lure, the majority of anglers at a national bass-fishing championship named the plastic worm. The lure is effective because of its tantalizing, lifelike action. And when inhaled by a bass, the worm's soft body feels like natural food.

Plastic worms work best in warm water. You can retrieve them through thick weeds or brush without snagging, float them over shallow cover or jig them along deep structure. Generally, worms are not as effective in cold water.

Some plastic worms resemble eels, salamanders, lizards or even small snakes. Others look like nothing a bass has ever seen.

Worms range from 4 to 12 inches. The 6- to 8-inch sizes work best in most situations. Use smaller worms in clear water or when bass nip at a lure, such as after a cold front. Some anglers crawl 12-inch, snakelike worms over heavy cover to catch trophy bass.

Experiment to find the best color. Purple and black worms will catch bass in almost any type of water. In murky water, solid, gaudy colors such as chartreuse or red may work better. Many worms have bright or fluorescent tails, called *firetails,* or metal flakes molded into the body for extra attraction in murky water. In very clear water, try translucent worms in soft colors such as blue, grape or red.

When fishing in heavy cover, rig a plastic worm Texas-style (page 65). Most fishermen use cone-

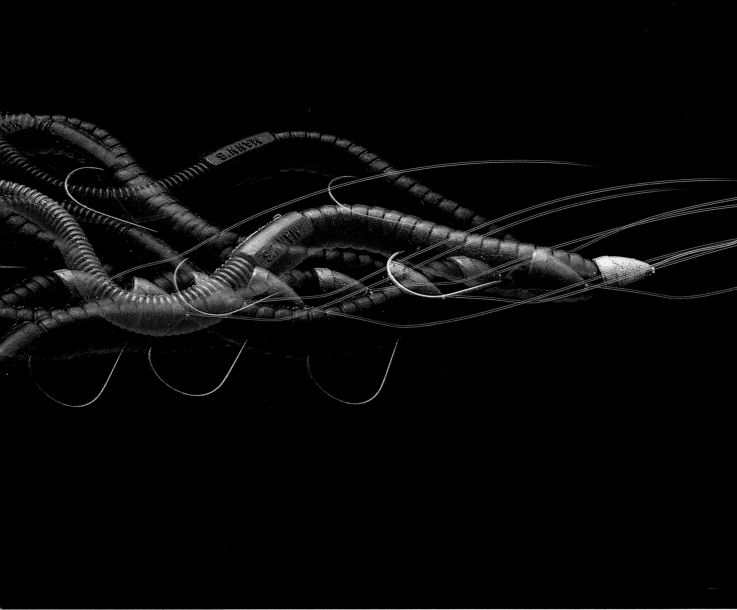

shaped slip sinkers. For better feel when fishing in brush or timber, some anglers *peg* the sinker to the line. Use a $\frac{1}{16}$- or $\frac{1}{8}$-ounce sinker in water less than 6 feet deep, $\frac{1}{8}$- or $\frac{1}{4}$-ounce in 6 to 12 feet, $\frac{1}{4}$- or $\frac{3}{8}$-ounce in 13 to 18 feet and $\frac{3}{8}$- or $\frac{1}{2}$-ounce in water deeper than 18 feet.

To rig a plastic worm for surface fishing, use a plain hook and no sinker. If the worm sinks, cut small slits in the body and imbed bits of styrofoam. Some manufacturers offer worms with extra flotation.

Where snags are not a problem, some anglers thread a worm on a plain jig head or on a plain hook ahead of a slip sinker.

For best results, rig plastic worms on large, long-shank hooks. Many worm hooks have barbs to keep the worm from sliding down the shank. If the shank does not have barbs, slide the worm over the eye of the hook and anchor it by pushing a toothpick

through the worm and eye. Then trim off the ends of the toothpick.

Hook size depends mainly on the size of the worm. Use a #1 or 1/0 hook with a 4-inch worm, a 2/0 or 3/0 with a 6-inch worm, a 4/0 or 5/0 with an 8-inch worm and a 5/0 or 6/0 with a 10-inch worm.

Worm-fishing demands a delicate touch. A strike, or *pick-up*, usually feels like a light tap. But sometimes the line moves off to one side or the worm suddenly feels weightless. Bass take a worm with a quick gulp. If you feel anything unusual, set the hook.

Use a rod heavy enough to drive the hook into a bass's tough jaw, yet sensitive enough to detect a subtle strike. A powerful hook-set places considerable stress on the line. Check it periodically to make sure it is free of nicks. Tie the line directly to the hook using a strong knot such as the World's Fair Knot (page 64).

How to Tie on a Plastic-worm Hook: The World's Fair Knot

WORLD'S FAIR KNOT is easy to tie and has a laboratory-tested strength of 95 percent. Fold the line against itself to create a double strand, then (1) push the doubled line through the eye and form a loop. (2) Bring the doubled line up through the loop. (3) Insert the free end into the space between the loop and the doubled line. (4) Push the free end through the new loop and pull the end tight. (5) Snug up the knot.

How to Fish a Texas-rigged Plastic Worm

CAST, then hold the rod tip high as the worm settles. Allow enough slack so the lure can sink, but keep enough tension so you can detect a strike.

RETRIEVE slowly with a lifting and dropping motion. Keep a tight line as you lower the rod, because bass often take a worm as it sinks.

DROP the rod tip when you detect a pick-up. Lean forward and point the rod at the fish. The bass should not feel any resistance at this crucial point.

How to Rig a Plastic Worm Texas-style

THREAD the line through a sliding cone sinker and tie on a plastic-worm hook. Insert the point about ½ inch into the worm's head.

PUSH the point through and slide the worm up the shank to cover the eye. Rotate the hook one-half turn and bury the point in the worm.

AVOID twisting the plastic worm before inserting the hook. If it does not hang straight, the worm will revolve and twist the line as it is retrieved.

SET the hook immediately with a powerful upward sweep of the rod. Jerk hard enough so the hook penetrates the worm and the bass's jaw. If the first hook-set does not feel solid, set the hook again.

KEEP the rod tip high and the line tight. The bass will lunge for cover the moment it feels the hook. Maintain steady pressure so the fish cannot wrap the line around weeds or brush.

Fishing for Largemouth Bass with Spinnerbaits

The outstanding success of the spinnerbait proves that a lure does not have to imitate natural bass food. A spinnerbait attracts bass with its flash, action and color. These qualities, combined with its semi-snagless design (page 68), make it a favorite among anglers who fish weedy or brushy waters.

The spinnerbait combines two excellent lures, the spinner and the jig. The wire shaft resembles an open safety pin. It has a lead-head jig on the lower arm and one or two spinners on the upper arm. Models with one blade are called *single-spins;* those with a pair of blades are called *tandem* spinnerbaits. The best spinnerbaits have ball-bearing swivels so the blades can turn rapidly. Most models have a plastic or rubber skirt that adds action and conceals the hook.

Many anglers customize their spinnerbaits to change the action or color. Carry a variety of skirts and blades, and keep switching until you find the combination that works best. Some manufacturers make spinnerbaits with straight skirts, but most anglers reverse the skirt for better action (page 69).

Spinnerbaits can be retrieved many different ways. Experiment to find the best retrieve for the situation at hand. Most fishermen use a steady retrieve. But you can buzz a spinnerbait across the surface or crawl it along bottom. The lift-and-drop technique (page 69) will sometimes trigger a strike when bass ignore other retrieves.

Tips for Customizing a Spinnerbait

CUSTOMIZE a spinnerbait by replacing blades or skirts, or by adding attractors. You can change blades easily if the spinnerbait has a snap-swivel on the upper arm. However, blades are not always interchangeable. A blade that is too large will cause the entire lure to revolve. You can add a plastic or pork rind attractor to the hook with the skirt in place, or you can remove the skirt and replace it with an attractor.

ADD a stinger hook by (1) sliding plastic tubing over the eye (arrow). Then thread the main hook through the tubing and eye of the stinger. Or (2) push plastic tabs onto the main hook, one on each side of the stinger.

CLAMP a split-shot, lead wire or pinch-on sinker to the lower arm of a spinnerbait to reach bass in deeper water. The weighted spinnerbait will sink faster, causing the blades to helicopter rapidly.

Three Basic Retrieves for Spinnerbaits

STEADY RETRIEVE. Reel a spinnerbait through weeds or brush, varying the speed and depth on successive retrieves. The hook lies directly behind the wire arms, which keep the hook from fouling in weeds.

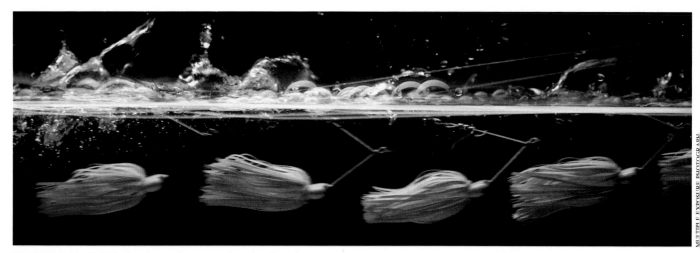

BUZZ RETRIEVE. Begin reeling a tandem-blade spinnerbait as soon as it hits the water. Keep the rod tip high and reel rapidly so the top blade barely breaks the surface. Try this retrieve in warm shallows over heavy cover.

Tips for Fishing With Spinnerbaits

RAP a spinnerbait against submerged brush, stumps or timber to give it an erratic action. Some anglers cast the lure past a visible obstruction such as a bridge piling or dock post, then retrieve to intentionally hit the object. The sudden change in the lure's speed and direction may trigger an immediate strike.

LIFT-AND-DROP RETRIEVE. Cast a spinnerbait, then let it slowly helicopter to bottom. Begin the retrieve by raising the rod to lift the lure. Reel in slack, then lower the rod slowly to ease the lure back to bottom.

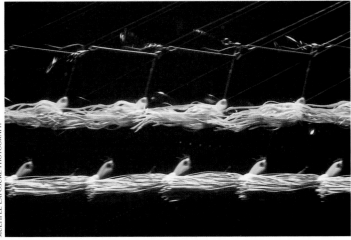

REVERSE the skirt to improve a spinnerbait's action. The reversed skirt on the upper lure flares out and wiggles more than the skirt on the lower spinnerbait.

TUNE a spinnerbait by bending the upper arm (arrow), to align with the hook (dotted line). A properly-tuned spinnerbait runs with its blades on top.

Fishing for Largemouth Bass with Crankbaits

Even the most stubborn largemouth finds it difficult to resist a crankbait wiggling frantically past its nose. Crankbaits work well for locating bass because you can cover a lot of water quickly.

Crankbaits are usually made of molded plastic, although some manufacturers use wood or even metal. Most anglers prefer the 3- or 4-inch sizes, but some use crankbaits up to 8 inches long. Crankbaits often have rattle chambers filled with tiny beads that create extra noise and vibration.

Crankbaits fall into three categories: minnow imitations that either float or sink, floating-diving plugs that float at rest and dive when retrieved, and vibrating plugs that sink. When selecting a crankbait, consider its action and the depth at which it is designed to run.

Floating crankbaits have metal or plastic lips that determine how much the lure wobbles and how deep it tracks. Larger lips give lures a more violent action and make them run deeper.

Large-lipped crankbaits run as deep as 15 feet with no added weight. To reach deeper water, attach a sinker to the line several feet ahead of the lure or rig it on a bottom-walker (page 81). You can make a crankbait run deeper by using lighter line. Thin-

diameter line offers little resistance when pulled through the water. The resistance pushes thicker line toward the surface. A faster retrieve will also draw a floating crankbait deeper.

Sinking crankbaits can be fished at any depth by using the countdown system. Cast the lure, then count while it sinks. Begin your retrieve at different counts until you find the right depth.

For best results, a crankbait should wobble freely. Attach the line to a split-ring or snap. Or tie on the lure with a loop knot such as a bowline (page 73). Snugging the knot directly to a fixed eye will reduce the lure's action, especially when using heavy line.

Most anglers carry a selection of crankbaits. To catch bass consistently, they experiment with different models and retrieves. In many cases, an erratic retrieve such as the stop-and-go-method (page 72) will catch more bass than a steady retrieve.

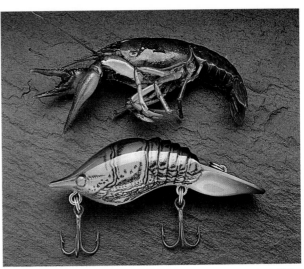

CRANKBAITS often look like crayfish and baitfish. Some manufacturers use a photographic process to give lures a lifelike appearance.

71

Basic Crankbait Shapes and Actions

BODY SHAPE and lip size determine a crankbait's action. Top to bottom are a minnow imitation, a floating-diving plug and a vibrating plug.

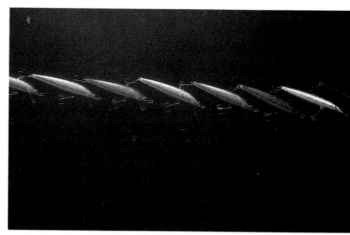

MINNOW IMITATIONS have a long, thin body and a small lip. The line attaches to the eye at the end of the nose. They roll gently from side-to-side.

How to Retrieve a Crankbait by the Stop-and-Go Method

REEL rapidly (left) to pull a floating-diving crankbait below the surface. Continue reeling to draw the lure deeper, then stop momentarily (right) to let it rise. Continue to reel, using the stop-and-go technique. This retrieve is effective when the water is warm and largemouths are active.

FLOATING-DIVING PLUGS usually have a fat body with a large lip that creates a violent, wobbling action. The eye is on the lip or nose.

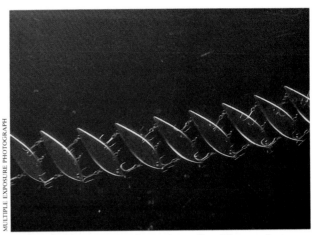

VIBRATING PLUGS do not have lips. The eye is on top and the forehead is usually flattened. These lures have a tight, wiggling action.

How to Tune a Crankbait

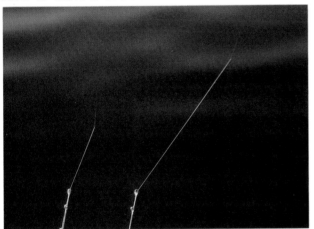

TEST a crankbait to see if it is running straight. The lure at left is working properly; the other is running on its side and tracking to the right.

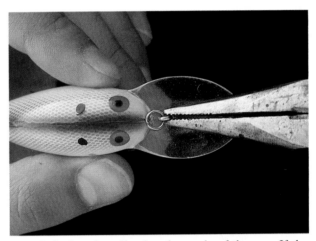

TUNE the lure by adjusting the angle of the eye. If the crankbait is tracking to the right, turn or bend the eye to the left.

How to Tie a Bowline Knot

A BOWLINE KNOT allows a crankbait to swing freely on a loop. (1) Thread the line through the eye and form a loop about 1 inch away. (2) Push the free end through the loop. (3) Wrap the free end around the standing line and push it through the loop again. (4) Snug up the knot by pulling on the free end.

Fishing for Largemouth Bass with Surface Lures

One of the most exciting moments in fishing is just after your surface lure hits the water. As the ripples die, you can almost sense the bass eyeing your lure. You know that the surface may erupt at any second.

Surface, or *topwater*, lures work best on calm summer mornings and evenings when bass are feeding in the shallows. They are not as effective in water below 60°F or when the surface is rough.

Topwater lures may be the only solution for catching bass nestled under thick mats of vegetation. The commotion often attracts bass even though they cannot see the lure. In this type of cover, anglers sometimes catch bass during midday.

Surface lures also work well for night fishing. Bass may not be able to see a deep-running lure. But they can detect the noise and vibration of a topwater lure. And when they move closer, they can see its silhouette against the moonlit sky.

Bass anglers use seven basic types of topwater lures:

PROPELLER-TYPE PLUGS have a long, thin body with a small propeller at one or both ends. Retrieve them by reeling slowly and steadily or in short twitches followed by pauses. Before buying a propeller-type plug, blow on the blades to make sure they turn freely.

POPPERS AND CHUGGERS have a concave face that creates a popping or gurgling sound when retrieved. Most models have a rubber or plastic skirt. A twitch and pause retrieve usually works best, but there are times when bass prefer continuous twitching.

BUZZ BAITS resemble spinnerbaits, but the blade revolves around a shaft rather than spinning on a swivel. The large aluminum blade generates turbulence as the lure churns across the surface. Some models have tandem blades.

TOPWATER CRAWLERS have a metal lip or arms that cause the lure to wobble widely from side to side. Most crawlers make a loud, gurgling sound when retrieved.

STICKBAITS resemble propeller-type plugs, but they lack propellers. Anglers must twitch the lure to give it action.

SURFACE WOBBLERS may look like a spoon or a lead-head jig with a large, upturned metal lip. They have plastic or rubber skirts to disguise the hook. Most have weedguards so they can be skittered across shallow weeds without fouling.

ARTIFICIAL FROGS are made of soft plastic so the legs wiggle enticingly. Most have weedless hooks.

Bass will sometimes follow surface lures repeatedly without striking. You may be able to see the wake just behind the lure. To coax a strike, stop reeling, let the lure rest for several seconds, then twitch it. Not every bass strikes with an explosive smash. Sometimes a strike is merely a gentle slurp. Set the hook immediately after a strike because bass can spit the lure quickly.

How to Retrieve Propeller-type Lures

CAST the lure, then wait for the ripples to die. Leave enough slack so the lure does not move forward.

TWITCH the rod tip slightly so the lure barely moves. Twitching against a slack line produces a sharper jerk.

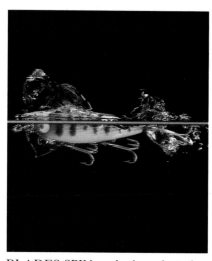

BLADES SPIN as the lure darts forward. Wait for a few seconds, then twitch the lure again.

How to Retrieve Poppers and Chuggers

WAIT for the ripples to subside after casting a popper or chugger. Sometimes bass will strike as the lure bobs on the surface or while it is motionless.

JERK the lure so it pops or chugs across the water. Lower the rod tip and keep the line tight, so you can set the hook the instant a fish strikes.

How to Retrieve a Buzz Bait

RIP a buzz bait across the surface. Its winged blade will churn the water, leaving a wake of bubbles. To make the lure noisier, bend the top arm so the blade clacks against either the shaft or lead head.

How to Retrieve Topwater Crawlers and Stickbaits

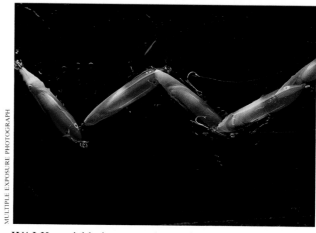

MULTIPLE EXPOSURE PHOTOGRAPH

MULTIPLE EXPOSURE PHOTOGRAPH

JERK a topwater crawler across the surface by twitching the rod tip as you reel steadily. Or reel a short distance, then stop while you twitch the lure. Topwater lures are often used at night.

WALK a stickbait across the surface. Reel slowly while twitching the rod tip. This type of retrieve is widely used by fishermen on southern reservoirs to bring largemouths up from deep water.

How to Retrieve Surface Wobblers and Artificial Frogs

RETRIEVE a surface wobbler slowly. Keep the rod tip high so the lure skims across the surface. These lures can be drawn across dense weeds and brush without snagging or fouling.

CRAWL artificial frogs through lily pads or other float-ing-leaved weeds. Largemouths often strike as the lure moves into a pocket. Some anglers pull the frog onto a pad, then hop it into the water.

VERTICAL JIGGING with a tailspin, vibrating blade or other heavy jigging lure is effective for largemouth bass in cold water. Work the lure close to heavy cover and vary the depth.

Fishing for Largemouth Bass with Jigging Lures

Bass that ignore fast-running plugs will often strike lures jigged vertically near their hiding spots. Jigging lures, including lead-head jigs, jigging spoons, vibrating blades and tailspins, are a good choice when fishing in deep water.

LEAD-HEAD JIGS have feathers, hair, rubber skirts or plastic attractors on the hook. Many anglers tip jigs with live bait. Or they add some type of pork attractor to make a *jig-and-pig* or *jig-and-eel*. Some jigs have nylon bristle weedguards. Jigs can be retrieved with a slow, steady motion, bounced along bottom or jigged vertically.

JIGGING SPOONS are made of heavy metal. Most have a hammered, unpainted finish. They work well during coldwater periods when bass hold tight in timber or along cliff walls. Most spoons are heavy enough to be jigged vertically in water 50 feet deep.

VIBRATING BLADES are made of thin metal. Tie a snap to your line, then attach it to a hole in the lure's back. Jig these lures vertically or retrieve by reeling rapidly. Some anglers use them for trolling. The action is much like a vibrating crankbait.

TAILSPINS have a heavy lead body and a spinner on the tail. They work best for vertical jigging, but can be hopped along bottom or retrieved steadily.

Detecting strikes may be difficult because bass normally strike a jigging lure as it sinks. Keep the line tight to feel the light tap. Set the hook immediately.

Tips for Fishing With Jigging Lures

HOP a jig along bottom when fishing in warm water. Vary the height of the hops to find the retrieve that works best. In cold water, use a slow, straight retrieve or slight twitches.

LOWER a jigging spoon, stopping to jig for a few seconds at different depths. Pause occasionally so the lure hangs motionless. Bass sometimes prefer a lure that is not moving.

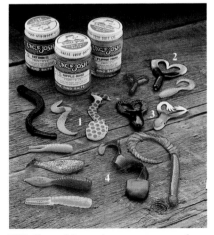

TIP jigs with pork attractors such as (1) eels, Ripple Rind and frogs. Or you can add (2) single- or double-tailed plastic grubs, (3) plastic frogs, or (4) a variety of plastic attractors.

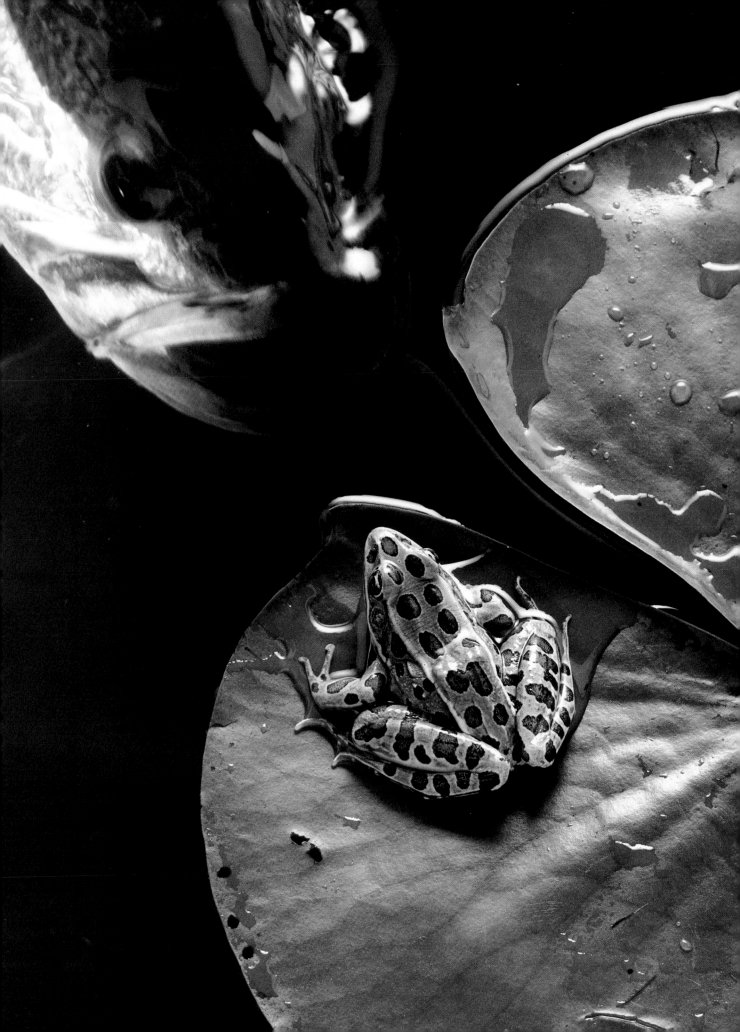

Fishing for Largemouth Bass with Live Bait

The overwhelming majority of bass fishermen use artificial lures. But there is no doubt that live bait works better in many bass-fishing situations.

Trophy bass hunters swear by live bait. A glance at the record book shows that the second largest bass, 21 pounds, 3 ounces, was taken on a crayfish and the third largest, 20 pounds, 15 ounces, was caught on a nightcrawler.

Largemouths are more apt to strike live bait after a cold front, or when the water temperature is above or below their active feeding range. Sluggish bass grab only slow-moving food. But some artificial lures lose their action at slow speeds. Live bait, however, can be inched along bottom or dangled from a bobber. Lethargic bass take more time to examine their food, so they are more likely to spot an imitation.

Bass in extremely clear water can recognize a fake quickly. To catch these wary fish, some fishermen switch to live bait. They use the lightest line possible and keep their boats well away from the fishing zone to avoid spooking bass.

When fishing is slow, anglers often tip their lures with live bait such as worms or minnows. This adds scent appeal to the lure. A lively bait can also add action to a jig, spinner or spinnerbait, although it will ruin the action of a crankbait.

Largemouth bass eat a wider variety of natural foods than most gamefish. They will strike almost any live bait, from an inch-long grasshopper to a foot-long baitfish. The best baits have a lot of action and will stay lively despite repeated casting.

The type and size of bait must suit the fishing conditions. For example, some anglers use a technique called *freelining* to catch bass in thick weeds. They allow the bait to swim into dense cover. This method requires a large bait with enough power to pull the line through the tangle. Big baits generally work best for big bass, especially when the fish are feeding actively. Smaller baits are better when bass are sluggish.

Nationwide, the most popular bass baits include waterdogs, frogs, crayfish and nightcrawlers.

Many experts consider the waterdog the number one bait for largemouth bass. The waterdog is the immature stage, or *larva,* of the tiger salamander. Once the larval salamander turns into an adult, it is less appealing to bass. Waterdogs can be purchased from bait shops or commercial growers in many areas of the country.

Some fishermen still rank frogs as the top bait for largemouth bass, but frog populations have plummeted as a result of disease and wetland drainage. Many anglers regard crayfish as the best bait for smallmouth bass, yet these crustaceans work equally well for largemouths. And while they rarely see earthworms, hungry bass will seldom ignore a gob of wiggling nightcrawlers.

Other live baits have gained popularity in certain regions. Bass in most estuaries prefer live shrimp to any other bait. In weedy lakes of Florida and Georgia, 8- to 12-inch golden shiners account for most trophy largemouths.

Fishermen along the Atlantic Coast are discovering that the American eel is a top bass producer. Known for their hardiness, eels will stay alive for days in a bucket of cool, damp grass.

The siren, a long, thin salamander found in south central and southeastern states, has an enticing, snake-like action. Other salamanders, called spring lizards, have been popular among generations of fishermen in the Southeast.

Hooking and Rigging Live Bait for Largemouth Bass

Even the most irresistible bass bait is worthless if not hooked and rigged properly. Choose the hook, sinker and line that best suits the conditions at hand.

When selecting a hook, consider the size of the bait and the type of cover. With a small hook and large bait, the bass is likely to steal your offering without getting hooked. If the hook is too large, the bait appears unnatural. Always use a weedless hook when fishing in heavy cover.

The size and type of sinker depends on water depth, cover and bottom material. A ⅛- or ¼-ounce sinker works well in water shallower than 15 feet, but deeper water requires more weight to keep the bait near bottom. A cone sinker is best for snaking baits through weeds and brush. A snag-resistant sinker such as a bottom-walker helps you to avoid constant hang-ups when fishing a rocky bottom.

When choosing line, keep in mind the water clarity, the potential for snagging, and the abrasiveness of the cover or bottom. Bass in clear water are most likely to strike live bait presented with clear, thin-diameter monofilament. Use heavier line in murky water or when snags are a problem. Hard-finish, abrasion-resistant line works best in tough weeds or in brush, timber or rocks.

Almost all of the baits and rigs shown on these pages are interchangeable. Anglers should experiment to discover the rigging methods and fishing techniques that work best in their favorite bass waters.

How to Rig Nightcrawlers

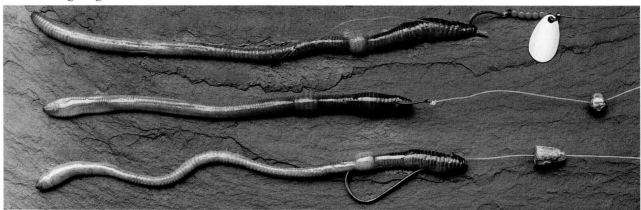

NIGHTCRAWLER RIGS include (top to bottom): #2 hook and spinner with a #8 stinger hook for catching short-striking fish; #4 hook with split-shot for working on a clean bottom; snag-resistant Texas rig with 2/0 hook and ¼-ounce sliding cone sinker for fishing in deep weeds, timber or brush.

How to Rig Minnows

HAIR JIGS tipped with minnows work well when casting or vertical jigging for largemouths along deep structure. Use a ¼-ounce or heavier jig in water deeper than 15 feet.

SPIN-RIGS are designed for tipping with a minnow or nightcrawler. Similar to a spinnerbait, a spin-rig can be retrieved through thick weeds or brush without fouling.

STINGER HOOKS increase your chances of hooking bass, especially when using large baitfish. Insert a 4/0 weedless hook through the lips and a #4 treble hook just ahead of the tail.

How to Rig Frogs and Salamanders

WEEDLESS HOOKS enable you to retrieve live bait through dense cover. Jigs with brushguards can also be tipped with live bait.

JIGS tipped with waterdogs catch bass along deep weedlines. A Pow-rr Head® jig (above) slides through weeds because of its tapered head.

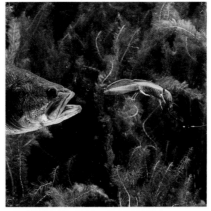

BAIT-SAVER TABS keep a water-dog on the hook. Punch tabs out of a plastic lid. Push on a tab, hook the bait through the lips and add another tab.

How to Rig Crayfish

FLOATING JIGS keep bait above a rocky bottom. Slide a walking sinker on the line, then tie on a swivel, 24-inch leader and #2 floating jig. Hook a crayfish in the tail.

BOTTOM-WALKER RIGS seldom snag on rocks. Tie a ⅛- to ⅜-ounce bottom-walker to your line. Add an 18-inch leader and #2 hook. Push the hook through the tail.

Basic Live Bait Techniques

CASTING enables you to drop live bait into a precise spot, such as a small pocket in the weeds, or the shade of a stump. It is the best technique for working a small area thoroughly.

BOBBER-FISHING works best where casting or trolling would be impossible, like in dense weeds. It is especially effective for sluggish bass in cold or warm water.

TROLLING allows you to cover a timberline, shoreline break or other long, straight edge quickly. Let out enough line so your sinker bounces along the bottom.

Smallmouth Bass

Smallmouth Bass Basics

Known for its aerial acrobatics and never-give-up determination, the smallmouth bass has a well-deserved reputation as the fightingest freshwater gamefish. After a smallmouth strikes, it usually makes a sizzling run for the surface, does a cartwheel in an attempt to throw the hook, then wages a dogged battle in deep water.

The smallmouth bass, *Micropterus dolomieui*, was originally found mainly in the eastern United States. Its range extended from northern Minnesota to southern Quebec on the north, and from northern Georgia to eastern Oklahoma on the south. It was not found east of the Appalachians. But owing to its tremendous popularity, the smallmouth has been widely stocked and is now found in every state with the exceptions of Florida, Louisiana and Alaska. It has also been stocked in most Canadian provinces and in Asia, Africa, Europe and South America.

The smallmouth is sometimes called *bronzeback* because of the bronze reflections from its scales. Other common names include black bass, brown bass, Oswego bass, redeye and green trout.

Like its close relatives the largemouth and spotted bass, the smallmouth belongs to the sunfish family. Smallmouth have been known to hybridize naturally with spotted bass, and biologists have created a smallmouth-largemouth hybrid nicknamed the *meanmouth* because of its aggressive nature.

APPEARANCE of smallmouth (top) differs from that of spotted bass (lower left) and largemouth (lower right). Smallmouth have nine dark vertical bars that come and go, and three bars radiating from the eye. Smallmouth lack the dark horizontal band present on largemouth and spotted bass, and normally have a darker belly. On spotted bass, the horizontal band consists of a row of diamond-shaped dark spots. They may have several rows of spots below the band. The band on largemouth lacks the diamond-shaped spots.

Although smallmouth bass are considered excellent eating, the modern trend in sport fishing is toward catch-and-release, especially in heavily fished waters. Where fishing pressure is heavy, the large smallmouth are quickly removed, leaving only the small ones. Catch-and-release fishing is the best solution to this problem.

On July 9, 1955, D.L. Hayes was trolling a pearl-colored Bomber around a shale point in Dale Hollow Lake, Kentucky. At about 10:00 a.m. he hooked a huge fish, and after a 20-minute fight landed what turned out to be the world-record smallmouth. It weighed 11 pounds, 15 ounces and was 27 inches long.

Smallmouth Bass Range

CHAMELEON EFFECT is shown by these two photos of the same smallmouth. The top photo was taken after the fish had been held in a light-colored tank; the bottom photo after it had been held in a dark-colored tank.

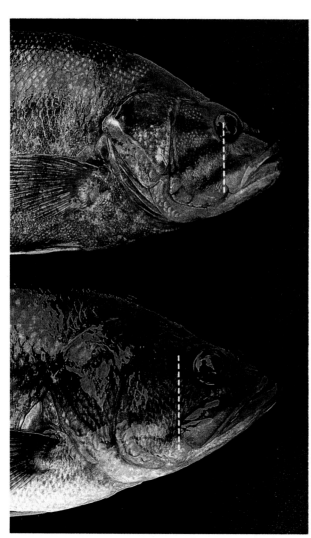

MOUTH SIZE clearly separates smallmouth bass (top) from largemouth bass (bottom). On a smallmouth, the upper jaw extends to the middle of the eye; on a largemouth, beyond the rear of the eye. The mouth of a spotted bass is intermediate in size.

Basswood Lake, Ont. (slightly bog stained)

Lake George, N.Y. (very clear)

Percy Priest Lake, Tenn. (greenish)

COLOR PHASE of smallmouth bass varies greatly in different waters, depending mainly on the color of the water. These photos show three of the many possible color phases. In murky waters, smallmouth often have pale, grayish coloration.

Smallmouth Bass Senses

To find food and escape danger, smallmouth rely on eyesight to a far greater degree than any of their other senses. As a result, good smallmouth fishermen generally use lures with a natural look. And they take great pains to avoid being seen by the smallmouth, especially when fishing in clear water.

Little scientific research has been done on the smallmouth's sensory capabilities, but some conclusions can be drawn based on field observation. For instance, smallmouth evidently have a well-developed lateral-line sense because they can detect lures that produce vibration in water where the visibility is only a few inches. They also have good hearing as evidenced by the fact that they are easily spooked by noise, especially noise that is transmitted directly into the water. Experienced smallmouth fishermen are careful to avoid slamming the live-well lid or dropping the anchor on the floor of the boat.

The sense of smell evidently plays some role in extremely turbid water, but in most other situations it appears to be less important than the other senses. Some smallmouth anglers believe that scent products, particularly crayfish scents, improve their success. But others who have tested scented lures alongside unscented ones have found no difference. Some scent manufacturers claim their products cover up foreign odors, like those of gasoline and human hands. But anglers who have deliberately soaked their lures in gasoline report that these lures catch smallmouth as well as any other lures, whether treated with scent or not.

Studies have shown that smallmouth bass are less line- and lure-wary than largemouth bass, and thus easier to catch. But the degree of wariness varies greatly in different waters, depending mainly on the amount of competition.

In waters where the smallmouth population is low and food plentiful, smallmouth can be extremely wary. Any sudden movement by a fisherman will scare them into deeper water, where they refuse to bite. The best policy is to keep a low profile and avoid throwing your shadow over the fish.

But if the population is high and food relatively scarce, smallmouth are not as wary and spooking is not as much of a problem. In fact, scuba divers have attracted smallmouth to within a few feet by tapping rocks on their air tanks.

*How the Senses of Smallmouth Bass Compare to Those of Other Gamefish**

FISH SPECIES	DAYTIME VISION	NIGHT VISION	LATERAL LINE	SMELL	HEARING
Smallmouth Bass	Excellent	Fair	Good	Fair	Good
Spotted Bass	Excellent	Good	Good	Fair	Good
Largemouth Bass	Good	Fair	Good	Fair	Good
Walleye	Fair	Excellent	Good	Fair	Good
Sauger	Fair	Excellent	Excellent	Fair	Good
Yellow Perch	Good	Poor	Fair	Fair	Fair
Crappie	Good	Good	Fair	Fair	Fair
Bluegill	Excellent	Fair	Fair	Good	Fair
Northern Pike	Excellent	Poor	Good	Poor	Good
Catfish	Fair	Fair	Excellent	Excellent	Excellent

*Ratings determined from a survey of prominent fish physiologists and fisheries biologists.

Smallmouth Bass Habitat Preferences

Smallmouth bass are fish of clear, clean waters. They are equally at home in streams and lakes, but are rarely found in small ponds, lakes shallower than 25 feet, or any water that is continuously murky or polluted.

To locate smallmouth, you should become familiar with their preferences in regard to the following environmental conditions:

TEMPERATURE. During the summer months, smallmouth in northern lakes are usually found at water temperatures from 67° to 71°F and seldom at temperatures above 80°. But smallmouth in south-ern reservoirs are often found at temperatures of 78° to 84°. This difference can be explained by the fact that the deeper, cooler water in the reservoirs lacks sufficient oxygen in summer.

Laboratory tests have shown that smallmouth pre-fer a temperature of about 82°F. But most of these tests were conducted using juvenile smallmouth, whose temperature preference is considerably high-er than that of the adults.

These findings have great significance for small-mouth fishermen. If you are fishing in shallow water and catching nothing but undersized smallmouth, you may be able to catch bigger ones by fishing several feet deeper.

During the cold months, smallmouth activity drops off. In laboratory studies, smallmouth fed very little at temperatures below 50°F and lay motionless on the bottom at temperatures below 40°. In their natu-ral surroundings, smallmouth respond to tempera-ture in much the same way.

OXYGEN. Smallmouth can tolerate an oxygen level of 2.5 parts per million, while largemouth can survive at 2.0. This slight difference may explain why largemouth are better able to tolerate stagnant water. But neither species fares well at oxygen levels this low. Feeding and growth are severely reduced if the level remains below 5 parts per million for an extended period.

In most smallmouth waters, the oxygen level is adequate throughout the depths that smallmouth prefer. So measuring oxygen levels will not help you locate the fish. But in highly fertile waters, smallmouth may be confined to shallow water in summer because the depths lack sufficient oxygen.

pH. Smallmouth are found in waters with a pH from 5 to 9. Although the best smallmouth populations are usually found where the pH is from 7.9 to 8.1, there is no research to indicate that smallmouth prefer any specific pH level. Canadian researchers found that smallmouth were unable to successfully reproduce at pH levels from 5.5 to 6.0.

Temperature Preferences and Oxygen Requirements of Various Freshwater Fish

SPECIES	PREFERRED SUMMER TEMP.	OXYGEN REQUIRE-MENT*
Smallmouth bass	67-71°F	2.5 ppm
Largemouth bass	68-78°F	2.0 ppm
Bluegill	75-80°F	3.5 ppm
Walleye	65-75°F	4.0 ppm
Northern pike		1.4 ppm
under 7 pounds	65-70°F	
over 7 pounds	50-55°F	
Brook trout	52-56°F	5.0 ppm
Rainbow trout	55-60°F	1.5 ppm
Black bullhead	78-84°F	less than 1 ppm

* Minimum requirement (in parts per million) for long-term survival at summertime temperatures. Oxygen requirements decrease at lower water temperatures.

CURRENT. Smallmouth prefer moderate current, usually in the range of 0.4 to 1.3 feet per second. This range is slower than that preferred by trout, but faster than that favored by largemouth bass. With a little experience, you will be able to recognize the right current speed.

In most streams, smallmouth are more numerous in pools with noticeable current than in pools where the water is completely slack.

In lakes, smallmouth often concentrate around river mouths or in areas with wind-induced current, such as a trough between two islands or a narrow channel between two major lobes of a lake.

DEPTH. Smallmouth are generally considered fish of the *epilimnion,* the upper layer of water in a lake that is stratified into temperature layers. They are most likely to be found in shallow areas adjacent to deep water. The depths offer smallmouth refuge from intense light and boat traffic.

In waters that have both smallmouth and largemouth, the smallmouth are usually slightly deeper. Generally, smallmouth stay deep enough that they are not visible from the surface.

In spring, summer and early fall, smallmouth are seldom found at depths exceeding 30 feet. But in late fall and winter, they often congregate in tight schools at depths down to 60 feet.

CLARITY. Although smallmouth will tolerate murky water for short periods, they rarely live in water that remains murky year-around. As a rule, waters where the usual visibility is less than 1 foot do not hold substantial smallmouth populations.

If the water is murky in one portion of a lake but clear in another, chances are that smallmouth will be most numerous in the clearer area. Similarly, smallmouth are usually more plentiful in a clear reach of a stream than in a muddy reach. And in extremely fertile lakes, smallmouth bite best in spring, before intense algal blooms cloud the water, and in fall, after the algae has died back.

BOTTOM TYPE. In most waters, smallmouth are found over a bottom consisting of clean rocks or gravel. This type of bottom is usually rich in smallmouth foods including crayfish and larval insects like dragonfly nymphs and hellgrammites. But in lakes where most of the basin consists of rock, smallmouth often prefer sandy shoal areas, especially those with a sparse growth of weeds. The sandy, weedy areas will hold fewer crayfish and insect larvae, but more baitfish.

SPAWNING HABITAT. To spawn successfully, smallmouth need a rock, gravel or hard sand bottom. Nests on silty bottoms are seldom successful. Stream smallmouth nest in light current, but avoid swift current. The best spawning areas have boulders or other large objects to protect one side of the nest. Waters that tend to remain muddy for long periods of time following a heavy rain are not well suited to successful smallmouth spawning. The suspended silt makes it difficult for the male to defend his nest, and silt deposited on the eggs prevents them from absorbing enough oxygen.

COMPETITOR SPECIES. Populations of other species that compete with smallmouth for food, living space or spawning habitat can greatly affect the size of the smallmouth population and the way the smallmouth behave. Compared to most other freshwater gamefish, smallmouth are poor competitors. If a body of water contains a large number of shallow-water predators like largemouth bass (right) or northern pike, chances are it will not support a dense smallmouth population.

Competition with other fish species can be a major factor in determining smallmouth location. Most reservoirs in the mid-South, for instance, have good populations of largemouth and spotted bass. If largemouth are numerous, smallmouth and spotted bass are normally found in the main-lake portion of the reservoir where the water is relatively deep and clear. Largemouth tend to dominate the upper portion where the water is shallower and the clarity lower. Largemouth also concentrate in shallow creek arms and wherever there is weedy or brushy cover. In reservoirs with fewer largemouth, the smallmouth and spotted bass may occupy the upper as well as the lower portion.

Smallmouth Bass Feeding & Growth

If you have ever caught a smallmouth and examined its stomach contents, chances are you found pieces of crayfish. Where crayfish are plentiful, they make up at least two-thirds of the smallmouth's diet.

Because crayfish inhabit the same rocky areas that smallmouth do, they make a convenient target for feeding bass. Other important food items include fish, adult and immature insects, and tadpoles.

The diet of smallmouth bass may vary from season to season, depending on the availability of food. In a five-year food-habits study conducted in Nebish Lake, Wisconsin, crayfish made up 83 percent of the smallmouth's diet in September, but only 14 percent in May. Insects made up 34 percent of the diet in May, but only 4 percent in July.

Smallmouth feed very little during cold-water periods. Normally, they begin feeding in spring when the water temperature reaches about 47°F. Food consumption peaks when the water reaches about 78°. When the water temperature drops below 40° in fall, practically no feeding takes place. However, in some high-competition waters, smallmouth continue to feed through the ice-cover season.

Smallmouth bass differ from most freshwater gamefish in that males and females grow at about the same rate. Smallmouth in lakes and reservoirs usually grow faster and reach a larger size than those in streams. And smallmouth in southern waters generally grow faster than those in the North. The table at right shows how growth rates vary. In Norris Lake, Tennessee, for instance, an age-6 smallmouth measures 18 inches (about 4 pounds); in Lake Opeongo, Ontario, a smallmouth of the same age measures only 12.2 inches (about 1 pound).

Although smallmouth grow much faster in the South, their maximum size varies less from North to South than would be expected. Smallmouth live as long as 18 years in the North, but seldom longer than 7 years in the South. Higher metabolic rates cause faster burnout (page 125) in southern waters.

Smallmouth weighing up to 11 pounds, 8 ounces have been taken from Canadian waters, and there are probably as many 5-pound-plus smallmouth caught in the North as in the South.

How to Select Lures Based on Stomach Contents

WHOLE CRAYFISH or crayfish parts mean a crayfish-colored crankbait may be effective.

SHINER MINNOWS mean that a small, silver-colored minnow plug would be a good choice.

IMMATURE INSECTS can be imitated with a dark-colored jig or a nymph.

ADULT INSECTS indicate that smallmouth will probably take a large dry fly or a bass bug.

Growth Rates of Smallmouth Bass at Different Latitudes

Lake Name and Latitude	Length in Inches at Various Ages									
	Age 1	2	3	4	5	6	7	8	9	10
Lake Opeongo, Ont. (46°N)	2.1	5.2	7.7	9.1	11.1	12.2	13.5	14.5	15.5	—
Northern Lake Michigan (45°N)	3.9	6.3	8.1	9.7	11.5	13.2	14.6	15.8	16.8	17.4
Lake Simcoe, Ont. (44°N)	4.2	6.3	8.6	10.9	13.0	14.6	15.8	16.9	17.0	—
Quabbin Lake, Mass. (42½°N)	3.5	6.7	10.2	12.9	14.7	16.1	16.7	17.1	17.3	17.5
Pine Flat Lake, Cal. (37°N)	5.5	8.9	12.5	14.7	16.6	17.9	18.3	—	—	—
Norris Lake, Tenn. (36°N)	3.1	8.9	13.3	15.8	17.4	18.0	18.6	20.9	—	—
Pickwick Lake, Ala. (35°N)	5.9	10.7	13.5	16.6	18.5	20.4	21.0	21.6	—	—

Smallmouth Bass Spawning Behavior

Smallmouth bass can spawn successfully in lakes or streams, and the areas they choose for spawning in streams differ very little from the areas they choose in lakes.

A typical spawning site is near an object like a rock or log which shelters it from strong current or wave action. Such an object also makes it easier for a male to guard the nest because predators cannot sneak in from behind. Nests are usually in water 2 to 4 feet deep, although they have been found in water as deep as 20 feet. Smallmouth almost always nest on sand, gravel or rubble and avoid mud bottoms.

Males begin building nests in spring, when the water temperature stabilizes above 55°F. The male uses his tail to fan out a circular nest with a diameter about twice as great as his own length. On a rubble bottom, he simply sweeps debris off the rocks. But on a sand or gravel bottom, he fans out a depression from 2 to 4 inches deep. A male nests in the same general area each year and will sometimes use the same nest.

Females move into the vicinity of the nest a few days later. When a male spots a female, he rushes toward her and attempts to drive her to the nest. At first, she swims away, but she returns again later. Eventually, the male coaxes her to the nest. Spawning usually occurs at a water temperature of 60° to 65°F, about 3 degrees cooler than the typical spawning temperature of largemouth bass.

As the spawning act begins, the fish lie side by side, both facing the same direction. Then the female tips on her side to deposit her eggs and the male simultaneously releases his milt. Females deposit an average of 7,000 eggs per pound of body weight.

The female leaves after spawning, but the male remains and vigorously guards the nest against any intruders. He will attack fish much larger than himself and may even bump a wading fisherman who gets too close. The amount of time required for hatching depends on water temperature. At 54°F, the eggs hatch in ten days; at 77°, two days. On the average, 35 percent of the eggs hatch.

The male guards the fry on the nest for 5 to 7 days and usually continues to guard them for another week or two after the school leaves the nest. Of the fry that leave the nest, only about 10 percent survive to fingerling size.

Fishermen can destroy smallmouth nests by stepping on them or by catching the guarding male. If panfish are numerous, they quickly consume the eggs or fry once the male is gone.

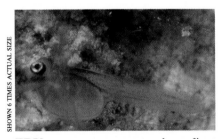

FRY are transparent when first hatched. They have a large, yellowish egg sac that nurtures them through the first 6 to 12 days of life.

BLACK COLORATION begins to appear within a few days after the fry hatch. This explains the origin of the term *black bass*.

FINGERLINGS are 3 to 5 inches long by the end of the first summer. The tail fin has a brownish-orange base and a distinct whitish margin.

MALES guard the fry (small black spots in foreground) to protect them against predators, particularly small panfish. In one study, a single bluegill ate 39 smallmouth fry when the male was momentarily driven away.

OBJECT FISHING is effective when smallmouth are in the shallows. Motor along slowly, looking for boulders, logs, stumps, brush piles or any other visible object that provides shade. Cast as close to the object as possible, making sure to work the shady side. Wear polarized glasses so you can see objects below the surface. Do not spend too much time in one spot; the active fish will usually bite on the first or second cast.

Smallmouth-Fishing Fundamentals

To catch smallmouth bass consistently, you must understand a few basic fishing principles that always apply, regardless of the technique you use.

· Smallmouth are object-oriented, meaning that they like to get next to something. Their favorite type of object is a large rock. They are sometimes found around weeds, but are not as weed-oriented as largemouth.

· In a given body of water, smallmouth can usually be found deeper than largemouth, but shallower than walleye.

· Smallmouth school by size, so if you are catching nothing but small ones, try a different area.

· Smallmouth have different personalities in different waters. In high-competition waters, they tend to be aggressive, so a variety of presentations will work. But in low-competition waters, they can be very finicky. Here, a slow, tantalizing presentation draws the most strikes.

· Small-sized smallmouth are more aggressive than large ones and generally inhabit shallower water.

· Smallmouth are prone to spooking, even in waters where they are normally aggressive.

· Most smallmouth are caught near the bottom, but you can also catch them on the surface. However, they are not as vulnerable to surface presentations as largemouth.

· In most waters, smallmouth bite best in early morning. In clear lakes, they may bite best at night, especially in summer.

SELECT small lures and baits when fishing for smallmouth bass. A smallmouth (top) would prefer a 4-inch plastic worm, for instance, while a largemouth (bottom) would prefer a 7-inch worm.

KEEP a low profile to avoid spooking smallmouth. Pay attention to the sun so you do not cast your shadow over the fish. Keep your movement to a minimum and do not drop anything on the bottom of the boat.

Fishing for Smallmouth Bass with Artificial Lures
How to Catch Smallmouth Bass with Jigs

If you were limited to only one lure for all of your smallmouth fishing, your best choice would undoubtedly be a lead-head jig. A jig will catch smallmouth in any type of water at any time of year. And you can work a jig through practically any type of cover and at any depth where smallmouth are likely to be found.

JIGGING BASICS. Jig fishing for smallmouth is much like jig fishing for largemouth or walleyes. Smallmouth generally strike as the jig is sinking, so you must keep a taut line at this critical stage. If you let the line go slack as the jig sinks, you will probably not feel the strike.

Even with a taut line, smallmouth strikes may be difficult to feel. In cold water or whenever a smallmouth is not in the mood to feed, it swims up to a jig and simply closes its mouth on it. You may feel a little extra weight, or the line may go slack or move slightly to the side. If you do not set the hook quickly, the smallmouth will spit the jig.

Detecting these subtle strikes is much easier with a sensitive rod. A 5¼- to 6-foot, fast-action, medium-power graphite spinning rod designed for 6- to 8-pound mono is a good all-around choice. For casting tiny jigs around shallow cover, many anglers prefer a 5- to 5½-foot ultralight graphite spinning rod with 4- to 6-pound mono.

The way you work your jig depends on the time of year and the mood of the smallmouth. During cold-water periods, a gentle twitch or slow lift is usually more effective than a sharp snap. But in warm water, a sharp snap may work better.

Because smallmouth prefer subtle colors, some expert fishermen use unpainted jig heads. The gray color has a natural minnow-like look, especially when the jig is tipped with a smoke-, amber- or motor oil-colored grub tail. Other popular jig colors are black, brown, white and green. Bright or fluorescent colors are used mainly in murky water and around spawning time.

In most situations, tipping your jig with live bait is not necessary. In fact, tipping may result in fewer smallmouth because they tend to strike short. But tipping will probably improve your success at water temperatures below 55°F, in low-competition waters and under cold-front conditions.

Instead of live bait, many experts use a 2-inch pork strip for tipping their jigs. A pork strip has a true-to-life action and is nearly impossible to tear off the hook. Most pork strips are designed for largemouth

How Smallmouth Take a Jig

STRIKES (left) often feel like a light tap, a sensation created when a smallmouth inhales the jig in vacuum-like fashion. If it detects something unnatural, a smallmouth expels the jig (right) within a fraction of a second. Experienced fishermen know they must set the hook instantly at any hint of a strike.

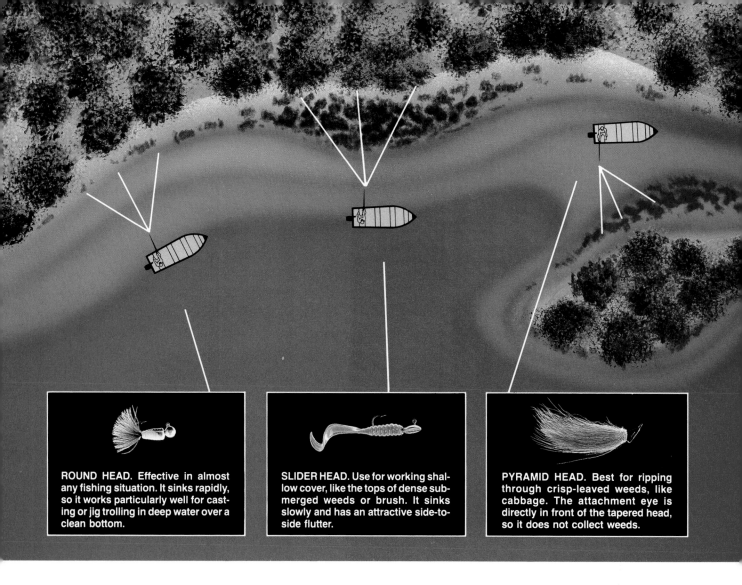

ROUND HEAD. Effective in almost any fishing situation. It sinks rapidly, so it works particularly well for casting or jig trolling in deep water over a clean bottom.

SLIDER HEAD. Use for working shallow cover, like the tops of dense submerged weeds or brush. It sinks slowly and has an attractive side-to-side flutter.

PYRAMID HEAD. Best for ripping through crisp-leaved weeds, like cabbage. The attachment eye is directly in front of the tapered head, so it does not collect weeds.

and are too big for smallmouth, so you have to cut them to size.

Versatile smallmouth fishermen use several different jig-fishing techniques, including casting, jig trolling and vertical jigging. Each technique has its advantages and disadvantages.

CASTING. Casting with a jig is extremely effective in a wide variety of smallmouth-fishing situations.

When smallmouth are holding in the shade of rocks, logs or other objects, cast a jig and let it sink into their hiding spot. Often, a smallmouth will grab the jig before it hits bottom.

To catch smallmouth in stream pools or eddies, cast a jig into the slack water. It will sink into the fish zone before the current sweeps it away.

When smallmouth are scattered along a breakline, drift or slowly motor along just out from it, cast a jig into the shallows, then retrieve down the drop-off.

To work a specific piece of structure, like a sharp point or small reef, anchor your boat and cast. If you suspect the smallmouth are in shallow water, anchor in deep water, cast into the shallows and retrieve downhill. You will need a long rope to make the anchor hold. If the fish are deep, anchor in the shallows and retrieve uphill, or anchor along the drop-off and retrieve parallel to the break.

For casting into shallow water, use a slow-sinking jig. A slower sink rate is more attractive to smallmouth and results in fewer snags. Use a $\frac{1}{16}$- to $\frac{1}{8}$-ounce jig in depths of 10 feet or less. Some fishermen use a slider-type jig with a buoyant dressing. Others mold their own jig heads using tin instead of lead. Smallmouth like the shine of the tin head and the sink rate is much slower than that of a lead head.

JIG TROLLING. This technique has not gained widespread popularity, but is one of the best ways to locate smallmouth. It enables you to cover a lot of territory while keeping your jig in the most productive depth range.

The technique works best in water of moderate depth, usually from 12 to 20 feet. In shallower water, jig trolling may spook smallmouth; in deeper water, you may have trouble maintaining bottom contact.

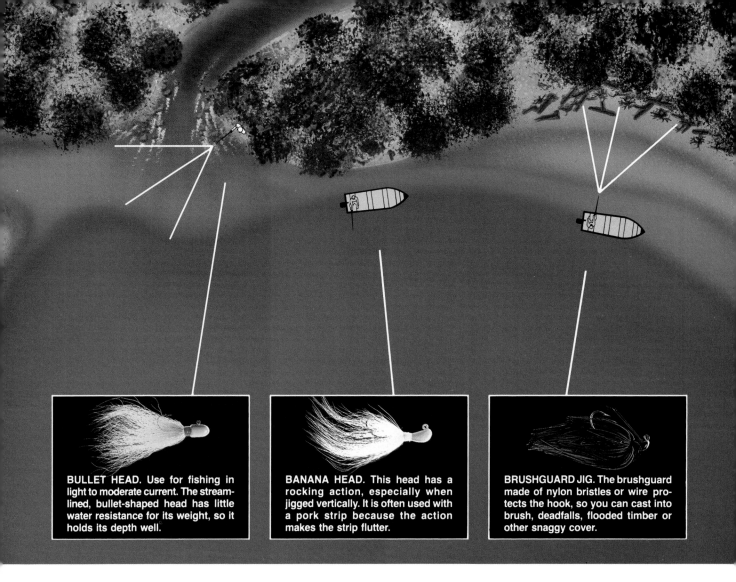

BULLET HEAD. Use for fishing in light to moderate current. The streamlined, bullet-shaped head has little water resistance for its weight, so it holds its depth well.

BANANA HEAD. This head has a rocking action, especially when jigged vertically. It is often used with a pork strip because the action makes the strip flutter.

BRUSHGUARD JIG. The brushguard made of nylon bristles or wire protects the hook, so you can cast into brush, deadfalls, flooded timber or other snaggy cover.

Jig trolling requires moving the boat very slowly while precisely following a contour. The best way to control your speed and depth is to backtroll with an electric motor.

To begin jig trolling, lower your jig to bottom. Let out only enough line so your jig can touch. Repeatedly lift the jig and lower it until you see the line go slack. Being able to see your line go slack after each jigging stroke is the key to successful jig trolling.

If you troll into deeper water, you will lose bottom contact, so the line will not go slack. Let out just enough line to reach bottom, then continue trolling. If you troll into shallower water, too much line will drag on bottom. You will not see your line go slack because the jig does not lift off bottom even though you are lifting your rod. The best solution is to reel in your jig, then start over.

A round-head jig is a good choice for jig trolling because it sinks rapidly, enabling you to feel bottom easily. Use a ⅛- to ¼-ounce jig in depths down to 20 feet. In deeper water or in windy weather, you may need a ⅜-ounce jig. Avoid using bulky bucktail or large soft-plastic dressings that reduce the sink rate, making it difficult to maintain bottom contact.

VERTICAL JIGGING. One of the best deep-water techniques, vertical jigging is especially effective in late fall and winter, when smallmouth commonly retreat to depths of 30 to 50 feet and form tight schools. In summer, vertical jigging works well in waters of low to moderate clarity.

Working a jig in deep water requires hovering over a specific spot while jigging straight up and down. On a calm day, keeping the boat stationary is no problem. But on a windy day, you must point the transom of your boat into the wind, put your motor into reverse, and adjust the throttle to compensate for the wind.

If you are accustomed to jig fishing and have a sensitive touch, you can get by with a jig as light as ¼ ounce. But most fishermen use ⅜- to ½-ounce jigs for vertical jigging.

Because of line stretch at these extreme depths, detecting strikes may be difficult. Low-stretch line makes it easier to feel a slight tap or nudge.

Fishing for Smallmouth Bass with Jigging Lures

When smallmouth are tightly schooled in deep water, a jigging lure is an excellent choice. You can hold your boat directly over the school and vertically jig so the lure is continually in the fish zone. And the constant jigging motion may irritate an uninterested smallmouth into striking.

Any jigging lure will catch smallmouth, but each type has its advantages and disadvantages.

Tailspins work well in water with few obstructions. The spinner blade on the tail turns as the lure is pulled forward and helicopters as it sinks. Helicoptering slows the sink rate, giving the fish extra time to strike. But tailspins are prone to snagging, so they are not a good choice in heavy cover.

The heavy lead body of a tailspin is ideal for long-distance casting. In clear water, for instance, you can cast to distant objects, yet keep your boat far enough away that you do not spook the fish. Retrieve the tailspin using the helicoptering technique shown on the opposite page.

Vibrating blades are a good choice in murky water, but they also work well in clear water. The rapid wiggling action produces intense vibrations that smallmouth can easily detect with their lateral line. Most vibrating blades have two or more holes on the back for attaching a round-nosed snap. Placing the snap in the front hole results in a tight wiggle; the rear hole, a looser wobble. Like tailspins, vibrating blades are prone to snagging in heavy cover.

Although vibrating blades are most commonly used for vertical jigging, you can also use them for casting or trolling, much the way you would use a crankbait.

Jigging spoons have an attractive fluttering action when they sink. To a smallmouth, the action probably resembles that of an injured minnow. Jigging spoons are effective in heavy cover, like flooded timber or brush. If you get snagged, twitch the rod tip to make the spoon dance up and down. The long, heavy body swings downward with enough force to free the hook from the snag.

KEEP your line tight as a jigging lure sinks, but not too tight. If the line goes slack, a smallmouth may grab the lure and eject it without your realizing you had a strike. If you keep too much tension on the line, the lure will lose its spinning or fluttering action because it cannot sink freely. To maintain the right tension, lower your rod tip at the same rate the lure sinks, watching for the line to twitch or suddenly go slack.

But the long, heavy body can be a problem when playing a smallmouth. If the fish jumps and shakes its head, it can easily throw the spoon. If you keep a tight line, however, the chances it will throw the spoon are greatly reduced.

Jigging lures commonly used for ice fishing will also catch smallmouth during the open-water season. A lead-bodied jigging minnow works especially well because it darts to the side when jigged vertically, covering more water than most other jigging lures.

The principles of fishing with a jigging lure are much the same as with a lead-head jig. Because smallmouth generally strike as the lure is sinking, you must keep enough tension on your line that the impulse of the strike telegraphs to your rod.

For ¼- to ⅝-ounce jigging lures, use 8- to 10-pound mono. For lures over ⅝ ounce, use 12- to 14-pound mono. Most anglers prefer a stiff 6- to 7-foot bait-casting rod. This type of rod works especially well for jigging vertically. You can snap the lure sharply, and if you drift into shallower water and develop slack line, the length still gives you enough sweep to set the hook.

JIGGING LURES include: (1) tailspin, which should be tied directly to the line; (2) jigging spoon, attached with split-ring or snap-swivel; (3) vibrating blade, attached with cross-lock snap; and (4) jigging minnow, tied directly to the line or attached with cross-lock snap.

LINE UP casting targets so you can work two or more with one cast. To work a tree line with a tailspin, cast beyond one tree, reel up to it, and let the lure helicopter alongside. Then, reel to another tree and repeat.

AVOID attaching a vibrating blade with a snap-swivel. When you jig, the hooks will tangle in the swivel and ruin the lure's action. If you attach the blade with a plain round-nosed snap, the hooks will not tangle.

Fishing for Smallmouth Bass with Plugs

Even though a smallmouth can throw a plug more easily than most other lures, plugs account for a surprising number of trophy-class smallmouth, including the current world record.

Experienced smallmouth fishermen prefer small plugs, generally 2 to 3 inches in length. Some anglers use plugs up to 6 inches long when fishing for big smallmouth, but a plug that long greatly reduces the number of strikes.

The best type of plug to use for smallmouth depends on the season, time of day, water and weather conditions, and mood of the fish. Effective types include surface plugs such as propbaits, stickbaits, chuggers and crawlers; and subsurface plugs such as minnow plugs, crankbaits and vibrating plugs.

SURFACE PLUGS. These plugs work best when smallmouth are in the shallows. They are most effective during the spawning period or at water temperatures above 60°F. They do not work well in rough water. The best times to catch smallmouth on surface plugs are early morning, around dusk or after dark.

In general, the best surface plugs for smallmouth are those which create the least surface disturbance. Smallmouth differ from largemouth in that they will not tolerate as much commotion.

Propbaits are probably the best all-around surface plugs for smallmouth. Use a twitch-and-pause retrieve, moving your plug just enough to make the blades spin. When smallmouth are spooky or not in the mood to feed, long pauses usually draw more strikes than short ones. Some fishermen wait as long as a minute between twitches. A steady retrieve seldom works for smallmouth.

Make sure your propbait is properly tuned by blowing on the blades. If they do not spin freely, bend them until they do.

Stickbaits are more difficult to use than propbaits, but they work better over deep water. If the water is clear, they may draw smallmouth from depths as great as 20 feet. When retrieved with short, sharp jerks, a stickbait dances enticingly from side to side, mimicking an injured minnow.

Chuggers are used mainly for largemouth, but they will catch smallmouth if worked properly. The most common mistake is to twitch the chugger too hard, causing a big splash and spooking the fish. Instead, work it with short, gentle twitches followed by pauses. Chuggers do not work well in current because they dig too much water.

Crawlers create a lot of surface disturbance and do not work as well as other surface lures during daylight hours. But they can be effective at night, when smallmouth are more aggressive and less easily spooked. Normally, crawlers are retrieved steadily so they produce a gurgling sound, but for smallmouth a reel-and-pause retrieve often works better.

Surface plugs should be tied directly to the line. A snap-swivel or steel leader may weight down the nose of the plug so it catches too much water when retrieved. A 5½- to 6-foot medium-power spinning or baitcasting outfit with 6- to 10-pound mono is adequate for most surface plugs.

SUBSURFACE PLUGS. These plugs will catch smallmouth under a much wider variety of conditions than surface plugs. They work well in rough water and at water temperatures as low as 50°F. Subsurface plugs can be fished by trolling as well as casting, and at any depth where smallmouth are likely to be found.

Minnow plugs come in floating and sinking models, but floaters seem to work best for smallmouth. Most floaters have short lips and run at depths of 5 feet or less. But long-lipped floaters run as deep as 12 feet.

When smallmouth are in very shallow water, twitch a short-lipped floater so it darts just beneath the surface then floats back up. Pause occasionally between twitches as you would with a surface plug. A hungry smallmouth finds this erratic retrieve difficult to resist.

In deeper water, use a steady retrieve with a periodic twitch to change the action. By attaching your minnow plug to a three-way swivel rig or adding a pinch-on sinker to your line, you can easily reach depths of 20 feet or more.

Minnow plugs are light for their size, so they are difficult to cast. To make casting easier, use 4- to

6-pound mono and a spinning rod with a light tip. To avoid dampening the plug's action, attach it with a loop knot or small, round-nosed snap. For extra wiggle, position your knot on the lower part of the attachment eye.

Crankbaits come in shallow- and deep-running models. Shallow runners have small, sharply sloping lips and track at 6 feet or less. Deep runners have lips that do not slope as sharply. They track as deep as 12 feet. Some extra-deep runners track as deep as 18 feet and reach depths of 25 feet when trolled.

Crankbaits can be cast a long distance and retrieved rapidly, so they will cover a lot of water. The large lip tends to deflect off obstructions, keeping the hooks from snagging. Because of their snag resistance, crankbaits are ideal for working the rocky shorelines and reefs where smallmouth are commonly found.

In cold water or whenever smallmouth are not in the mood to feed, a slow, stop-and-go retrieve is more effective than a fast, steady retrieve. But in warm water, the reverse is sometimes true.

Trolling a deep-running crankbait along a breakline or over a deep reef is an excellent technique for locating smallmouth. If you find a school of smallmouth but they quit biting, you can switch to a slower method like jig or live-bait fishing.

Whether you are casting over a 5-foot flat with a shallow-running crankbait or trolling a 15-foot reef with a deep runner, try to keep the crankbait's lip digging bottom or bumping obstructions. The interruption in the action triggers more strikes.

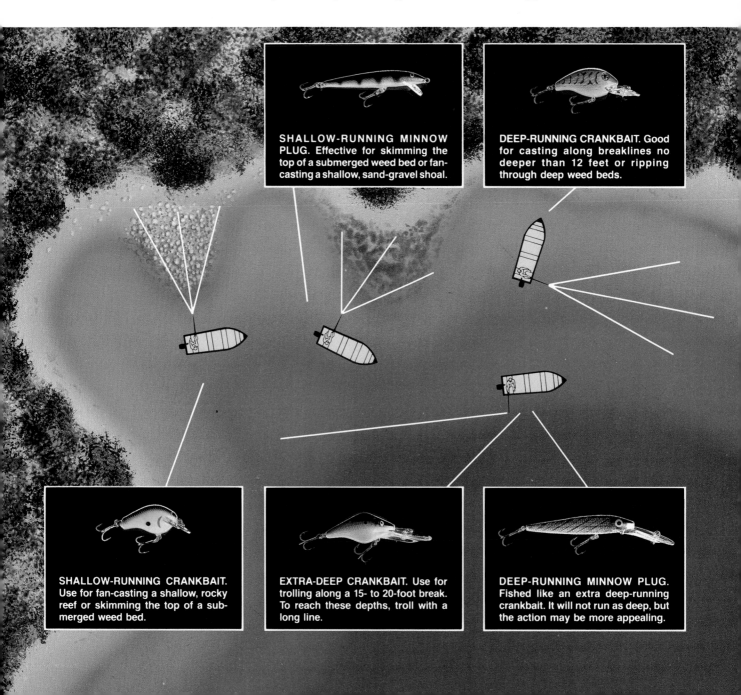

SHALLOW-RUNNING MINNOW PLUG. Effective for skimming the top of a submerged weed bed or fan-casting a shallow, sand-gravel shoal.

DEEP-RUNNING CRANKBAIT. Good for casting along breaklines no deeper than 12 feet or ripping through deep weed beds.

SHALLOW-RUNNING CRANKBAIT. Use for fan-casting a shallow, rocky reef or skimming the top of a submerged weed bed.

EXTRA-DEEP CRANKBAIT. Use for trolling along a 15- to 20-foot break. To reach these depths, troll with a long line.

DEEP-RUNNING MINNOW PLUG. Fished like an extra deep-running crankbait. It will not run as deep, but the action may be more appealing.

Deep-running crankbaits have a lot of water resistance, so most veteran anglers prefer medium-power baitcasting or spinning gear with 8- to 14-pound mono. For most shallow runners, light- to medium-power spinning gear with 6- to 10-pound mono is adequate. If your crankbait comes with a split-ring or snap, tie your line directly to it. If not, attach the lure with a small, round-nosed snap or a loop knot.

Minnow plugs and crankbaits must be properly tuned for peak performance. If the plug veers to the side, it is out of tune. To make it run straight, bend or turn the attachment eye in the direction opposite the way the plug is veering.

Vibrating plugs have a tight wiggle that appeals to smallmouth. They work best when retrieved at medium to high speed.

The vibrating action makes them especially effective in murky water. Models with beads or shot inside a rattle chamber create even more vibration and noise. But vibrating plugs do not have lips, so they snag more easily than crankbaits.

You can fish vibrating plugs at practically any depth. To fish in the shallows, begin your retrieve as soon as the plug hits the water. To fish in deeper water, feed enough line to let the plug reach bottom before beginning your retrieve. Keep the lure near bottom by pausing occasionally to let it sink.

Vibrating plugs, especially those with lead shot, are easy to cast. A medium-power spinning or baitcasting outfit with 6- to 10-pound mono works well in most situations. Attach a vibrating plug the same way as a crankbait.

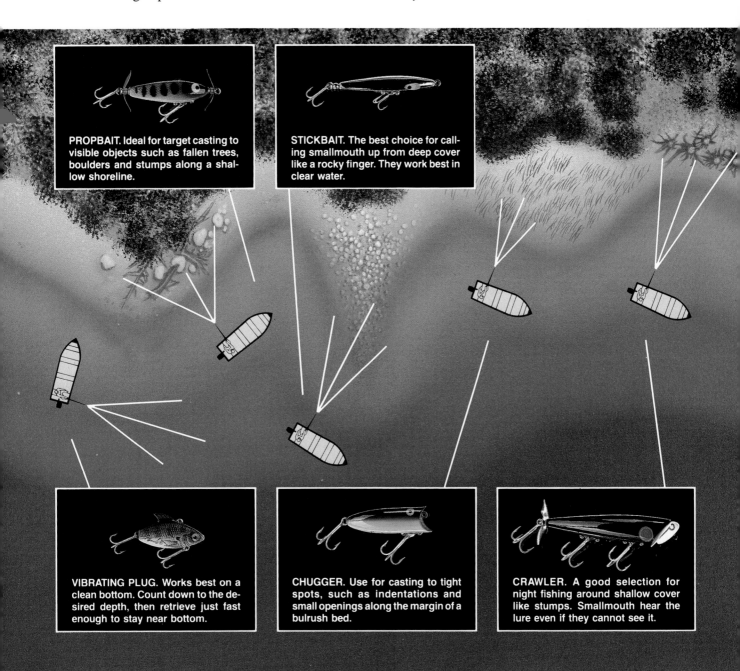

PROPBAIT. Ideal for target casting to visible objects such as fallen trees, boulders and stumps along a shallow shoreline.

STICKBAIT. The best choice for calling smallmouth up from deep cover like a rocky finger. They work best in clear water.

VIBRATING PLUG. Works best on a clean bottom. Count down to the desired depth, then retrieve just fast enough to stay near bottom.

CHUGGER. Use for casting to tight spots, such as indentations and small openings along the margin of a bulrush bed.

CRAWLER. A good selection for night fishing around shallow cover like stumps. Smallmouth hear the lure even if they cannot see it.

Fishing for Smallmouth Bass with Spinners

Smallmouth are quick to notice any unusual flash or vibration. Spinners produce a good deal of both, explaining why they are so effective.

Spinners commonly used for smallmouth fishing include spinnerbaits, standard spinners, weight-forward spinners and buzzbaits.

SPINNERBAITS. A spinnerbait is a good choice when smallmouth are in heavy cover. Its safety-pin design makes it relatively snagless. It can be fished in shallow or deep water, and is one of the best lures for night fishing.

Smallmouth prefer spinnerbaits smaller than the ones normally used for largemouth. Most smallmouth anglers use $\frac{1}{8}$- to $\frac{1}{4}$-ounce models, but some use panfish models weighing as little as $\frac{1}{32}$ ounce. Spinnerbaits are usually fished without live bait or other attractors, although some fishermen add pork trailers or twister tails to reduce the sink rate.

To fish a spinnerbait in shallow water, cast well past an obstruction like a boulder or stump, then reel steadily. Keep your rod tip high so the spinner

blades bulge the surface. Try to make the lure bump the obstruction. The change in action often triggers a strike.

In deeper water, let the spinnerbait helicopter to bottom, reel a short distance, then let it helicopter to bottom again. Using this technique, you can *walk* it down a drop-off or keep it at a constant depth.

For night fishing, use a fairly large spinnerbait, from ¼ to ½ ounce. A large blade sends out more vibrations than a small one, making it easier for smallmouth to find the lure. And smallmouth seem more aggressive at night, so the large size does not discourage strikes. Large spinnerbaits also work well during the nesting period and in late fall, when smallmouth begin their pre-winter feeding spree.

A medium-power spinning outfit with 6- to 8-pound mono works best for fishing small spinnerbaits. But a medium to medium-heavy power baitcasting outfit with 12- to 20-pound mono is better suited to heavy spinnerbaits or to fishing in dense cover.

STANDARD SPINNERS. A favorite of many old-timers, the standard spinner is not as widely used for smallmouth as it once was. Nevertheless, it is still an excellent smallmouth lure. Its decline in popularity is probably due to the increasing popularity of other smallmouth lures, like crankbaits.

Standard spinners work best in shallow water, especially for casting to rocks, stumps and other visible cover. Simply toss the spinner a little past your target, then retrieve steadily, just fast enough to

107

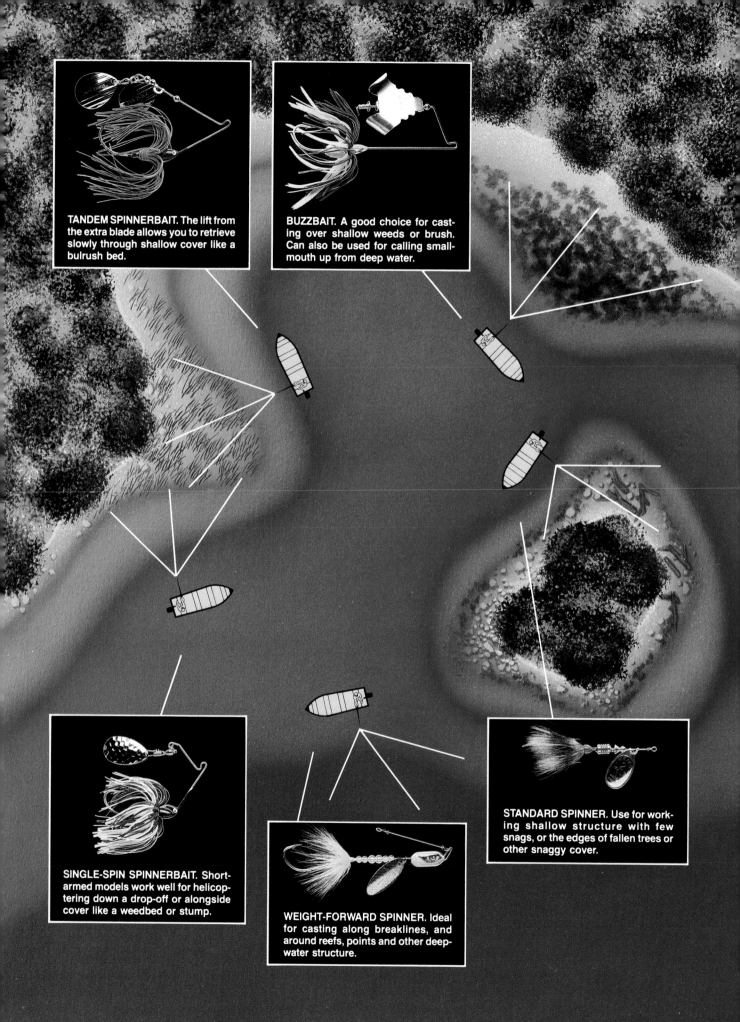

TANDEM SPINNERBAIT. The lift from the extra blade allows you to retrieve slowly through shallow cover like a bulrush bed.

BUZZBAIT. A good choice for casting over shallow weeds or brush. Can also be used for calling smallmouth up from deep water.

SINGLE-SPIN SPINNERBAIT. Short-armed models work well for helicoptering down a drop-off or alongside cover like a weedbed or stump.

WEIGHT-FORWARD SPINNER. Ideal for casting along breaklines, and around reefs, points and other deep-water structure.

STANDARD SPINNER. Use for working shallow structure with few snags, or the edges of fallen trees or other snaggy cover.

make the blade turn. To make the spinner run a little deeper, attach split-shot to your line about a foot ahead of the lure.

A spinner with a blade no larger than size 3 works best. Some fishermen tip their hook with a leech, a piece of nightcrawler or a small minnow.

For maximum sport, use an ultralight spinning rod with 4- to 6-pound mono. To avoid line twist, attach the spinner with a ball-bearing swivel.

WEIGHT-FORWARD SPINNERS. These lures work better than standard spinners in deep water or current. They sink faster than other types of spinners, and hold their depth well.

Weight-forward spinners are normally tipped with some type of live bait, usually a minnow, leech or piece of nightcrawler. But tipping is not always a good idea. If smallmouth are striking short, you may hook more of them by removing the bait.

To fish a weight-forward spinner, make a long cast, then keep your line taut as the lure sinks. The blade turns as the lure drops, so smallmouth may strike before it hits bottom. When you feel bottom, lift the lure a foot or so with an upward sweep of your rod, then begin your retrieve. Reel just fast enough to keep the lure near bottom, occasionally sweeping the rod to change the spinner's action.

When fishing over a snaggy bottom, count the lure down to the right depth rather than letting it sink to bottom and snag.

Weight-forward spinners used for smallmouth range from ¼ to ½ ounce. A medium-power spinning outfit with 6- to 8-pound mono is ideal for these lures. Weight-forward spinners will not twist your line, so you do not need a swivel.

BUZZBAITS. Like most other surface lures, buzzbaits work best when the surface is relatively calm. Although buzzbaits are normally used for catching largemouth in dense or matted weeds, they also can be effective for smallmouth in some situations.

At night, when smallmouth may have trouble seeing a lure, they cannot help but notice a buzzbait's noisy, sputtering action. Buzzbaits also work well in early morning and around dusk, when smallmouth are feeding in the shallows. Although they are normally fished over depths of 10 feet or less, there are times when they will draw smallmouth from depths as great as 20 feet, particularly in clear water. A spinnerbait buzzed across the surface will also draw smallmouth from deep water.

Smallmouth prefer buzzbaits ranging in size from ¼ to ½ ounce. Use the same tackle you would when fishing with spinnerbaits.

Tips for Fishing with Spinners

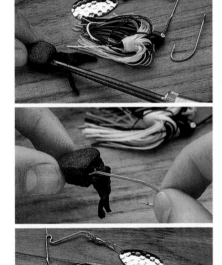
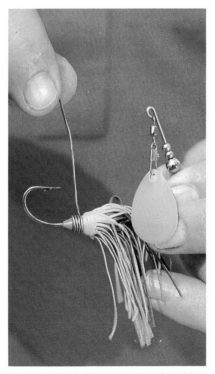

MAKE a trailer-hook attractor by punching a hole in a pork chunk (top), inserting a trailer (middle) and forcing the main hook through the pork and the trailer eye (bottom).

WRAP thin-diameter lead solder around the body of your spinner to increase its weight without increasing its size. With the extra weight, the lure casts easier and runs deeper.

ADD an extra blade to a spinnerbait to increase its lift so you can retrieve more slowly. Attach a swivel to the extra blade and clip it to the snap-swivel on the main blade.

Fly Fishing for Smallmouth

Anyone who has battled a big smallmouth on a fly rod would be quick to agree that few other types of fishing are as exciting. When a smallmouth smashes a fly and catapults into the air, even an experienced angler has a tough time maintaining his composure.

Not only is fly fishing for smallmouth a lot of fun, it is extremely effective. Flies imitate natural smallmouth foods more closely than most other lures. The most popular smallmouth flies are subsurface types including streamers, crayfish and leech imitations, and nymphs; and surface types including bugs and dry flies.

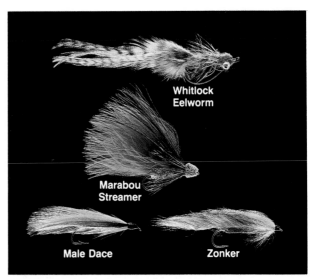

STREAMERS. The elongated shape of a streamer usually imitates that of a baitfish. Among the top streamers for smallmouth are jigging flies. They work better than other types of streamers in still water, because the weighted head makes them move with an appealing up-and-down action; in addition, they work well in current. Marabou streamers also are effective in still or moving water. They have a long, flowing wing that gives them an attractive breathing action. Hackle-wing and bucktail streamers are most effective in current; they lack sufficient action in still water.

Many streamer patterns are tied in both weighted and unweighted versions. A few have monofilament weedguards. Streamers in sizes 2 to 6 are most popular for smallmouth fishing.

When fishing a streamer in current, quarter your cast upstream, then let the streamer sink and drift naturally until it swings below you. If a curve or *belly* forms in your line during the drift, use your rod tip to *mend* the line. Flip the line into the air and straighten it without lifting the fly from the water.

When the fly has swung below you, retrieve it with short jerks to imitate a minnow struggling against the current. Strikes may come at any time during the drift or retrieve.

Cast well upstream of cover like a boulder or log, so the streamer will have time to sink before reaching it. An unweighted streamer fished on a floating line is the best choice where the current and depth are moderate. Use a weighted streamer or a sink-tip line in deeper or faster water.

In long, still pools or in lakes, cast around likely cover, let the streamer sink and then retrieve it with foot-long pulls to imitate a darting baitfish. At times, a steady retrieve or a series of short twitches may work better.

For fishing in still water at depths less than 5 feet, a floating line is usually best. For depths from 5 to 10 feet, switch to a sink-tip line. For greater depths, you will need a sinking line.

Streamer fishing requires the same basic equipment used for most other types of fly fishing. In streams, most fishermen prefer 6- or 7-weight rods and lines; in lakes, 7- or 8-weight. All lines should be weight-forward tapers. With floating lines, use 7½- to 9-foot leaders; with sink-tip or sinking lines, 3- to 4-foot leaders. Leader tippets range from 6- to 12-pound test, depending on the size of the fly and the type of cover. For maximum action, attach your fly with a loop knot.

CRAYFISH AND LEECH FLIES. These flies mimic some of the smallmouth's favorite foods. Crayfish flies have realistic claws made of hair or feathers. Leech flies have a long tail made from marabou or a strip of chamois. Marabou leech patterns in dark brown or black also make excellent

hellgrammite imitations. Many crayfish and leech flies are weighted, and some have mono weed-guards. Sizes 2 to 6 work best for smallmouth.

Drift a crayfish fly in current much as you would a streamer. When the drift is complete, crawl the fly back along the bottom, or swim it just above bottom with a series of short pulls. Crayfish flies that sink rapidly can be fished in current with a floating line; those that sink slowly require a sink-tip line.

In lakes, crayfish flies take smallmouth on rocky points, reefs, ledges and other places where crayfish are found. Make the longest cast you can, let the fly sink to bottom, then retrieve it slowly with short pulls. Choose your line according to depth, as you would in lake fishing with streamers.

Crayfish and leech flies require the same basic fly-fishing equipment used with streamers.

NYMPHS. Big nymphs rank among the top lures for river smallmouth. They also work well in lakes. Nymphs resemble immature forms of aquatic insects, an important part of the smallmouth's diet. They are effective whether or not a hatch is in progress. Nymphs that imitate hellgrammites or the larvae of dragonflies and damselflies are most popular for smallmouth. Sizes 6 to 10 work best.

Different types of aquatic insects move through the water in different ways, so you can use a wide variety of presentations when fishing nymphs. You can let them drift with the current, or retrieve them with long, slow pulls or gentle twitches followed by pauses. A weighted nymph sometimes works best if you let the current roll it along bottom, like an immature insect tumbling or crawling over the rocks.

Strikes may be hard to detect when fishing with nymphs. Sometimes a smallmouth swims up and simply closes its mouth on the nymph. Anytime you feel a tick or notice the tip of your line twitch or stop moving, set the hook.

Nymph fishing is done with the same basic tackle used for streamer fishing.

BUGS. Sometimes called bass bugs, these floating flies generally work best in early morning and around dusk, when smallmouth are feeding in the shallows. They are most effective in calm water.

Bugs have bodies of hard cork or plastic, or of clipped deer or elk hair. Hard-bodied bugs are more durable, but hair bugs feel more like real food. A smallmouth will hold a hair bug slightly longer, giving you an extra instant to set the hook.

Before you fish a hair bug, treat it with a paste-type floatant. If it starts to sink, dry it with a powdered dessicant and then reapply the floatant.

Smallmouth prefer bugs in sizes 1 to 6. For fishing in heavy cover, select a bug with a monofilament weedguard. Bugs have a lot of wind resistance, so they require a heavy rod and line, usually 7 to 8 weight. Your rod should be 8 to 9 feet long. Use a bug-taper line, which will lay a bug out faster and easier than an ordinary weight-forward line.

The following types of bugs work best for smallmouth fishing:

Poppers — The cupped or flattened face produces a popping or gurgling sound. Most poppers imitate frogs, mice or insects. Many have rubber legs, which give them a remarkably lifelike look.

Most poppers are designed for still water. The face will dig into a current, creating too much disturbance and making it difficult to lift the popper off the water for a new cast.

In most cases, the best retrieve consists of slight twitches that produce only moderate pops or no pops at all. Pause a few seconds between twitches. If you jerk the popper too hard, you will pull it away from the cover too soon, and the loud popping may spook the fish. If a twitch-and-pause retrieve does not produce, try twitching the popper more rapidly with no pauses.

Pencil poppers, which are long and very thin, should be fished with a darting retrieve to imitate an injured minnow. Because of their slender shape, they work as well in current as in still water.

How to Handle Fly Tackle for Smallmouth

CAST the fly just to the side of a log, brush pile, rock, or other cover likely to hold a smallmouth. Aim the cast parallel to the water, or slightly below parallel. If you aim the cast too high, the line and leader will be slack when they settle on the water.

LOWER your rod tip close to the water as the last few feet of line shoot to the target and unroll. The rod, line and leader should point directly at the target, with no slack. This way, you can set the hook instantly should a bass strike when the fly hits the water.

Sliders — Designed to imitate a minnow struggling on the surface, these flies have a bullet-shaped body which makes them easier to cast than a popper.

Sliders do not create as much surface disturbance as poppers, so they sometimes work better when smallmouth are spooky. They do not dig like a popper, so you can fish them in current or still water.

You can retrieve sliders with a twitch-and-pause technique or a slow, steady pull. Occasionally, smallmouth prefer them skittering across the surface and kicking up spray.

Divers — The head design causes these flies to dive when pulled forward, much like a frog. Most have a long wing made of feathers or a fur strip. Divers work well in either still or moving water.

When retrieved with a short pull followed by a pause, a diver plunges beneath the surface, emitting a stream of air bubbles, then floats back up. If you strip in line rapidly without pausing, a diver will stay underwater. And when fished with gentle twitches and pauses, it reacts much like a slider.

Because of its surface and subsurface action, a diver will often take smallmouth when other types of bass bugs fail.

Other bugs — A wide variety of bugs are shaped like frogs, moths, mice, dragonflies or other smallmouth foods. Generally, they have less action than other types of bugs. As a result, they cannot attract fish from much distance. They work best when cast precisely to a rise or to shallow cover. These bugs are normally retrieved slowly, with slight twitches followed by long pauses.

DRY FLIES. A dry fly can be identified by its prominent hackle collar, which helps keep it afloat. Although dry flies are not as popular for smallmouth as bugs, they sometimes work very well in rivers, especially when a hatch of large mayflies or stoneflies is in progress. Under these conditions, dry flies in sizes 4 to 6 are the best choices.

The most productive way to work a dry fly for smallmouth is to angle your cast downstream, allow the fly to drift over a likely spot, then skate it there by holding your rod tip high. Smallmouth nearly always prefer the skating action to a dead drift.

Like hair bugs, dry flies should be treated with a floatant before fishing. Paste floatants last longer than liquid types and should be applied sparingly with the fingertips.

For skating a dry fly, use a 9- to 9½-foot rod matched to a 6-weight floating line, and a 9- to 12-foot leader with a 7- to 10-pound tippet.

HOLD the line against the rod handle with the forefinger of your right hand. Strip in line with your left hand, letting it slip beneath your finger. Between pulls, pinch the line securely against the handle in case a fish should strike. Keep your rod tip low throughout the retrieve.

SET THE HOOK by sharply lifting the rod with a stiff wrist. At the same time, pull the line down with your left hand. Keep the rod nearly parallel to the water; raising the tip high would not increase your hooking power and could tangle the line on the rod if you miss the fish.

Fishing for Smallmouth Bass with Soft Plastics

Modern soft-plastic baits appeal to smallmouth because of their natural look and lifelike texture. Soft-plastic worms, salamanders, lizards, crayfish and frogs in 3- to 4-inch sizes are more effective than the larger soft plastics used for largemouth.

You can rig soft plastics Texas style for fishing in weeds, brush or other dense cover. Or, you can rig them with an exposed hook for fishing on a clean bottom. Your hooking percentage will be higher with the hook exposed.

Soft plastics are normally weighted with a cone sinker or split-shot, or with an egg sinker rigged to slip. They can also be fished on a jig head, either with the hook exposed or buried in the plastic. Some jig heads, such as the *keeper* style, are designed specifically for soft plastics.

Normally, soft plastics are retrieved with a jigging action, much as you would retrieve a lead-head jig. Smallmouth usually grab the lure as it sinks, so you must keep your line taut to detect a strike. But when smallmouth are not feeding, you may have better success by simply crawling the lure on the bottom. This *do-nuthin'* retrieve works best with a 3½- to 4-inch plastic worm rigged with two exposed hooks.

When fishing soft plastics rigged Texas style, use a medium- to heavy-power baitcasting outfit with 12- to 14-pound mono. You need a fairly stiff rod to drive the hook through the soft plastic and into the fish's mouth. A medium-power spinning outfit with 6- to 8-pound mono works better when using soft plastics with exposed hooks.

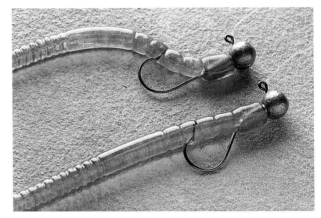

TREAT your soft plastics with worm oil to keep them soft and pliable. Store them in a zip-lock bag; if you store them in a tackle box, they may get wet and their colors may turn milky. Do not mix different colors in the same bag. In time, the colors will bleed together.

BEND your jig hook when you intend to bury it in a soft-plastic lure. If not bent (top), the hook penetrates the worm at an extreme angle, causing missed strikes. With the hook bent (bottom), the point will come through straighter so you are more likely to hook the fish.

Fishing for Smallmouth Bass with Live Bait

How you present your bait depends mainly on the depth of the water you are fishing. When smallmouth are at depths of 10 feet or less, simply tie on a hook and pinch a split-shot or two about 18 inches up the line. In deeper water, a slip-sinker rig is a better choice. You will need more weight to reach bottom, so if your sinker is not rigged to slip, smallmouth may feel too much resistance and drop the bait.

Slip-bobber rigs work well for fishing tight schools, especially when smallmouth are not in the mood to feed. And you can set your depth so the bait rides just above rocks or other snags.

Another technique that is less popular, but very effective, is free-lining. This is the most natural of all live-bait presentations because the bait swims freely, with no drag from a sinker.

With any live-bait technique, the most important consideration is to present the bait to make it look natural. This means using as little weight as possible, small hooks, and light, low-visibility line with no heavy leader. Many live-bait specialists use clear 4-pound-test monofilament for practically all of their fishing.

A 6- to 7-foot medium-power, slow- to medium-action spinning rod is a good choice for most types of live-bait fishing. A slow-action rod reduces the odds of snapping the bait off the hook when you cast and is more forgiving should you mistakenly tighten the line when a smallmouth is biting.

Split-shot Fishing for Smallmouth Bass

This technique is ideal for smallmouth because they spend so much of their time in relatively shallow water. A split-shot rig takes only seconds to tie and is easy to use.

The most important consideration in using a split-shot rig is the amount of weight. Too much, and the rig will sink quickly and wedge in rocks or other snags. Too little, and a lively bait will keep it from sinking. By using just enough shot to barely sink your bait, you can swim the rig along bottom without snagging, yet the bait can move freely and keep its natural look. To use a split-shot rig properly, follow steps 1 through 5.

1. LOB-CAST a split-shot rig (inset) past the spot you want to fish, then let it sink to bottom. A sweeping sidearm motion reduces the chances of snapping the bait off the hook when you cast.

2. POINT your rod tip in the direction of the rig while reeling up any slack line. Do not begin your retrieve until you are sure all of the slack has been removed.

3. SLOWLY LIFT your rod to nearly vertical. Then lower it to horizontal, reeling to keep the line taut. Continue to lift and lower, watching the line and rod tip.

4. DROP your rod tip when you notice any twitch, sideways movement or excess drag. Point the rod at the fish and feed line when it runs with the bait. When it stops running, tighten the line until you feel resistance.

5. SET THE HOOK with a powerful snap of the wrists. For maximum hook-setting leverage, keep your elbows close to your body and pull sharply with your forearms instead of extending your arms full length.

Slip-sinker Fishing for Smallmouth Bass

When a smallmouth swims away with the bait, it feels no resistance because the line slides freely through the sinker.

Normally, you can use a ¼-ounce slip sinker for depths of 20 feet or less. But you can also use a heavier one because the sinker slips on the line. The extra weight allows you to keep your line more nearly vertical, so you will feel bites more easily and get fewer snags.

You can fish a slip-sinker rig in shallow water, much like a split-shot rig. But slip-sinker rigs are usually trolled along a breakline. You can cover a lot of water and easily fish as deep as 40 feet.

Most fishermen backtroll when using a slip-sinker rig. Because of the slower speed and better boat control, you can keep your bait in the fish zone more easily than you could by forward trolling.

Keep your bail open and hold the line with your finger when slip-sinker fishing. A smallmouth often makes a fast run after it grabs the bait. If your bail is closed, you cannot release your line in time.

When the fish stops running, reel up the slack until you feel some resistance before setting the hook. Smallmouth may swim a long distance and put a lot of slack in the line. If you do not reel up the slack, you will not have enough leverage to set the hook.

SMALLMOUTH often rocket toward the surface after grabbing the bait. With a slip-sinker rig (inset), the sinker stays near the bottom, resulting in a lot of slack. If the fish takes more than 10 feet of line and continues to run, quickly reel up the slack and set the hook.

How to Hook Bait for Split-shot and Slip-sinker Fishing

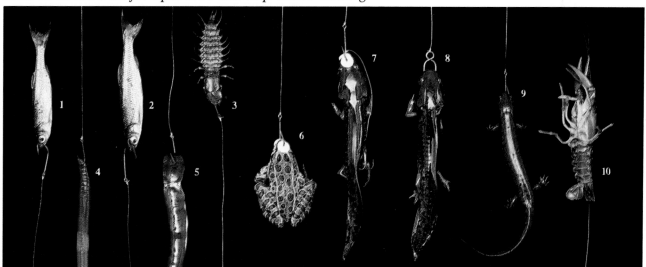

HOOK a minnow (1) through the lips or (2) eyes with a size 2 to 6 hook; a hellgrammite (3) under the collar with a size 4 or 6 hook; a nightcrawler (4) through the head with a size 6 or 8 hook; a leech (5) near the sucker with a size 6 or 8 hook; a frog (6) through the lips with a size 2 or 4 hook and bait-saver tabs (page 118); a waterdog (7) through the lips with a size 2 or 4 hook, tabs and a size 12 stinger, or (8) with a size 2 Super Hook pinched over the head; a spring lizard (9) through the lips and out the eye with a size 2 or 4 hook; and a crayfish (10) through the tail and out the belly with a size 2 or 4 long-shank hook.

Slip-bobber Fishing for Smallmouth Bass

A slip-bobber rig is a good choice when smallmouth are not in the mood to feed. Even a full-bellied smallmouth will take a nip at a stationary bait if it wiggles in front of his nose long enough.

You can adjust your slip-bobber knot to keep your bait dangling just off bottom, so the rig works well over rocks or other snags. And, when smallmouth are tightly schooled, a slip-bobber rig enables you to keep your bait in the fish zone more of the time than you could with any other method.

When your bobber goes down, wait a few seconds, tighten your line until you feel weight, then set the hook. If you wait too long, the smallmouth will feel resistance and let go.

ADJUST your slip-bobber rig (inset) so the bait dangles 6 to 12 inches off bottom. Slide the bobber stop (arrow) up the line the same distance you want the bait to hang below the surface. About 18 inches above the hook, pinch on enough split-shot so the bobber barely floats.

HOOK a leech (1) through the middle with a size 6 hook; a minnow (2) below the dorsal with a size 4 hook; a crayfish (3) through the tail with a size 2 or 4 hook; a hellgrammite (4) under the collar with a size 4 or 6 hook; and a crawler (5) through the middle with a size 6 hook.

Tips for Fishing with Live Bait

KEEP shiners alive in warm weather by adding ice to your minnow bucket to chill the water. Try to keep the water at about the same temperature it was at the bait shop.

CARRY your leeches in a specially designed bucket that enables you to change water easily. When you lift the inner bucket, water drains through the holes, but the leeches stay in.

HOLD your bait on the hook and keep it from covering the hook gap by threading on tabs made from a (1) rubber band or (2) plastic lid. Or, tie rubber bands on the shank (3).

Freelining for Smallmouth Bass

Freelining allows you to present your bait more naturally than you could with any other technique. Simply tie on a hook and let the bait swim about with no sinker to restrict its movement.

Lob-cast your bait so it alights over a shallow rock bar, or alongside a boulder, log or some other type of shallow-water cover. Let the bait swim freely, but keep your line just tight enough so you will feel a bite. After a minute or two, twitch the bait or move it a short distance, then let it swim again.

Use a fine-wire hook and 4- to 6-pound mono for freelining. A thick-shanked hook will weight down the bait and heavier line will prevent it from swimming naturally.

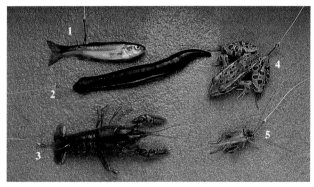

HOOK a minnow (1) in the tail with a size 4 hook; a leech (2) in the sucker end with a size 6 hook; a crayfish (3) through the tail with a size 2 hook; a frog (4) through the hind leg with a size 2 hook; and a grasshopper or cricket (5) under the collar with a size 6 hook.

KEEP some tension on your line when freelining with a crayfish. If you allow the crayfish to move about as it pleases, it will crawl under a rock or log and hide. Some fishermen remove the pincers to keep the crayfish from holding onto objects on the bottom.

ADD some type of attractor when smallmouth refuse a plain bait. Popular attractors include: (1) a spinner, clevis and beads; (2) a small *corkie*, which slides freely on the line; (3) a piece of yarn snelled onto the hook; and (4) a small live-rubber skirt.

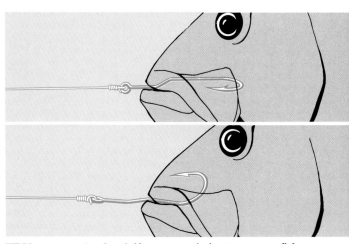

TRY a *cam-action* hook if you are missing too many fish. When a smallmouth clamps down on the bait, the hook lies flat on its side (top). But when you set the hook, the cam design causes the point to rotate up or down so it will penetrate the fish's jaw (bottom).

119

Walleye

Black area at
lower rear of dorsal

Dorsal
lacks spots

No spot
on pectorals

White corner on
lower lobe of tail

Walleye Basics

The elusive nature of the walleye has intrigued generations of fishermen. Anyone who has spent much time fishing walleyes knows that they can bite like mad one day, then disappear for the next week for no apparent reason. And when walleyes decide to quit biting, almost nothing can change their minds.

But despite their unpredictable behavior, walleyes rank among the nation's most popular gamefish. Some anglers pursue walleyes for the challenge, others because walleye fillets make prime table fare.

Originally, walleyes were found only in a triangular area extending across Canada and south to Alabama. But as a result of widespread stocking, they are now found in almost every state and province. Few attempts have been made to introduce walleyes outside North America.

Two subspecies of walleyes have been identified in North America: the yellow walleye, *Stizostedion vitreum vitreum,* and the blue walleye or blue pike, *Stizostedion vitreum glaucum.* The yellow walleye, commonly referred to simply as walleye, is the only remaining subspecies.

Yellow walleyes (above photo) usually have an olive-green back, golden sides and a white belly. Distinctive markings include a milky-white tip on the lower lobe of the tail and a black blotch at the rear base of the spiny dorsal fin.

Blue walleyes had a steel-blue back, silvery sides and larger eyes. They were found only in lakes Erie and Ontario. But due to severe water pollution and excessive commercial fishing, they are now thought to be extinct.

In many waters, fishermen mistake the walleye for its close relative, the sauger. But saugers have a distinctly different coloration and do not grow as large. To further complicate matters, walleyes and saugers sometimes hybridize, producing a fish called the *saugeye* with characteristics intermediate between those of the parents. Except perch and darters, walleyes have no other North American relatives. However, walleyes are closely related to the European zander, or pike-perch. The two look remarkably similar, but walleyes distribute their eggs at random while zanders are nest-builders.

The walleye's common names lead to much confusion among fishermen. In much of Canada, walleyes

SAUGERS have several rows of distinct black spots on the dorsal fin. The pectoral fins have a dark spot at the base. The overall coloration is grayish to brownish with dark blotches. There is no black area at the lower rear of the dorsal. The tail may have a thin white band at the bottom. The body is slimmer than that of a walleye.

SAUGEYES usually have a spotted dorsal fin, but the spots are not round like those of a sauger. There may be a small black area at the lower rear of the dorsal. The sides are often tinged with gold and may have faint dark blotches. The tail resembles that of a sauger, with no prominent white corner on the lower lobe.

are called pickerel, jackfish or doré, the French name for the species. In the United States, they are often called walleyed pike. But that term is a misnomer because walleyes belong not to the pike family, but to the perch family.

Walleyes are strong but not spectacular fighters. They do not jump like bass or make sizzling runs like northern pike. Instead, they wage a dogged, head-shaking battle, stubbornly refusing to be pulled from deep water.

The world-record walleye weighed 25 pounds and was caught by Mabry Harper in Old Hickory Lake, Tennessee, on August 2, 1960. Harper caught the huge walleye on a big minnow while fishing for catfish. His tackle included a 6/0 hook and 75-pound-test line.

Several other walleyes exceeding 20 pounds have been caught in southeastern reservoirs, causing biologists to speculate that these waters contain a unique, fast-growing strain (page 125).

Walleye Range

COLORATION of walleyes varies greatly in different waters. In waters that are relatively clear, walleyes have the typical golden hue (top). But in bog-stained or coffee-colored waters, they are noticeably darker and often have yellowish bellies (middle). In extremely turbid waters, walleyes usually have a grayish coloration (bottom).

Walleye Senses

Much of the seemingly mysterious behavior of walleyes can be explained by their acute night vision, finely tuned lateral-line sense and sharp hearing. They also have a good sense of smell, but it does not appear to play a prominent role in their life.

VISION. The *tapetum lucidum,* a layer of reflective pigment in the retina, gives walleyes a built-in advantage: they can see well in dim light, but their prey cannot. This highly developed night vision explains why walleyes do most of their feeding in dim light.

Because of their light-sensitive eyes, walleyes will not tolerate sunlight. If the water is clear and there is no shade in the shallows, they may go as deep as 40 feet to escape the penetrating rays. But in dark or choppy waters, walleyes can remain shallow all day.

Walleyes can see color, but they cannot see as many hues as fish like largemouth bass and northern pike. Any animal with good color vision has two types of color discriminating cells: red-green cells and blue-yellow cells. But a walleye lacks the blue-yellow cells, so its color vision is similar to that of the rare human beings with blue-yellow color blindness. In other words, walleyes most likely see all colors as some shade of red or green.

The color bars below provide some clues to the lure colors walleyes can see best, but water color and depth can change the way a lure appears to the fish. In addition, the best lure colors may differ from one body of water to the next because the walleyes are eating different foods. As a result, the only sure way to find the best color is to experiment.

Electronic color selectors were developed based on tests conducted on largemouth bass. But walleyes see color differently than bass, so it is unlikely that these devices will improve your walleye fishing.

LATERAL LINE. These ultra-sensitive nerve endings along each side of the body can detect minute vibrations in the water. The lateral-line sense enables walleyes to single out an erratically swimming baitfish from the rest of a school. The lateral line also enables them to locate an artificial lure in deep or murky water where they could not possibly see it.

HEARING. Seasoned fishermen know that walleyes in the shallows will not tolerate any commotion. Even the slightest noise will drive them into deep water. As a rule of thumb, when walleyes are in water of 10 feet or less, it pays to anchor your boat and cast to them. Avoid trolling over them, especially with an outboard motor.

Expert ice fishermen avoid drilling or chopping holes during peak fishing periods. They know that the sound of an auger or chisel will drive the fish off their feeding reefs.

SMELL. Laboratory tests have shown that fish can detect extremely dilute odors. Yet the sense of smell does not seem to have much influence on walleye feeding behavior. If smell were important, the evidence should be most obvious in low-clarity water, where walleyes cannot see well enough to feed. But in this type of water, live bait does not work as well as artificial lures, especially lures that produce vibrations. This evidence indicates that the lateral-line sense is more significant.

How the Walleye's Eye Responds to Different Colors

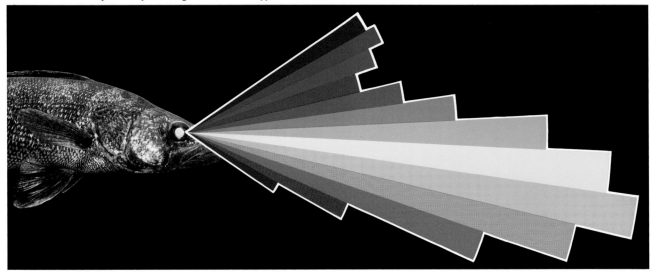

COLOR VISION of walleyes was tested in a laboratory experiment in which a tiny probe was placed inside individual *cones,* or color receptors in the retina. The probe measured the amount of reaction to light of different colors. The length of each color bar represents the relative level of response generated by each color.

YELLOW PERCH make ideal prey. They have poor night vision and cannot see an approaching walleye. At night, perch rest with their fins touching bottom. Scuba divers have caught resting perch with their hands.

Walleye Feeding & Growth

Like most other predatory fish, walleyes are opportunists. They eat whatever foods nature provides them. In many mesotrophic lakes, walleyes feed primarily on yellow perch, often stalking them at night on shoals less than 5 feet deep. In the Missouri River reservoirs of North and South Dakota, walleyes frequently eat smelt, which they sometimes follow into water over 100 feet deep. In southern reservoirs, walleyes commonly suspend to feed on gizzard or threadfin shad, pursuing them in wide expanses of open water.

Although small fish make up the bulk of the diet in most waters, there are times when walleyes feed almost exclusively on insects, both immature and adult forms. Occasionally, walleyes eat snails, leeches, frogs, mudpuppies, crayfish and even mice.

The abundance of natural food is the major factor that determines how well walleyes bite. When food is scarce, they spend much of their time moving about in search of a meal, so the chances are greater that they will take your bait or lure. But when food is plentiful, the opposite is true.

Most species of baitfish spawn in spring. The young they produce are usually too small to interest adult walleyes until midsummer. Because yearling or adult baitfish are often scarce in spring, walleyes are hungry and fishing is usually good. The action slows down in summer when they begin to feed on the newly available crop of young baitfish. A commonly heard old wives' tale is that walleyes refuse to bite in summer because they have sore mouths. But in reality, they are consuming more food than at any other time of year. Fishing picks up again in fall when predation and other natural mortality have substantially reduced the crop of young baitfish.

Fishing success in a given body of water can change dramatically from year to year, depending on whether or not there is a good baitfish hatch. Occasionally, baitfish become so abundant that walleyes are almost impossible to catch in midsummer. When baitfish are this plentiful, fishing usually remains slow through the winter months, and may stay slow through the next summer.

RECURVED TEETH make a walleye an efficient predator. A baitfish or other prey caught by a walleye has little chance of escaping.

GROWTH RATES of walleyes are reflected by the size of the head compared to that of the body. A fast-growing walleye (top) has a relatively small head and a short, chunky body. A slow-growing walleye (bottom) has a relatively large head and a long, slim body.

Growth Rates of Walleyes at Different Latitudes

Lake Name and Latitude	Length in Inches at Various Ages									
	Age 1	2	3	4	5	6	7	8	9	10
North Caribou Lake, ONT (53°N)	4.3	6.7	8.5	10.2	12.0	12.4	14.6	16.1	17.0	18.0
Lake of the Woods, MN (49°N)	5.6	8.0	10.0	11.6	12.8	14.4	15.7	17.2	18.7	19.6
Trout Lake, WI (46°N)	5.3	9.7	13.7	16.6	19.0	20.7	21.7	22.3	23.1	23.3
Spirit Lake, IA (43°N)	7.2	11.1	14.4	17.5	19.9	22.0	23.7	24.9	26.0	27.8
Pymatuning Lake, PA (42°N)	7.9	13.6	17.4	20.7	23.3	25.2	26.7	27.8	28.8	29.0
Claytor Reservoir, VA (37°N)	8.1	13.9	18.4	22.6	25.5	27.4	30.0	32.2	—	—

In some years, adverse weather prevents baitfish from spawning successfully. As a result, forage is scarce and walleyes bite well through the summer and into the winter.

How fast walleyes grow depends on the availability of food and the length of the growing season. In southern reservoirs, where shad are super-abundant and the growing season is 8 to 9 months long, walleyes can reach weights exceeding 15 pounds in only 7 years. But in the deep, cold lakes of the Canadian Shield, where baitfish are less abundant and the growing season lasts only 3 to 4 months, a walleye reaches a weight of just 2 pounds in the same amount of time.

Despite this great difference in growth rate, walleyes in northern waters can reach sizes rivaling those in the South. This phenomenon can be explained by a factor that could be called *warmwater burnout*. Fish in cold northern waters grow more slowly, but have a much longer life span than fish in warmer southern waters. Walleyes in the North have been known to live as long as 26 years, although walleyes older than 15 years are rare; in the South, a life span of 10 years would be unusual. So even though walleyes in the North do not grow as fast, their longevity results in an average size not much smaller than that in the South.

There is evidence to support the theory that a fast-growing strain of walleyes exists in rivers and reservoirs in the southeastern United States. Apparently, this strain spawns exclusively in rivers. When dams were built to create the reservoirs, long stretches of river habitat were lost. In most cases, the walleyes eventually disappeared from the reservoirs.

Many of these reservoirs were then stocked with northern-strain walleyes. This strain can spawn in rivers or lakes, but evidently does not grow as fast as the southern strain. In Center Hill Reservoir, Tennessee, southern-strain walleyes sampled in 1964 averaged 30.6 inches (about 10½ pounds) at age 7. They eventually disappeared from the reservoir, so it was stocked with northern-strain walleyes. When the northern fish were sampled in 1976, they averaged only 23.3 inches (about 4½ pounds) at age 7.

Female walleyes grow much faster, live longer and attain much larger sizes than males. In most waters, male walleyes exceeding 4 pounds are unusual.

Walleyes concentrate around the mouth of an inlet stream because of the reduced clarity.

Walleyes prefer a firm bottom, usually sand, gravel, rock or a combination of these materials.

No walleyes on soft, mucky bottom, even though it is in the right temperature zone.

Walleye Habitat Preferences

Compared to most other freshwater fish, walleyes can tolerate an exceptionally wide range of environmental conditions. This explains why they are found from northern Canada to the southern United States. Most of the habitat preferences of the walleye are described below. Another important factor, light level, is discussed on pages 130-131.

TEMPERATURE. The walleye is a *coolwater* species, meaning that it prefers intermediate temperatures when compared to warmwater fish like bass and coldwater fish like trout. In summer, walleyes are commonly found at temperatures from 65° to 75°F, but they will leave this zone to find food or to avoid intense light. At other times of year, they will usually seek the water closest to their preferred summer range. Walleyes are seldom found at temperatures above 80°F.

WATER CLARITY. Walleyes prefer water of relatively low clarity. They are most abundant where suspended silt or algae, or bog stain, limits visibility to about 3 to 6 feet. Tannic acid and other dissolved organic materials are responsible for the bog-stained, or coffee-colored, appearance of many lakes in the North.

Differences in clarity within the same body of water may affect walleye location. In a clear lake, researchers found that walleyes were 10 times more abundant in the turbid zone near a river mouth than in other parts of the lake. But in low-clarity lakes, walleyes generally avoid highly turbid areas.

BOTTOM TYPE. Given a choice, walleyes generally select clean, hard bottoms rather than bottoms of silt, muck or other soft materials. Walleyes favor bottoms with a combination of sand, gravel and rock. This type of bottom produces a great deal of insect and other invertebrate life which in turn attracts baitfish.

In fertile lakes, the bottom is often covered with a thick layer of soft sediment. Experienced anglers know that if they can find an exposed rock pile or gravel bar, it will usually hold walleyes.

A study conducted on the Mississippi River revealed that walleye populations declined as shoreline protected by riprap, or large rock, was covered with sand from Corps of Engineers dredging. Popu-

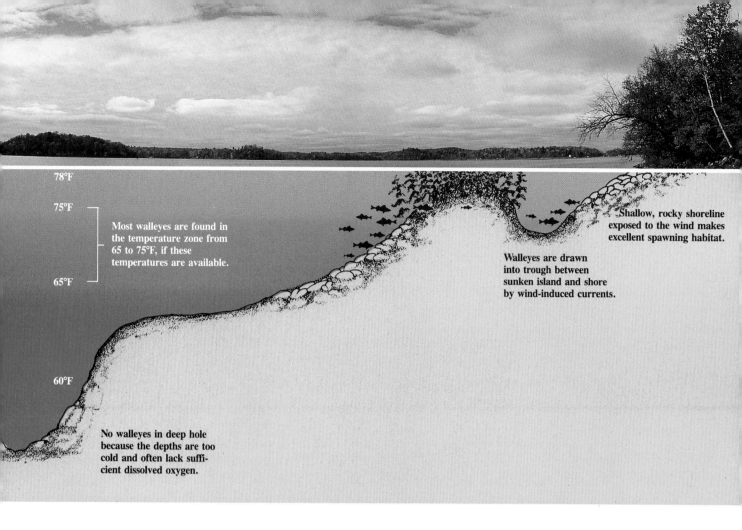

78°F

75°F

Most walleyes are found in the temperature zone from 65 to 75°F, if these temperatures are available.

65°F

Shallow, rocky shoreline exposed to the wind makes excellent spawning habitat.

Walleyes are drawn into trough between sunken island and shore by wind-induced currents.

60°F

No walleyes in deep hole because the depths are too cold and often lack sufficient dissolved oxygen.

lations remained stable where the riprap banks were still exposed.

SPAWNING HABITAT. Shallow, rocky shorelines and reefs make ideal spawning habitat. The eggs fall into crevices between the rocks where they are safe from crayfish and other egg-eating predators. Spawning is most successful in large lakes because the spawning habitat is exposed to the wind. Some wave action is necessary to prevent the eggs from silting over and keep them aerated. So it is not surprising that lakes of this type have the highest walleye populations. Walleyes can also spawn in rivers and streams, if there is enough rocky bottom.

Many fertile lakes and reservoirs lack suitable spawning areas. A few walleyes may spawn along shorelines where homeowners have placed rocks to protect the bank, or on flooded gravel roadbeds. Unless these waters are stocked, they seldom contain many walleyes.

OXYGEN. Walleyes avoid water with a dissolved oxygen content below 4 ppm (parts per million). But contrary to popular belief, they do not seek out areas with higher oxygen levels. It is true that wind-swept portions of a lake draw the most walleyes. However, the fish are attracted by lower light levels and a concentration of food, not by higher oxygen.

Walleyes can tolerate oxygen levels as low as 1 ppm for short periods. It is not unusual for walleyes to move into deep water with a low oxygen level, especially when there is an easy source of food in the depths or water in the shallows becomes too warm.

CURRENT. Walleyes are native to most major river systems in the North, so they are accustomed to living in current. Given a choice, lake-dwelling walleyes will seek areas of light current rather than stay in slack water. The highest walleye concentrations are often found around inlet streams, in narrows separating two basins of a lake or in areas with wind-induced currents.

pH. This is a term used to denote the acidity or alkalinity of the water. pH is measured on a scale from 1 to 14, with 1 the most acidic and 14 the most alkaline. A pH of 7 is neutral. Fishing waters usually have pH levels ranging from 6 to 9. If the pH drops below 5.5, walleye eggs do not develop properly, so the fish eventually disappear.

Canadian researchers have found that adult walleyes avoid pH levels below 6 or above 9. But within that range, pH has no effect on walleye behavior. Because the walleye's pH comfort range corresponds to the range found in most waters, there is no need to concern yourself with pH.

MALE walleyes bump the sides of the female during the spawning act, emitting milt while she drops her eggs. Sometimes several males bump a single female. A female deposits 50,000 to 300,000 eggs, usually in a single night.

Fertilized eggs fall between the rocks where they are safe from egg-eating predators. Parents abandon the eggs after spawning. On a rocky bottom, up to 25 percent of the eggs will hatch; on soft muck, less than 1 percent.

Walleye Spawning Behavior

In early spring, as the days grow longer and the water temperature rises, walleyes know that the time has come to abandon their winter haunts and begin their annual spawning migration.

Walleyes can spawn successfully in natural lakes, reservoirs and rivers. In many cases, some walleyes spawn in the main body of a lake or reservoir while others spawn in tributary streams.

Spawning areas are usually 1 to 6 feet deep, with a bottom of gravel to baseball-sized rock. Because the eggs require constant aeration, walleyes in lakes and reservoirs deposit their eggs on shoal areas exposed to the wind. River walleyes usually spawn in areas with moderate current. Seldom will walleyes spawn in a sheltered bay or backwater.

Male walleyes are the first to move into the vicinity of the spawning area. Large numbers of males gather even though the water temperature may be only a few degrees above freezing, and spawning time is a month or more away. Females begin moving in several weeks later, when the water temperature reaches the upper 30s to low 40s.

Walleyes remain relatively deep until spawning time approaches. A week or two before spawning, they move shallower and begin to feed more heavily. On warm evenings, they mill about in the spawning area, then drop back to slightly deeper water when the sun comes up. These nighttime movements become more frequent as spawning time nears.

The exact water temperature at which walleyes spawn depends on latitude. Walleyes in the North may spawn at temperatures as much as 15 degrees lower than in the South. In the extreme northern part of their range, walleyes generally spawn at temperatures from 40° to 44°F; in the South, from 50° to 55°F.

Spawning times can differ by as much as two weeks in waters in the same area. A shallow lake, for instance, warms much faster than a deep one, so walleyes spawn much sooner.

Because offshore waters warm more slowly, spawning on reefs may take place as much as two weeks later than spawning on shorelines and in tributaries.

The spawning period generally lasts from one to two weeks. But if the water warms rapidly, walleyes spawn at temperatures higher than normal and all spawning is completed in a few days. If the water warms slowly, they start to spawn at temperatures lower than normal and spawning activity may continue for three weeks or more. A severe cold snap during the spawning period may interrupt spawning for several days. After repeated cold snaps, walleyes may reabsorb their eggs and not spawn at all.

Although an individual female usually drops all of her eggs on the same night, not all females ripen at once. This explains why some walleyes are just beginning to spawn when others have been finished for a week or more.

After spawning is completed, males stay near the spawning area up to a month and continue to feed. Females begin to move toward their early-summer locations soon after spawning. When recuperating, they refuse food for about two weeks. But after recuperation, they begin a period of heavy feeding that lasts for several weeks. Anglers who know where to find them during this post-spawn feeding spree enjoy some of the best fishing of the year, particularly for trophy-class walleyes.

FRY emerge from the eggs in one to two weeks, depending on water temperature. They live off the egg sac for the first few days of life. On the average, only one fry in a thousand survives to fingerling size.

FINGERLING size, 4 to 8 inches, is reached by the end of the summer. About 5 to 10 percent of the fingerlings survive to catchable size, although survival rates vary greatly in different types of waters.

SCOUT potential walleye structure by sounding with your flasher while motoring at high speed. This enables you to cover a lot of water quickly. Adjust your transducer so it will give you a good reading at high speed.

Recognizing Good Walleye Structure

One of the big mysteries of walleye fishing is why certain spots consistently hold fish, but other seemingly identical spots do not. The answer lies in some slight variation that may not be noticeable to a fisherman but makes a big difference to a walleye.

Learning to evaluate structure quickly and recognize these slight variations is the key to walleye-fishing success. A skillful presentation will do you no good if you cannot locate the fish.

The following factors influence whether or not walleyes will use a particular piece of structure.

BOTTOM TYPE. Walleyes generally prefer a firm bottom, but which bottom material is best varies in different waters. As a rule, walleyes look for something different from the rest of their surroundings. In a lake where the bottom is mainly sand, for instance, rocky reefs draw large numbers of walleyes. But in a rocky lake, sandy, weed-covered sunken islands are often better than rocky reefs.

In waters with large expanses of mucky bottom, a patch of sand, gravel or rock is usually a prime walleye spot, even if there is no change in depth.

MINIMUM DEPTH. The depth at which a piece of structure tops off (illustration at upper right) can determine whether or not it holds walleyes. Because they prefer to feed on a relatively flat shelf rather than a drop-off, they spend a good deal of time on

How Depth and Slope of Structure Affect Seasonal Walleye Location

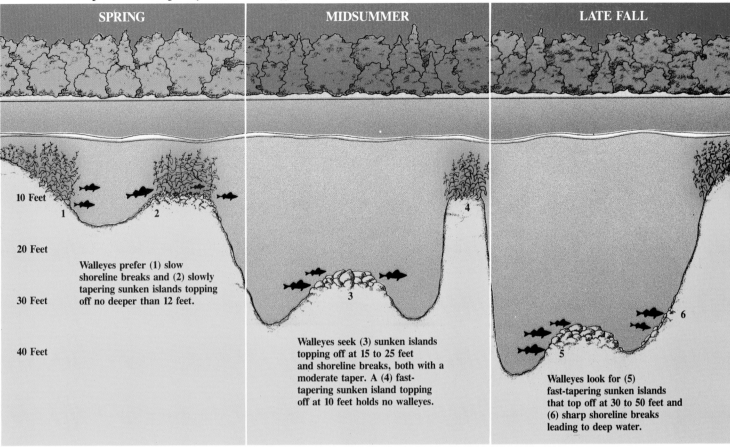

SPRING

Walleyes prefer (1) slow shoreline breaks and (2) slowly tapering sunken islands topping off no deeper than 12 feet.

MIDSUMMER

Walleyes seek (3) sunken islands topping off at 15 to 25 feet and shoreline breaks, both with a moderate taper. A (4) fast-tapering sunken island topping off at 10 feet holds no walleyes.

LATE FALL

Walleyes look for (5) fast-tapering sunken islands that top off at 30 to 50 feet and (6) sharp shoreline breaks leading to deep water.

10 Feet · 20 Feet · 30 Feet · 40 Feet

LOOK for structure with different slopes and minimum depths in different seasons. In a typical stratified meso-trophic lake, the type of structure preferred by walleyes in different seasons is shown above.

top of the structure. In a stratified lake, they select structure that tops off in the zone where the water temperature is most comfortable.

DEPTH OF NEARBY WATER. Walleyes will seldom cross a wide expanse of deep water to reach an isolated piece of structure. They prefer to follow migration routes in their normal depth range. As a result, you would be more likely to find walleyes on an offshore reef connected to another reef by a saddle than on an offshore reef surrounded on all sides by deep water.

Structure connected to the shoreline is generally the best choice in spring. After spawning, walleyes remain near shore where the temperature is warmest. But when inshore temperatures rise to the low 60s, many of them move to offshore structure that offers easy access to the depths. If there is no offshore structure, walleyes select areas of the shoreline break adjacent to deep water.

DEGREE OF SLOPE. Early in the year, walleyes seek out structure that slopes very gradually (illustration above). Because they remain in relatively shallow water all day, they have no need for a sharp

drop-off. By midsummer, most of them have moved to structure with a more pronounced slope. The sharper drop-off makes it easy to move deeper when the sun comes up. In late fall, they move to structure with an even steeper slope. This way, they can grab a quick meal in the shallows, then quickly retreat to warmer water in the depths.

In shallow lakes that lack noticeable structure, walleyes relate to subtle depth changes. A sunken island that rises gradually to a height of 2 feet above the surrounding bottom may attract large numbers of fish. In a lake with more structure, they would probably not relate to such a minor depth change.

BREAKLINE CONFIGURATION. Structure that has an irregular breakline with numerous points and inside turns will generally hold more walleyes than structure that has a straight breakline.

SIZE. All other factors being equal, a large piece of structure is more likely to hold walleyes than a small one. Walleyes would soon drive the baitfish off a small reef, exhausting the food supply. But on a big reef, baitfish that escape would move a short distance away, then gradually filter back.

BIG REEFS that slope gradually into deep water are especially productive in summer. Reefs with firm bottoms and cover such as rocks or scattered weed clumps hold more walleyes than soft-bottomed humps with no cover.

ROCK PILES on an otherwise smooth bottom draw walleyes all year. Algae on the rocks attracts crustaceans and baitfish, which in turn draw walleyes. Rocks also provide shade and give the walleyes something to relate to.

POINTS AND INSIDE TURNS along a shoreline break are consistent walleye producers, particularly in spring. The best breaklines have a wide, shallow feeding shelf extending from shore.

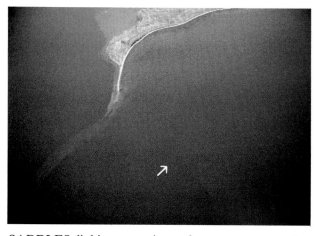

SADDLES linking one piece of structure to another concentrate walleyes. A saddle (arrow) serves as an underwater highway, so walleyes following this shoreline break would be naturally drawn to the offshore hump.

LONG FINGERS projecting from any type of structure also concentrate walleyes. They generally hold just off the tip, then use the finger as a path when moving into shallower water to feed.

SHADED STRUCTURE holds walleyes on bright days. Submerged weeds several feet high will cast a significant shadow. Fishing along a breakline is usually best where there is a shadow on the deep side of the weeds.

Low-percentage Walleye Structure

SMALL HUMPS that drop rapidly into deep water generally draw few walleyes. The small flat surface on top does not make a good feeding shelf and the sheer sides do not provide a comfortable resting area.

SAND FLATS with no weeds, rocks or other cover seldom hold walleyes. The sterile sand bottom produces little if any invertebrate life. As a result, these flats draw few baitfish.

SHORT-LIPPED POINTS are less likely to hold walleyes than points that project a long distance. Because these points usually lack a shallow feeding shelf, walleyes have little reason to use them.

LONG, NARROW POINTS may lack a feeding shelf, even though they project a long distance. Points that rise rapidly from deep water, then immediately plunge back down usually hold few walleyes.

SHEER DROP-OFFS rarely attract walleyes, even in late fall when the fish prefer sharp-tapering structure. Walleyes often rest with their fins touching bottom, an impossibility along an underwater cliff.

STRAIGHT BREAKLINES may have a few walleyes, but the fish are seldom as concentrated as on the points and inside turns of an irregular breakline. But in bowl-shaped lakes, a straight breakline may be the only choice.

Fishing for Walleye with Live Bait

Fishing surveys show that live bait accounts for at least two-thirds of all walleyes caught on hook and line. Even the staunchest artificial-lure advocates switch to live bait or add live bait to their lures when walleye fishing really gets tough.

The best live baits for walleyes include minnows and other small fish, nightcrawlers and leeches. There are times when other kinds of baits, such as water-dogs and frogs, will also produce. But they seldom work better, and are usually less effective. Your choice of live bait depends mainly on availability and the time of year.

Some baits are not available year around. Leeches, for example, cannot be caught in early spring because they are not active enough to swim into traps. Many bait shops do not carry shiner minnows in summer. At typical summer water temperatures, they are difficult to keep alive in a bait dealer's tank or in your minnow bucket.

Walleyes favor different types of bait in different seasons. Nightcrawlers rank among the best summertime baits, but in most waters, they do not work well in early spring. Minnows are a good choice in spring and again in fall, but may not be as effective in summer.

At times, the species of minnow can make a big difference. In spring, shiners often produce when nothing else will. But in fall, other minnows like redtail chubs may outfish shiners. Different types of minnows are effective in different waters, so it pays to ask your bait dealer what works best in the body of water you plan to fish.

Many anglers consider ribbon leeches to be the best all-around walleye bait. They swim enticingly at water temperatures of 50°F or higher. But leeches are not a good choice in cold water because they often curl around the hook, forming a useless ball.

Whatever the bait you choose, make sure that it is lively. When walleyes are really biting, you can often get by with a dead minnow or chewed-up nightcrawler, but a struggling minnow or squirming crawler will normally catch many more fish.

POPULAR LIVE BAIT includes: (1) golden shiner; (2) spottail shiner; (3) redbelly dace, or *rainbow*; (4) horny-

head chub, or *redtail* chub; (5) fathead minnow, or *tuffy* or *mudminnow*; (6) madtom, or *willow cat*; (7) larval tiger salamander, or *waterdog*; (8) ribbon leech; (9) night-crawler; and (10) leopard frog.

Slip-sinker Fishing for Walleyes

Slow-trolling with slip-sinker rigs probably accounts for more walleyes than any other technique. It is simple yet extremely effective, enabling you to present live bait so it stays lively and appears natural. Because the line slides freely through the sinker (above photo), a walleye feels no resistance when it grabs the bait and swims off. With a fixed sinker, a walleye may feel the tension and let go.

Slip-sinker rigs are versatile. They work well for walleyes hugging the bottom or suspended well above it. They can be fished over any bottom material or through dense weeds. And they are effective at depths from less than 10 feet to over 50.

You can purchase pretied slip-sinker rigs, but many anglers prefer to make their own to suit their style of fishing. When buying or assembling a slip-sinker rig, consider the following:

TYPE OF SINKER. The size of your sinker depends mainly on the water depth. As a general rule, you will need about ⅛ ounce of weight for every 10 feet of depth. At a depth of 20 feet, for instance, you would need a ¼-ounce sinker. But you may have to use more weight when fishing in wind or current.

In clear water, you may have to use a sinker lighter than normal and let out more line to prevent spooking the fish.

Sinker style is dictated by the type of bottom. On a clean, smooth bottom, any sinker will do as long as the line slips through freely. On a weedy bottom, a cone sinker works best because it will not catch vegetation. On a rocky bottom, a snag-resistant or pull-off sinker is the best choice. Many anglers prefer removable sinkers so they can switch weights without untying the rig.

How to Make a Slip-sinker Rig

COMPONENTS include: hooks such as (1) Mustad 9523, (2) Eagle Claw 84A, (3) VMC National Round; sinkers such as (4) egg, (5) Snap-Loc, which is removable, (6) walking-type; stops such as (7) barrel swivel, (8) swivel clip, (9) split-shot, (10) plastic bead.

TIE a slip-sinker rig by threading on the sinker, adding a barrel swivel or other type of stop, then attaching a leader and hook.

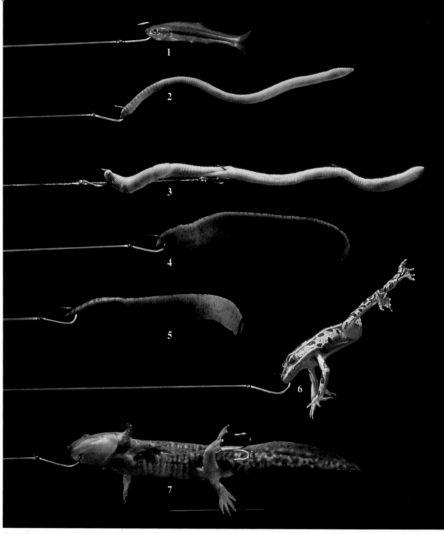

HOOK a (1) minnow through the lips; a (2) nightcrawler through the head or (3) on a harness; a (4) leech through the sucker or (5) the neck, which has tough skin, making it hard for panfish to steal the bait; a (6) frog and (7) waterdog through the lips. Use a stinger hook with a waterdog.

TYPE OF HOOK. The hook should be small enough that a walleye can swim off and swallow the bait without detecting anything unusual. Select a hook with an extremely sharp point, a relatively short shank and either a straight or turned-up eye. Most anglers prefer a size 6 to 8 hook for leeches and nightcrawlers; size 2 to 4 for minnows. You may need a larger hook for big minnows.

To keep your bait above a snaggy bottom or to reach suspended walleyes, use a hook with styrofoam, cork or hollow plastic molded around the shank for flotation. Called *floating jig heads,* these hooks usually have a fluorescent-colored body. You can also float your hook by attaching a small cork or styrofoam ball to the leader.

You can add color to your slip-sinker rig without using a floating jig head by threading a small piece of fluorescent yarn through the knot used to attach your hook. Some fishermen add a spinner blade ahead of the hook (page 143). At times, the extra color or flash makes a big difference.

TYPE OF LEADER. When walleyes are near bottom, there is no need for a long leader. An 18- to 36-inch leader works well in this situation. But when the fish are suspended, you may need a leader over 10 feet long.

Use a light, low-visibility mono leader, especially when fishing in clear water. Many commercial rigs have leaders much too heavy. Walleyes are more likely to see a heavy leader, so you will get fewer bites. A 6-pound leader is adequate in most situations, but you may need an 8- to 10-pound leader on a snaggy bottom. In extremely clear water or when the walleyes are sluggish, a 4-pound leader may improve your success.

TYPE OF STOP. To prevent the sinker from sliding down to the hook, you will need a stop. The simplest stop is a split-shot pinched onto the line at the desired position. But if the sinker snags, the split-shot may slip and fray your line. The most common stop is a barrel swivel. A swivel allows you to use a leader that is lighter than your main line. Then, if the hook becomes snagged, you can break it off without losing your entire rig.

A handy stop which enables you to adjust your leader length is a slip-bobber knot (page 144) with a bead to keep the knot from slipping through the sinker. Or, use only the bead and loop the line around it. To adjust the leader, loosen the loop and move the bead.

To troll a slip-sinker rig effectively, you must learn to control your boat in wind or current. To detect pickups, which are often extremely subtle, keep your line as short as possible. This means you must move the boat very slowly. And once you locate the walleyes, you must be able to follow the contour so you stay at the precise depth. If you move your bait too fast or wander back and forth across the structure, you will catch few walleyes.

How to Troll with a Slip-sinker Rig

LOWER the rig until the sinker touches bottom. Let out no more line than necessary; if you let out too much, you will have trouble feeling bites. Continually adjust the amount of line as the depth changes.

TROLL with your bail open, holding the line with your index finger. If you feel resistance, pull back very gently with your rod tip. A shake or any other sign of life indicates a fish; a dead pull is probably a stick or weed.

DROP the line off your index finger immediately when you determine that you have a bite. If you fail to release the line in time, the fish will detect too much resistance and let go of your bait.

You can also cast and retrieve a slip-sinker rig from an anchored boat or from shore. Many fishermen troll until they locate some walleyes, then anchor away from them and cast into the school. This technique works well in shallow water where continually trolling over the fish would spook them.

Effective slip-sinker fishing requires a sensitive rod with a flexible tip. Most experts use a medium-action graphite or boron rod from 5½ to 6 feet long. A flexible tip offers less resistance than a stiff one should you fail to release the line when a walleye swims off with the bait.

Keep your spinning reel filled with line. When a walleye moves with the bait, line will flow easily from the spool. If the spool is not filled, the line may catch and cause the fish to drop the bait.

FEED line as long as the fish continues to run. If you are right-handed, use your left hand to strip line from the reel. This is a precaution to assure that the line does not catch on the spool.

REEL RAPIDLY to take up slack once the fish stops running. Continue reeling until you feel weight. You may have to reel up more line than you think; a walleye may double back rather than move straight away.

SET THE HOOK with a sharp snap of the wrists when you feel the weight of the fish. Attempting to set the hook before all of the slack is removed is the most common mistake in slip-sinker fishing.

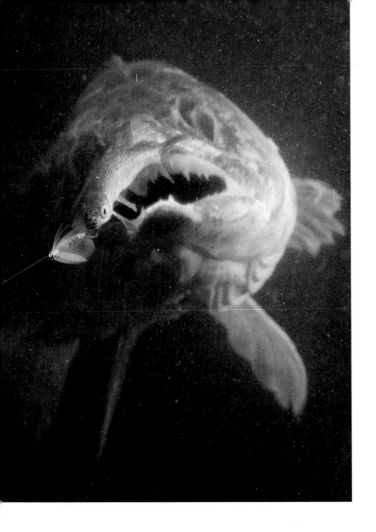

Fishing for Walleyes with Spinner - Live Bait Combinations

Spinner-live bait rigs have ranked among the top walleye baits for decades, and they remain just as effective today. Vibration and flash from the spinner blade attract a walleye's attention. And live bait increases the odds that the fish will bite. Spinner-live bait rigs work best in low-clarity water, but will catch walleyes anywhere.

The amount of vibration a spinner produces depends on the style and size of blade. A Colorado blade turns at about a 50-degree angle to the shaft; an Indiana blade, about 40 degrees; and a willow-leaf blade, about 25 degrees. The greater the angle and larger the blade, the stronger the beat.

Blades that produce a strong beat work well in low-clarity water or at night because walleyes can

Basic Spinner-Live Bait Rigs

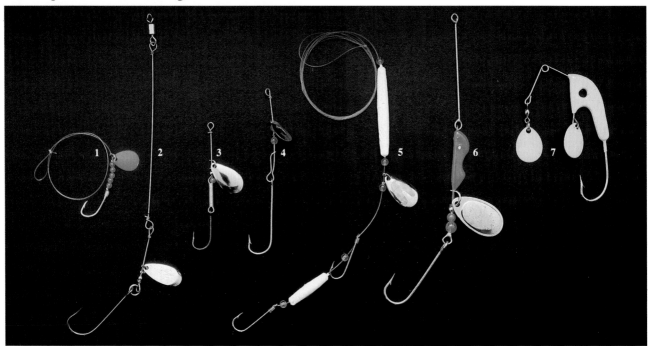

POPULAR SPINNERS for use with live bait include (1) mono-leader type, the best all-around choice; (2) steel-leader type, which runs slightly deeper but is more visible to fish; (3) sliding-spring type, which lets you change hooks easily; (4) june-bug type, with a steel shaft and an easy-turning blade; (5) floating type, with styrofoam floats to keep the rig above obstructions; (6) weight-forward type, with a lead body ahead of the blade for easy casting; (7) spinnerbait, with wire arms to prevent weeds and brush from catching on the hook.

detect the vibration with their lateral-line sense even if they cannot see the spinner. In this situation, a large Colorado blade would most likely be the best choice. But in clearer water, walleyes seem to prefer a less intense vibration, so a small willow-leaf blade may be more effective.

Colorado blades work well in spring, when walleyes prefer a slow-moving bait. Because these blades have more water resistance than others, they require less speed to make them spin. Willow-leaf blades are effective in summer and early fall, when walleyes are more willing to chase fast-moving baits. These blades have the least water resistance and require the most speed to make them turn. Indiana blades have intermediate qualities, making them a good all-season choice.

Spinners can be used in combination with almost any type of live bait, but minnows, nightcrawlers and leeches are most popular.

Spinner-live bait rigs are usually fished by trolling or drifting along a breakline. But they also work well for fishing over weedtops. The spinning blade functions as a weedguard and provides enough lift to keep the rig skimming over the vegetation.

Weight-forward spinners and spinnerbaits have lead bodies, so they work well for casting. They are effective for suspended walleyes because you can count them down to a precise depth and retrieve them at that level. Spinnerbaits can be retrieved through dense vegetation. The wire arms deflect weeds, and keep them from fouling the hook.

Most spinners, except weight-forward types and spinnerbaits, require a sinker to reach the desired depth. Many fishermen use a bead-chain or keel sinker to prevent line twist, but some prefer a slip sinker so they can feed line when a fish bites. When fishing over rocks, logs or brush use some type of snag-resistant sinker.

Many spinner-live bait rigs come with a two- or three-hook harness. With the trailing hook in the tail of the bait, you can set the hook immediately when you feel a strike. You can also set immediately with a single hook, if you feel a hard strike. But if you feel only a gentle tug, drop your rod tip back, hesitate a few seconds to let the fish take the bait, then set the hook. A long rod, from 6½ to 7 feet, enables you to drop the tip back farther and gives you a longer sweep for setting the hook.

Mono-leader type spinners should be tied with the lightest line practical, to avoid spooking the fish. Eight- to 10-pound line is usually adequate, but you may need 15-pound line in timber or brush.

How to Select and Tie Spinners

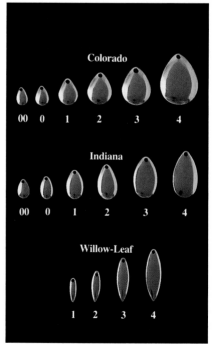

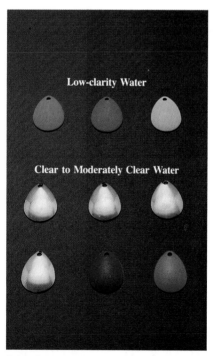

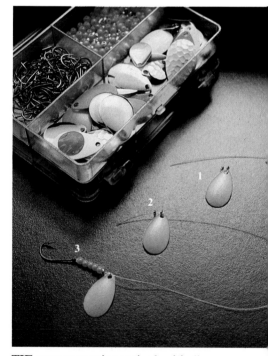

BLADE SIZE. Small blades in sizes 00 to 1 work well in cold or clear water; larger blades in sizes 2 to 4 are more effective in warm or low-clarity water or at night.

COLOR. Fluorescent orange, red and chartreuse are the best colors for fishing in low-clarity water. Silver, copper, gold, brass, blue and green are better choices in clearer water.

TIE your own spinner rigs by (1) slipping the blade onto a clevis. (2) Thread the clevis onto your line with the convex side of the blade forward, then (3) add beads and tie on a hook.

Slip-bobber Fishing for Walleyes

The idea of using a bobber for walleyes may draw a snicker from some anglers, but there are times when slip-bobber fishing will take more walleyes than any other technique.

Slip-bobber rigs work well in situations where walleyes are suspended at a specific depth or holding over a snaggy bottom. They are also effective when walleyes are not in the mood to feed. After a cold front, for instance, walleyes refuse to chase anything moving too rapidly, but may strike a bait dangling in front of them.

Because a slip-bobber rig seldom snags, you can use lighter line than with most other bait rigs. Six-pound-test mono is a good choice for most situations. Heavier line slides through the bobber more slowly and is more visible to the fish.

To set the depth, simply slide your bobber stop up the line the same distance as you want your bait to hang below the surface. The stop should slide freely so that it does not scuff your line when you want to change depth. But it should not be so loose that it slips while you reel in your line. You can buy a variety of bobber stops or make your own stop using a slip-bobber knot (shown below).

When you get a bite, wait a few seconds, then gently tighten your line until you feel weight. Failure to tighten the line at this point is the most common reason for losing fish. The bobber creates an angle between you and the walleye, so there will be slack line if you attempt to set the hook without performing this crucial step. A long, stiff rod is best for taking up slack and sinking the hook.

You can also improve your hooking percentage by waiting until the fish stops moving or begins to swim away from you. This gives you a better angle for setting the hook than if the fish were swimming toward you.

TERMINAL TACKLE for slip-bobber fishing includes: (1) various bobber stops; (2) beads; (3) size 4 to 6 bait hooks; (4) assorted split-shot; (5) various slip-bobbers; (6) lighted slip-bobber and batteries, for night fishing. You can substitute a 1/16-ounce jig for a plain hook.

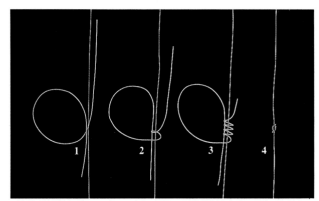

TIE a slip-bobber knot by (1) making a loop with a piece of braided dacron, then holding the loop alongside the mono. (2) Pass one end of the dacron through the loop and around the mono. (3) Continue until three or four wraps are completed. (4) Snug up the knot and trim.

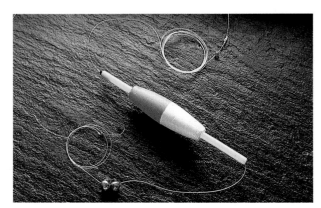

ATTACH the bobber stop, then add a bead so the stop does not slip through the bobber. Thread on the bobber and tie on your hook. About 18 inches above the hook, attach enough split-shot so the bobber just floats.

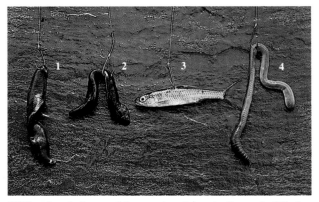

RIG a leech by pushing a size 6 hook through (1) the sucker end or (2) the middle; a (3) minnow with a size 4 hook through the back; a (4) nightcrawler with a size 6 hook through the middle so both ends dangle free.

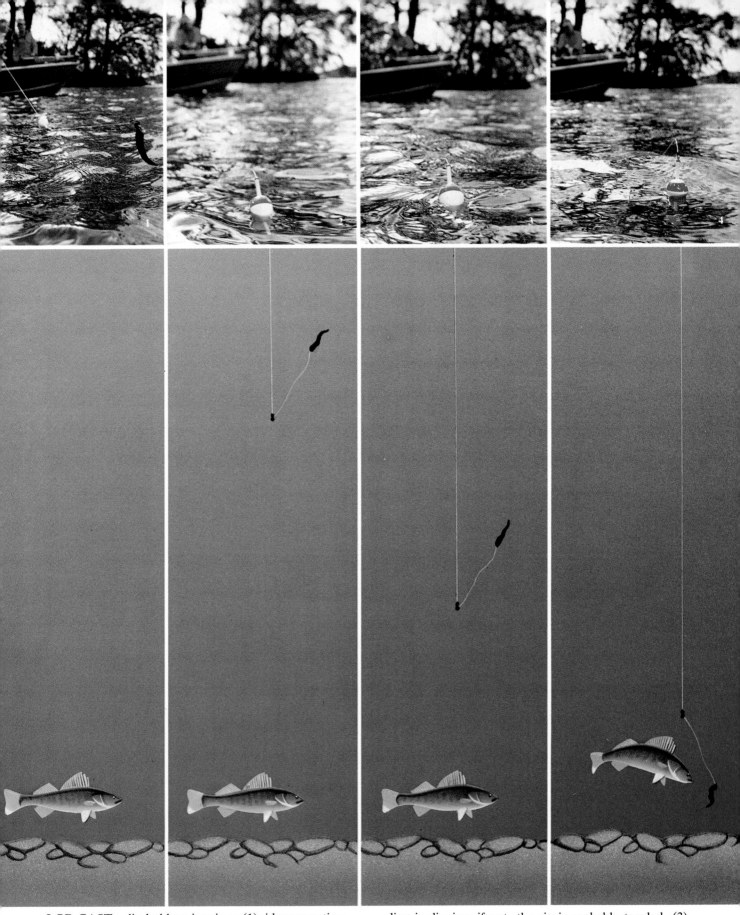

LOB-CAST a slip-bobber rig using a (1) sidearm motion. If you snap your wrist, the hook may tangle around the bobber. (2) Pay out line after the cast so that it can slip through the bobber freely. Watch carefully to be sure the line is slipping; if not, the rig is probably tangled. (3) Continue paying out line. When the bait reaches the right depth, the knot will prevent the line from slipping any farther, causing the bobber to (4) stand upright.

Fishing for Walleye with Artificial Lures
How to Catch Walleyes with Jigs

No other artificial lure will catch walleyes as consistently as a lead-head jig. A jig is a natural choice for walleyes because it is easy to keep on bottom where the fish spend most of their time.

Among the most versatile of artificial lures, jigs can be fished in many different ways. You can cast from an anchored or drifting boat, jig vertically while drifting with the wind or current, or troll slowly while bumping the jig along bottom. And, you can fish a jig plain when walleyes are biting, or tip it with live bait when fishing is slow.

CASTING. The most widely used jig-fishing technique, casting works well in shallow water. When walleyes are in the shallows, drifting or trolling over them, or even anchoring nearby, will probably spook them. But you will not disturb them if you anchor at a distance and cast.

To work a shallow reef, for instance, anchor in deep water so the wind pushes you into position for casting to the desired area of the reef. If nothing bites in a few minutes, pull up the anchor and reposition in a different spot. Continue moving until you find the fish. Anchoring and casting also works well for fishing eddies, pools and pockets in rivers.

When walleyes are scattered along a breakline, let your boat drift just off the break and cast into the shallows. Use your electric motor or outboard to keep the boat drifting parallel to the breakline. If you catch a walleye, toss a marker and work the spot more thoroughly.

To catch walleyes suspended off bottom, count your jig down to a different depth after each cast, then begin your retrieve. When you get a strike, repeat the count on the next cast.

Details on casting and retrieving a jig for walleyes are shown in the photo sequence on pages 148-149.

VERTICAL JIGGING. Use a jig heavy enough that you can keep your line nearly vertical. Bounce the jig along bottom while drifting with the wind or current, continually adjusting your line length as the depth changes. Keep your bail open and hold the line with your finger so you can easily let out a little more line when the water gets deeper. When it gets shallower, reel in the slack so the jig does not drag.

When walleyes are in deep water, vertical jigging generally works better than casting. Because of the greater line angle, you can hop the jig higher and give it more action. The extra action often triggers walleyes to strike, especially in low-clarity water.

Another advantage of jigging vertically: you can feel strikes more easily. Because you are using a minimum of line, stretch does not diminish the feel of a strike as much as it would with a longer line.

Vertical jigging is effective in lakes or rivers. In a lake, jig vertically while letting the wind push your boat over likely structure. In a river, let the boat drift with the current, keeping it at a likely depth.

JIG TROLLING. This technique combines vertical jigging with backtrolling. Lower your jig to bottom, then troll slowly in reverse while following a breakline or exploring a reef. Twitch the jig to hop it off bottom, then lower it back with a taut line. Continually adjust your line length as you would when jigging vertically.

The key to success in jig trolling is to move very slowly. If you troll too fast, your jig will lose contact with the bottom. And because you will have to let out more line, strikes will be harder to detect. For slower speed and better boat control, always troll against the wind.

With any of these techniques, the way you work your jig depends on the season and the mood of the walleyes. In spring and fall, when the water is cool, small hops generally work better than big ones. But in summer, larger hops often catch more fish. In late fall and winter, walleyes sometimes prefer a jig dragged slowly on bottom, with no hopping action. Because the walleyes' mood can change from day

How to Select a Jig

POPULAR HEAD STYLES include: (1) ball, a good all-around choice; (2) bullet, which cuts easily through current; (3) banana, with a sharp kicking action for vertical jigging; (4) pyramid, which slides easily through weeds; (5) stand-up, for snaggy bottoms; (6) mushroom, good for soft-plastic tails; (7) pony or spinner-type, and (8) propeller-type, both with extra flash and sound; and (9) wiggler, with a strong swimming action.

POPULAR DRESSINGS include: (1) curlytail; (2) paddle-tail grub; (3) split-tail grub; (4) shad; and (5) grub with marabou tail, a good choice for tipping because the tail does not cover the bait. These soft plastics feel like real food so walleyes hold on longer, giving you more time to set the hook. (6) Bucktail is durable and sinks slowly. (7) Marabou has a unique breathing action. (8) Chenille-and-feather jigs are also good for tipping.

to day, it pays to vary your retrieve until you find the action that works best.

Jig fishing demands intense concentration and a sensitive touch. When a walleye grabs a jig, what you feel ranges from a sharp tap to merely a gradual tightening of the line. An active fish inhales a jig by sucking in water and expelling it through the gills. This type of strike produces the sharp tap sensation. When a walleye is not actively feeding, it simply swims up and closes its mouth over the jig, causing the line to tighten.

Beginning jig fishermen fail to set the hook on a high percentage of their strikes. They expect to feel a sharp tug, as they would if using a crankbait or spinner. But a walleye usually grabs a jig as it sinks, not as it moves forward. So if you wait for a sharp tug before setting the hook, you will seldom catch a walleye on a jig.

The best policy is to set the hook whenever you feel anything unusual. If you hop the jig off bottom, but it does not sink as you would expect, a walleye has probably grabbed it. What seems like excess drag from a weed may turn out to be a walleye. And a slight peck that feels like a perch bite could be the trophy of a lifetime.

The secret to detecting subtle strikes is to keep your line taut while the jig is sinking. If you twitch your rod tip, then drop it back rapidly as the jig sinks, slack will form and you will not feel the strike. Instead, lower the jig with tension on the line, as if you were setting it gently on bottom.

You will detect more strikes if you carefully watch your line and rod tip. Many times, you will see a strike that you cannot feel. If you see the line twitch where it enters the water, or if the line moves slightly to the side, set the hook.

How to Cast and Retrieve a Jig for Walleyes

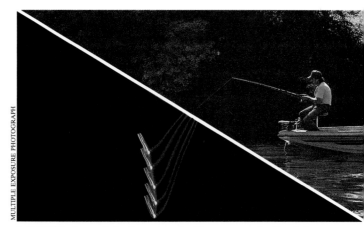

LIFT the jig with a slight twitch of the rod tip after letting it sink to bottom. How high you hop the jig depends on the mood of the fish. When they are lethargic, a steady retrieve may work better than a hopping retrieve.

LOWER the rod tip, keeping the line taut as the jig sinks. If you do not keep tension on the line, you will not feel the strike. Continue to lift and lower, reeling up a few inches of line after each hop.

How to Tip a Jig with Live Bait

TIP a jig with a minnow by (1) pushing the hook through the lips, from the bottom up. To keep a minnow on the jig longer, (2) hook it through the eye sockets. The most secure method of attaching a minnow is to (3) push the

hook of a plain jig into the mouth and up through the back. Hook a leech (4) through the sucker end. Attach a nightcrawler by (5) hooking it through the tip of the head; (6) hooking it through the middle so that both ends trail;

148

One of the big problems in jig fishing is noticing strikes on a windy day. The wind forms a belly in your line and buffets your rod tip, so a slight twitch often goes unnoticed. To keep the problem to a minimum, hold your rod tip low. The size of the belly will be much smaller, and the rod tip will not whip around as much.

Selecting the proper rod is vital to successful jig fishing. Most experts prefer a sensitive graphite or boron spinning rod to detect delicate strikes. A rod about 5½ feet long with a light tip and stiff butt is a good all-around choice. The light tip responds to a subtle tap, yet the powerful butt enables you to sink the hook with a slight snap of the wrists.

Line is also important. Limp, premium-grade monofilament from 6- to 8-pound test works well in most situations. Stiffer or heavier line comes off your reel in coils, so it is almost impossible to keep your line tight. Many anglers prefer fluorescent mono for jig fishing because it is easy to see. But in clear water, fluorescent line will result in fewer strikes. You can see your line better if you wear polarized glasses.

Attach your line to a jig with some type of clinch knot or with a loop knot (page 155). A loop knot lets the jig pivot freely at the attachment eye, maximizing the action. Do not use a heavy snap, a snap-swivel or a steel leader. They add weight and are more visible than plain mono.

One of the most common mistakes in jig fishing for walleyes is using a jig that is too heavy. A light jig sinks more slowly, so walleyes have more time to grab it. As a rule, use the lightest jig you can keep on bottom. In most cases, you will need about ⅛ ounce for every 10 feet of depth. You will need a heavier jig to stay on bottom when fishing in wind or current.

STRIKES come on the drop. If the fish inhales the jig (above), you will feel a sharp tap and the rod tip will twitch noticeably. If the fish hits gently, the line will tighten slightly or the jig will not sink as expected.

SET THE HOOK immediately when you feel anything unusual; a walleye spits a jig quickly. A flick of the wrists results in a faster hook set than a long sweep of the arms, but you will need a stiff rod to sink the hook.

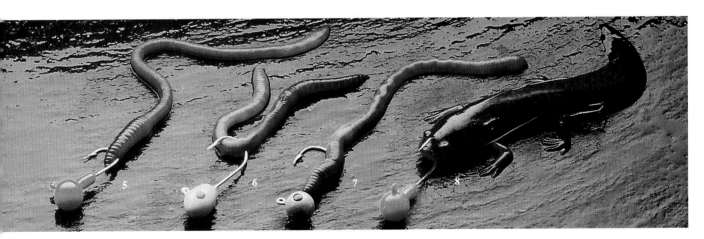

or (7) threading it onto a plain jig, pushing the night-crawler head as far up the shaft as possible. (8) Hook a waterdog through the lips with the jig hook and push a stinger, usually a size 10 treble hook, into the tail (page 150). Note: All the baits shown above have been hooked on plain jig heads so the hooking method is clear. But each of these methods except numbers 3 and 7 will also work with any short-tailed jig.

When and How to Use a Stinger

CHECK your minnow for teeth marks or ripped skin if you had a strike but failed to hook the fish. Damaged skin on the rear half of the minnow means that walleyes are striking short and that you should tie on a stinger.

ATTACH a stinger to a (1) hair or feather jig by tying the mono to the bend of the hook; to a (2) plastic-bodied jig by tying the mono to the eye of the jig. This method lets you change the body without removing the stinger.

TIE an adjustable stinger so that you can change the length of the mono to suit minnows of different lengths. Begin by (1) tying a size 10 treble to a length of mono with a Duncan loop (page 155). (2) Attach the loose end to the bend of the jig hook using your favorite fishing knot. (3) Shorten the mono to fit a small minnow by sliding the knot closer to the jig hook. (4) Lengthen the mono to fit a larger minnow by sliding the knot toward the stinger.

Other Jig-fishing Tips

STORE jig heads and soft plastic tails in small zip-lock bags. The bags are watertight, so the jig hooks will not rust. Tails stored this way will not discolor and can be treated with worm oil so they stay pliable.

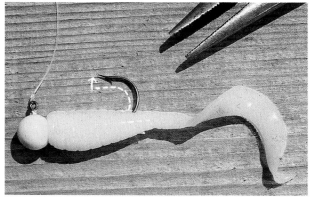

BEND the point of the jig hook slightly outward if you are having trouble hooking walleyes. The extra clearance between the hook point and the head of the jig will improve your hooking percentage.

Fishing for Walleyes with Jigging Lures

Of all the artificial lures used for walleyes, jigging lures may be the most underrated. Although commonly used on reservoirs and big rivers, these lures are seldom seen on natural lakes.

Unlike most jigs, jigging lures have built-in action. A vibrating blade wiggles rapidly; a tailspin has a spinner blade on the rear that rotates as the lure moves forward and as it sinks; a jigging spoon rocks when pulled upward and tumbles erratically when it settles toward bottom.

These lures usually work best when jigged vertically. Walleyes strike a jigging lure as it sinks, much the same way they strike a jig, so a taut line is crucial if you are to detect a strike. You can also troll or cast with jigging lures. Make long, fast sweeps with your rod tip, then let the lure settle back.

Vibrating blades are often more effective than jigs in murky water. Walleyes detect the wiggle with their lateral-line sense even if they cannot see the lure. Because vibrating blades sink rapidly, they work well in deep water or swift current. These qualities make them perfectly suited to the swift, murky water of most rivers.

Attach a vibrating blade with a plain, round-nosed snap inserted through one of the line-attachment holes on the back. You can change the amount of wiggle by attaching the snap in different holes. The rear hole produces the widest wiggle; the front hole the narrowest.

Tailspins work best in water that is relatively clear. The added flash and vibration of the spinner blade may trigger a walleye that is not interested in a jig. Tie a tailspin directly to your line.

Jigging spoons will take walleyes when jigged vertically in flooded timber. They can also be used for walleyes suspended in open water. Attach a jigging spoon to your line with a split-ring.

You can use the same tackle when fishing with jigging lures as you would when fishing with jigs. But many anglers prefer a slightly longer and stiffer rod, such as a 6-foot bait-casting rod, and heavier line, usually 8- to 10-pound mono.

BASIC STYLES of jigging lures include (1) vibrating blade, (2) tailspin and (3) jigging spoon. Some jigging spoons have a hook dressed with bucktail (above) or a soft plastic curlytail, to slow the sink rate.

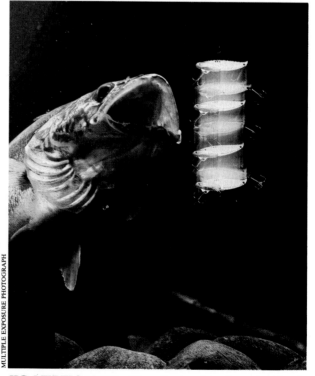

MULTIPLE EXPOSURE PHOTOGRAPH

JIG VERTICALLY with a jigging lure by sweeping it sharply upward, then letting it settle with a taut line. As it settles, watch your line for a twitch, sideways movement or slack. Then set the hook immediately.

151

Fishing for Walleyes with Plugs

Plugs are a recent addition to the arsenal of many walleye fishermen, but the idea of using plugs to catch walleyes is not exactly new. In fact, past generations of walleye anglers relied almost exclusively on trolling plugs.

As live bait became more widely used, plugs lost popularity. But with the introduction of many new plug types and the improvement of existing types, plugs have regained favor with walleye anglers.

Walleyes normally prefer plugs from 3 to 6 inches long, although big walleyes will take plugs as long as 8 inches. The plugs most commonly used in walleye

fishing are minnow plugs, crankbaits, vibrating plugs and trolling plugs.

MINNOW PLUGS. The long, slender shape of these plugs has a special appeal to walleyes because it resembles the shape of perch, ciscoes, shiners and other common walleye foods. And the tight wobble, even at a slow retrieve speed, gives minnow plugs a remarkably lifelike appearance.

Minnow plugs come in the following styles for fishing under various conditions:

- Short-lipped floating models run at depths of 5 feet or less. They work best for casting or trolling over shallow shoals and weedbeds.

- Long-lipped floating models dive as deep as 12 feet, and are generally used for trolling along deep structure or over deep weedbeds.

- Sinking models can be trolled in deep water, or counted down to a specific depth and retrieved at that level.

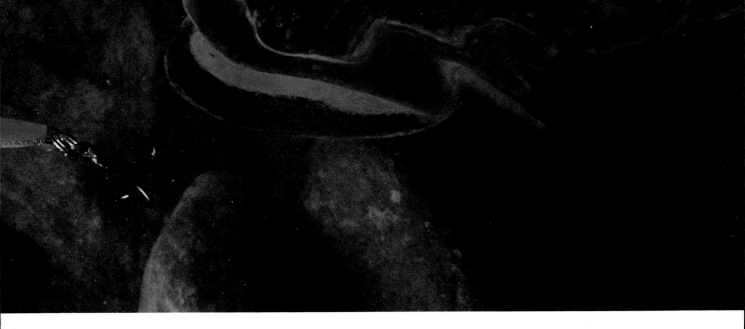

• Neutrally buoyant models can be retrieved very slowly without floating to the surface or sinking. When walleyes are inactive, a neutrally buoyant plug may work better than a floating or sinking type. Because neutrally buoyant plugs can be retrieved so slowly, they catch walleyes at water temperatures down to 40°F. Other types of minnow plugs become effective at about 45°F.

Walleyes seem to favor the action of short-lipped floaters. When fishing in deep water, many anglers attach sinkers ahead of short-lipped floaters instead of using diving or sinking models.

Minnow plugs are light for their size, so they are difficult to cast. But you can improve your casting distance by using light line, usually 6-pound test, and a 6½- to 7-foot spinning rod with a light tip. The long rod provides good casting leverage and the tip flexes enough to propel the light lure.

CRANKBAITS. These plugs have a stockier shape and more pronounced wobble than minnow plugs.

Most are relatively heavy and have an aerodynamic shape, so they are much easier to cast. Crankbaits are designed to tip sharply downward at the nose when retrieved, so the lip protects the treble hooks from fouling.

Crankbaits come in the same four styles as minnow plugs. Comparable styles of crankbaits and minnow plugs are fished under much the same conditions. Crankbaits, however, generally require a faster retrieve to achieve their intense wobble. As a result, they work best at higher water temperatures, usually above 55°F.

Before attempting to fish with a crankbait, test it to make sure it is properly tuned. If the plug is out of tune, it will not track straight and cannot run at maximum depth. To tune a crankbait, simply bend the attachment eye away from the direction in which the plug veers.

A 5½- to 6-foot spinning outfit with 8- to 10-pound mono is adequate for most crankbait fishing, but a stiff bait-casting rod works better for deep divers that have a strong pull.

VIBRATING PLUGS. The rapid wiggle of these plugs sets up vibrations that attract walleyes even in the murkiest water. Many have internal shot or beads to produce sound.

Most vibrating plugs sink, so you can fish them at virtually any depth. Like crankbaits, they must be retrieved rapidly to attain maximum action, so they are most effective at temperatures above 55°F.

Vibrating plugs have little wind resistance, so they cast easily. Models with internal shot will cast even farther and sink more quickly, so they are a good choice for casting or trolling along deep structure.

Vibrating plugs are normally fished with rods, reels and line similar to those used with crankbaits.

TROLLING PLUGS. Most of these plugs have broad foreheads which produce a wide wobbling action. But the broad forehead also adds wind resistance, making them difficult to cast.

Without added weight, trolling plugs run at depths ranging from 5 to 20 feet. Some are designed for slow trolling, others for speed trolling. Models used for speed trolling, like the Hellbender, work best at temperatures of 70°F or higher.

Medium-power spinning or bait-casting gear with 8- to 10-pound mono performs well with most trolling plugs. But for speed trolling, you will need a stiff bait-casting rod with low-stretch mono of at least 12-pound test.

For best action, attach all plugs with a split-ring, a round-nosed snap or a loop knot (shown at right). If you snub your knot directly to the attachment eye, you will dampen the plug's action.

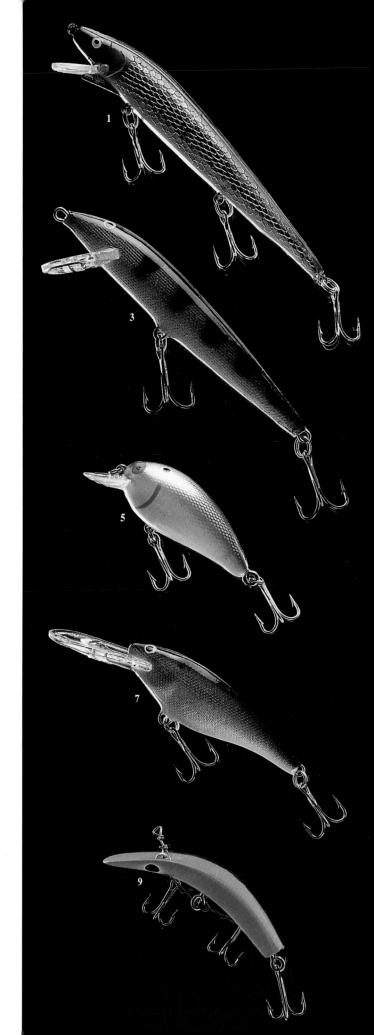

POPULAR PLUGS for walleyes include (1) short-lipped floating minnow plug, (2) long-lipped floating minnow plug, (3) sinking minnow plug, (4) neutrally buoyant minnow plug, (5) short-lipped crankbait, (6) long-lipped crankbait, (7) neutrally buoyant crankbait, (8) vibrating plug, (9) trolling plug and (10) speed-trolling plug.

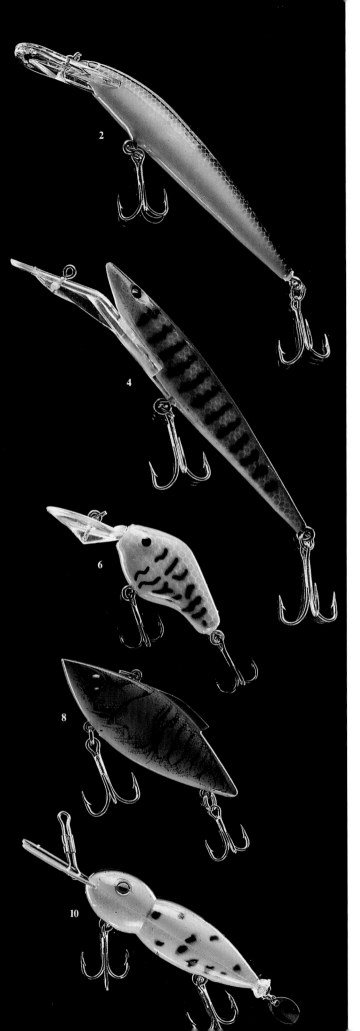

A Fast Method for Tying a Duncan Loop

THREAD the line through the eye of your plug, then hold the standing line in your left hand and the tag end in your right. The tag end should be about 10 inches long.

BEGIN wrapping the tag end around your left index finger, making sure the wraps are to the left of the plug.

COMPLETE four to six wraps.

SLIP the wraps off your finger, then thread the tag end through the loops, from right to left.

SNUG UP the knot by first moistening it, then gradually tightening it by pulling on the tag end. If the knot starts to bunch up, straighten the wraps, then continue snugging.

PULL on the standing line to reduce the size of the loop; trim. The loop may close when you catch a fish, but you can reopen it with your fingernails.

Basic Plug-fishing Techniques

CAST your plug downwind (arrows) while drifting over a shoal or weedbed or along a breakline. If necessary, use an electric motor to control your drift. Casting with the wind gives you more distance and keeps you from casting into water through which your boat has drifted.

LOCATE walleyes by trolling parallel to a breakline. To cover a wide range of depths, one fisherman trolls a deep-diving plug on the outside, another trolls a shallow-running plug on the inside and a third casts a shallow runner over weeds or rocky shoals.

TROLL against the wind or current whenever possible. Walleyes generally prefer a slow-moving plug, and trolling this way reduces your speed. If you troll with the wind or current, precise steering will be difficult. And trolling with the current will also cause your plug to lose action.

Tips for Fishing with Plugs

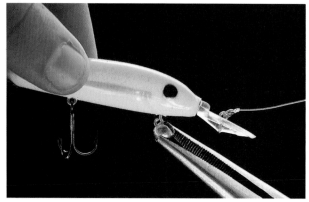

PINCH a split-shot on the front screw-eye after removing the treble hook. The shot makes the plug cast easier and run deeper. If the shot is the right size, the plug will be neutrally buoyant. Removing the treble also reduces tangling on the cast and snagging on the retrieve.

VARY the action and speed of a plug by periodically sweeping your rod tip forward, then dropping it back. The change often triggers a strike from a walleye that has been following the plug. This technique works equally well for casting or trolling.

Other Artificial Lures for Walleyes

A walleye will, on occasion, strike any type of artificial lure. Muskie fishermen sometimes hook trophy-class walleyes while pitching foot-long jerkbaits. Bass anglers often catch walleyes while fishing along weedlines with plastic worms. Bluegill fishermen have even taken walleyes on tiny wet flies.

Although jigs, jigging lures and plugs are the most widely used artificials, others like spinners and flies may be equally effective.

Weight-forward spinners can be used at a variety of depths. They are well-suited to unstratified waters, where walleyes may range from 5 to 30 feet deep. Most weight-forward spinners come with a plain hook for use with nightcrawlers or other live bait, but some have tail dressings of hair, feathers or soft plastic, making bait unnecessary. The best sizes for walleyes are ¼ to ⅝ ounce.

Standard spinners work well in spring, when walleyes are in the shallows. Models with size 2 or 3 blades are most effective.

Spinnerbaits are more snag-resistant than other types of spinners. Models weighing ⅛ to ¼ ounce will catch walleyes that are buried in weeds or brush.

Streamer flies produce walleyes in spring. They imitate baitfish, so a walleye cruising the shallows in search of food finds a streamer hard to resist.

STREAMER FLY. Cast a streamer over a shallow feeding shoal beginning at dusk. Retrieve with a darting motion. Use a sink-tip fly line, a tapered leader with an 8- to 10-pound tippet, and a size 2 or 4 fly that resembles a baitfish, such as a white marabou muddler.

How to Use Other Artificial Lures

SPINNERBAIT. Toss a spinnerbait into pockets in flooded brush or emergent weeds and let it helicopter downward before starting your retrieve. This method works best in rivers and reservoirs, where rising spring-time water levels drive walleyes into shoreline vegetation.

STANDARD SPINNER. Cast a standard spinner into the shallows when walleyes are cruising rocky or gravelly shorelines in early spring. Reel just fast enough to keep the lure above bottom. To avoid severe line twist, always attach a standard spinner with a snap swivel.

Ice Fishing for Walleyes

Catching walleyes, especially big ones, is seldom easy. And it becomes even more challenging when ice prevents you from exploring as you normally would at other times of the year.

Nevertheless, ice fishermen account for a major share of the big walleyes taken in many lakes. Where baitfish populations are high, anglers rarely catch the well-fed trophies in summer. The big fish start to bite in late fall when predation begins to reduce the baitfish crop. They continue biting into the winter.

You can greatly improve your chances of catching walleyes through the ice by learning when and where to fish for them. Most ice fishermen spend too much time fishing where there are no walleyes or at times when they simply will not bite.

The best time to catch walleyes is just after the ice becomes thick enough for safe fishing. In shallow lakes, walleyes continue to bite for three to four weeks. Then, action usually slows as the fish gradually become more dormant. Fishing picks up again in late winter, especially after the snow begins to thaw. Meltwater running into the lake seems to rejuvenate the fish.

In deeper lakes, walleyes also bite best at first ice, but good fishing usually continues later into the winter. So, if you plan to fish walleyes in mid- to late winter, your odds are generally better on a deep lake than a shallow one.

Weather and time of day affect walleye activity in winter much the same way they do at other times of year. Because walleyes feed most heavily in dim light, fishing is generally better at dawn and dusk than at midday, and better on overcast days than on sunny days. They bite best during periods of stable weather, although the rapidly decreasing light levels that accompany an approaching winter storm often trigger a feeding spree.

Ice-fishing success can vary greatly from year to year. A lake may be crammed with walleyes, but if too much forage remains at the end of the open-water season, they will not bite. As a rule, if fishing was good in fall, it will be good in winter.

Where you begin your search depends on the type of lake and the time of year. Wintertime walleyes in clear lakes generally inhabit deeper water than those in low-clarity lakes. Look for them in water from 10 to 15 feet deep at first ice; from 20 to 40 feet in midwinter; and again in 10 to 15 feet in late winter. In low-clarity lakes, they usually stay at depths of 6 to 15 feet through the entire winter.

Structure is as important to walleyes in winter as in summer. Prime wintertime spots include rock piles, sunken islands and shoreline points. But walleyes may be anywhere along a drop-off, especially around inside or outside bends. If a lake has both shoreline and mid-lake structure, the shoreline structure normally holds the most walleyes in early and late season; the mid-lake structure in midwinter.

In lakes with little structure, walleyes sometimes relate to weedbeds or submerged timber. Rather than fishing directly in the weeds, try to find the deep edge or an opening among the weeds.

If you know a spot that produces walleyes in summer, there is a good chance you will find them there in winter. When you find a good spot in summer, look for landmarks that will put you in the area once the ice forms. Then, you can sound through the ice with a portable depth finder to pinpoint the spot.

In most waters, walleyes stay within a foot of the bottom in winter. They seldom suspend, except in fertile lakes. There, the oxygen supply declines in deep water as the winter wears on, so the walleyes must suspend or move to the shallows.

Effective scouting requires drilling a lot of holes, and many anglers are not willing to work that hard. A successful ice fisherman seldom sticks with an unproductive hole for more than an hour. He may try dozens of holes before finding the fish.

Ice-fishing Equipment

Some fishermen invest a small fortune in equipment to help them catch walleyes through the ice. They race to their spots in high-powered snowmobiles and spend the day fishing in elaborate ice shacks with gas heat, lights and even television sets.

Snowmobiles and fancy shacks are optional, but you should have the following equipment:

• An ice chisel, or *spud,* for testing thin ice, chipping holes before the ice becomes too thick, and widening the bottom of your hole so you can land fish more easily.

• An auger-type ice drill, either manual or gas-powered, at least 7 inches in diameter. If there is a chance of catching walleyes over 8 pounds, the drill should be 8 to 9 inches in diameter.

• An extra set of blades for your drill and an Allen wrench for changing them. A slight bit of rust or a few nicks can render your old blades useless.

• A perforated scoop to clear ice from your hole.

• A portable flasher to measure the depth before drilling a hole.

• A jigging rod and reel with 8- to 10-pound mono (photo at right).

• Several tip-ups, possibly including wind tip-ups (photo at right). They should be spooled with 20- to 30-pound dacron line, ice-fishing line or fly line. Monofilament tangles too easily.

• An assortment of hooks, split-shot and leader material for rigging tip-ups and a clip-on weight for setting the depth.

• A thick-walled styrofoam minnow bucket. Styrofoam is an excellent insulator, so the water does not freeze as quickly as it would in a metal or plastic bucket.

• A molded-plastic minnow scoop. Mesh scoops soon become caked with ice in cold weather.

• A gaff for landing large fish.

Many walleye anglers use portable canvas shacks, but experts often fish in the open because shacks reduce their mobility. With a good snowmobile suit, felt-lined boots and warm mittens, you can stay comfortable at temperatures well below zero. Other handy items include a towel for keeping your hands dry, a 5-gallon plastic pail which stores gear and doubles as a seat, and a plastic sled for hauling gear to your spot.

TIP-UPS consist of a (1) plastic or wooden frame that rests on the ice, (2) an underwater reel that will not freeze up, (3) some type of release mechanism that springs a (4) flag when a fish pulls line off the reel. The best tip-ups have a (5) shaft filled with anti-freeze.

WIND TIP-UPS have a (1) metal plate that catches the wind, causing the bait to bob up and down enticingly. The (2) reel is above water, so the line may freeze in the hole during cold weather. The (3) spring rests on the reel so the (4) flag pops up when the reel begins to turn.

JIGGING RODS should be 2½ to 3 feet long and moderately stiff. Guides should be large, so ice cannot block them. To keep your hands warm, choose a rod with a foam handle instead of a metal one. Use a closed-face spinning reel with a trigger and a smooth drag. The closed face allows you to set the rod down without snow and ice collecting on the spool. And a trigger-operated reel hangs below the rod, so the outfit is ideally balanced for jigging.

JIGGING LURES for ice fishing include (1) Jigging Rapala® and (2) Sonar™, both of which are usually fished without bait. The (3) Swedish Pimple®, (4) Do-Jigger, (5) Russian hook and (6) plain lead-head jig are generally fished with a minnow or a perch eye.

POPULAR BAITS include (1) golden shiner, (2) fathead minnow, (3) spottail shiner and (4) redbelly dace. In most instances, 2½- to 3½-inch minnows are the best choice. But if you are fishing for big walleyes, a minnow 5 inches or longer will often work better.

Ice-fishing Techniques for Walleyes

Dangling a minnow beneath a float probably accounts for more walleyes than any other ice-fishing technique, but there are times when other techniques will take more fish.

When walleyes are feeding, you can often catch more on a jigging lure than on a minnow. You can switch holes more easily, and after catching a fish, you can drop your lure back down immediately without taking time to put on fresh bait.

Tip-ups enable you to cover more water than you could with a minnow and float. A flag can be seen from several hundred feet away. Most states and provinces allow at least two lines for ice fishing, so a group of anglers could scatter tip-ups over a large area to locate the fish.

Most tip-ups have underwater reels, so it makes no difference if the hole freezes over. A float quickly freezes in on a cold day, so you must continually scoop ice out of the hole.

When selecting tip-ups for walleye fishing, look for those with a carefully machined release mechanism, a reel that turns freely, and a main shaft filled with a freeze-proof liquid. Cheap tip-ups do not trip as

easily, so walleyes may feel the resistance and drop the bait. If the main shaft is not sealed, water can seep in and freeze the release mechanism.

A wind tip-up gives your minnow extra action and often increases the number of bites. But the reel is above water, so the line may freeze in the hole. To help solve this problem, place a cover of black cardboard or plywood over the hole, leaving a slit for the line. The black cover absorbs heat from the sun and keeps snow from blowing into the hole. To prevent your line from freezing on the spool and to reduce tangling, use line that sheds water, such as plastic-coated tip-up line or fly line.

Many fishermen make the mistake of arriving at their spot late in the afternoon, just when the walleyes move in, then drilling holes. The noise is sure to drive the walleyes out of the area. Instead, get to your spot and drill your holes at least an hour before they normally start to move in.

Another common mistake is fishing in a crowded area, thinking that a concentration of anglers means the fish are biting. But a group of fishermen driving snowmobiles, chopping holes, dropping equipment on the ice or merely walking around may spook the fish, especially if the water is shallow.

Your odds are better if you take the time to find a spot away from the crowd. Try to locate areas that produced during the previous summer, and keep moving to find a productive hole.

How to Use a Tip-Up

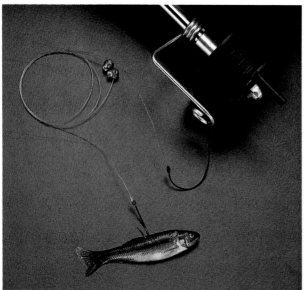

RIG your tip-up by filling the spool with 30-pound test dacron line. Tie on a 2-foot leader of 8- to 10-pound mono, pinch on split-shot and attach a size 4 short-shank hook. Push the hook through the minnow's back just ahead of the dorsal fin.

SET the flag arm under the *T*-shaped spindle after lowering your bait to the desired depth. For walleye fishing, set the arm under the smooth side of the spindle so it will trip easily. If you set the arm under the grooved side, it will take a stronger pull to trip the flag.

JIGGING LURES often trigger strikes from walleyes that refuse plain minnows. The tantalizing up-and-down motion arouses a walleye's curiosity, causing it to move in for a closer look. The fish almost always bite after the lure settles to rest. Some fishermen tip their lures with a small minnow, part of a minnow, or a perch eye for extra attraction, but the added weight may dampen the action of a delicately balanced lure like a Jigging Rapala®.

WATCH for a flag signalling a bite. If the spindle (inset) or spool is turning, wait for it to stop. Do not try to hook the fish while it is running; you will probably miss it.

SET the hook with a sharp snap of your wrist. Before you jerk, gently pull on the line until you feel resistance; walleyes sometimes double back after making a run.

KEEP a gaff handy for landing large walleyes. Try to gaff the fish below the chin or under the gill flap. Do not attempt to lift a good-sized walleye out of the hole with your line.

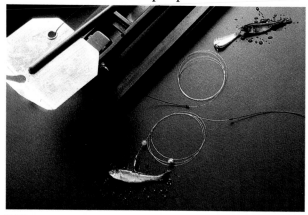

RIG a wind tip-up by threading tip-up line through the hole in the metal plate. Tie on a leader, attach a jigging lure and tip it with a minnow (top). Or, use an attractor rig with a bead that slides up and down as the tip-up bobs (bottom), or a standard minnow rig (page 162).

BEND the metal plate upward so it catches more wind if you want the bait to bob more intensely. The tension of the coil spring (arrow) also regulates the action. Loosen the wing nut, then slide the spring downward for more action; slide it upward for less action.

Wind Direction

POSITION the tip-up so that the wind blows parallel to the arm and from the back side, for maximum action. Pack slush around the base. Let out enough line so that your bait or lure just touches bottom when the arm dips to its lowest point.

MULTIPLE EXPOSURE PHOTOGRAPH

SET the flag by bending the thin metal flag spring so that it presses against the back side of the spool. Pressure from the spring prevents the spool from turning and fixes the depth. When a fish bites, friction from the turning spool springs the flag.

WATCH the tip-up to make sure it continues bobbing. If ice forms in the hole or the wind changes direction, the bobbing may stop. Walleyes usually prefer a bobbing action that covers a vertical distance of 6 to 12 inches, but an 18-inch distance sometimes works better.

How to Use a Willow Rig

PACK the butt of a flexible willow, 3 to 4 feet long, into a pile of the slush you scooped from your hole. Position the willow at an angle of about 30 degrees to the ice. The tip should be centered above the hole. Trim off any buds at the end of the branch.

MAKE a loop in your line and hang it over the tip of the willow. Position the loop so the minnow is about a foot off bottom. Attach a small bobber or piece of red cloth just below the loop so you can see if the line has been pulled off the willow.

WATCH for the willow to bend. The wind or the swimming motion of the minnow will cause the willow to bob slightly, but a walleye will pull it down much farther. The resistance offered by the willow is rarely enough to make a walleye drop the bait.

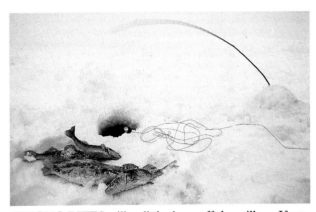

STRONG BITES will pull the loop off the willow. If you cannot see the bobber or red cloth, you probably have a bite. Be sure to keep some loose line piled on the ice so that the fish will not feel resistance when it runs off with the bait.

How to Use a Slip-bobber Rig for Ice Fishing

DETERMINE the depth by attaching a clip-on weight to your hook, then letting out line until the weight hits bottom. To mark the depth, keep the weight on bottom, then reel until the rod tip is at water level. Attach your slip-bobber knot (page 144) about a foot below the rod tip.

USE slip-bobber rigs only in above-freezing weather or in a heated shack. In cold weather, ice build-up prevents the line from sliding through the center tube. Slip-bobbers work better than fixed bobbers in deep water, because they allow you to reel in your line when you hook a fish.

RIG your tip-up with a night-fishing light (inset). As long as the string is seated between the metal contacts, the light remains off. But when a fish bites, the string pulls free and the light turns on. The light not only signals a bite, it helps you see while playing a fish or baiting up.

Tips for Catching Walleyes through the Ice

You can make your ice fishing more enjoyable and more successful if you learn some of the tricks used by veteran ice fishermen.

For example, a plywood box with an internal stove or lantern makes a good fishing chair and takes away the chill. Another handy device for keeping warm is a pail filled with charcoal briquets on top of a layer of sand. Hands and feet are the first to chill, so it pays to wear chopper mittens and felt-lined boots. Gloves and mittens lined with Gore-Tex™ are excellent for ice fishing because they will not soak up water when you handle fish or put on minnows.

A dull ice auger can take all the fun out of ice fishing. Carry an extra set of blades or learn to sharpen your old ones. Most removable blades can be sharpened by realigning the edges with a sharpening steel.

Once your holes are drilled, you face the constant problem of keeping them clear of ice and slush. You can reduce the problem by using a hole cover (page 162). Or, you can drill a hole a few inches deep next to your fishing hole. Chip out a channel between the two holes with your chisel. Put a can of charcoal briquets into the shallow hole; warm water will circulate into the fishing hole.

How to Make a Buzzer System for Detecting Bites

MOUNT a buzzer on your ice shack wall to signal a bite. Wire it to a pair of metal strips, then make a loop in your line and insert it between the strips. When a fish takes line, the strips make contact and the buzzer sounds.

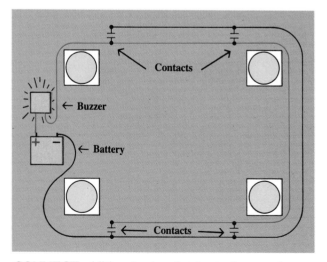

CONNECT additional pairs of strips to the same buzzer when fishing in several holes. Wire the system as shown in the above diagram. Then, a bite in any of the holes will set off the buzzer.

DETERMINE the depth where walleyes are feeding by drilling a line of holes perpendicular to a drop-off. Try jigging in each hole for a few minutes until you get a bite. Then set all of your lines at that depth.

PREVENT your line from freezing in the hole by threading it through a small plastic pipe inserted through a piece of styrofoam. Attach your terminal tackle, then drip mineral or vegetable oil into the pipe.

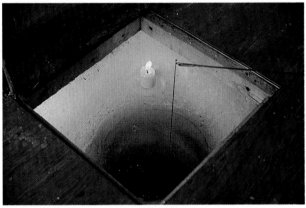

PLACE a candle alongside the hole and pack snow around the shack so wind does not blow out the flame. The candle gives off enough heat to keep the hole free of ice and enough light so you can see your line.

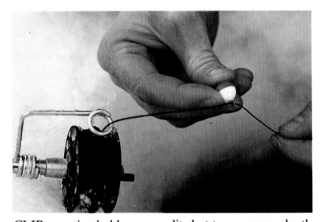

CLIP on a tiny bobber or a split-shot to serve as a depth reference for resetting your tip-up. On a regular tip-up, the bobber should be clipped to the line just below the spool; on a wind tip-up, just below the metal plate.

USE a *jingle reel* when fishing in a shack. The core of the reel contains several round bells. The reel turns easily when a fish takes the bait, causing the bells to tumble and alert the fisherman.

WARM your hands with a propane heater. You can also use the heater to melt ice from your line guides, auger blades and scoop. After dark, the heater provides enough light for unhooking fish and baiting up.

Northern Pike

With its snake-like body, huge head and razor-sharp teeth, the northern pike has a fearsome appearance and a reputation to match. It is not uncommon for a pike to strike a large bass or walleye struggling on a fisherman's line. In some instances, pike have re-fused to let go, even as they were guided into a landing net.

In North America, three members of the pike family are of interest to fishermen. They include the northern pike, muskellunge and chain pickerel. Grass and redfin pickerel are caught occasionally, but they rarely exceed 12 inches in length.

Known regionally as *jack, pickerel* or *snake,* northern pike are found across the northern United States and into Canada. They have also been stocked in waters as far south as Texas. In some areas of Alaska and Canada, pike are considered rough fish and fishermen kill them rather than return them to the water. But wherever they exist in

the United States, northerns are extremely popular with fishermen.

Lakes with shallow, weedy bays or connecting marshes are ideal for pike. Northerns spawn soon after ice-out, beginning when the water reaches about 40°F. They scatter their eggs onto dense vegetation in shallow bays or marshes. They refuse to bite just before and during spawning, but begin feeding actively soon after.

In most waters, northern pike reign supreme. They may feed on muskrats, mice, turtles, salamanders, small ducks and other birds, though most of their food is fish. Often they strike fish one-half their body length.

Pike are persistent. They sometimes follow a lure, hitting it repeatedly until hooked. Because they are easily caught, large northerns can be readily skimmed off a population. Today, most pike weighing over 20 pounds are taken in remote northern lakes and rivers where fishing pressure is light. The world-record northern pike, 46 pounds, 2 ounces, was caught in Sacandaga Reservoir, New York in 1940. However, many larger pike have been caught by fishermen in Scotland, Ireland and Germany.

Northern Pike Range

When and Where to Catch Northern Pike

Locating small northern pike is easy. They spend nearly all of their time in shallow, weedy water from 2 to 15 feet deep. But finding big northerns is not as simple. They are found along with small pike in spring, but when the shallows warm in summer, they move into 15- to 30-foot depths. Fishing becomes more difficult because the big pike are scattered. Summer angling is also difficult if the water becomes too warm. If pike cannot find water cooler than 75°F, they eat very little.

Northerns bite best during daylight hours. Night fishing is seldom worthwhile.

Mature northerns tend to stay in one spot, usually hiding in weedy cover. Typically, a northern lies motionless in the weeds or alongside a log, where it can make short lunges at passing fish.

The northern pike is one of the most adaptable fish species. As shown in the photos below, they live in nearly every type of freshwater environment.

GREAT LAKES' BAYS concentrate large numbers of pike. The bays offer warmer water and more food than the open waters of the main lake.

SHALLOW RESERVOIRS often produce large northerns. Most pike are found in weedy cover, though flooded timber holds a few fish.

WEEDY BAYS of large lakes hold northerns most of the year. Pike lie near weedlines or in small pockets within weedbeds.

BACKWATERS of large rivers are haunts for northern pike. Those with deep areas adjacent to shallow weedbeds have the most fish.

CANADIAN SHIELD lakes can grow trophy northerns, provided that fishing pressure is light enough for pike to survive and grow.

MARSHES are too shallow for most gamefish and are prone to winterkill. Pike can usually survive because they tolerate low oxygen levels.

Bobber Fishing for Northerns

A northern cannot resist a big minnow dangling from a bobber. Though a pike may stare at the struggling baitfish for a long time, sooner or later it curls its body into a Z and then attacks. All the angler has to do is cast the bobber rig near a likely weedline, drop-off, sunken island or point, then sit back and wait.

If large minnows are not available at a local bait shop, some anglers head for the nearest creek to catch their own suckers, chubs or redhorse.

FIGHTING a big pike tests the angler's tackle and skill. Often, a northern puts up little resistance until several feet from the boat. Then, without warning, it makes a strong run, its tail churning the water surface.

BOBBER RIGS are made with a 12-inch steel leader and a #1 or 1/0 hook. Attach a 1½- to 2-inch diameter bobber to the line. Add sinkers or split-shot for balance. Hook a large minnow in the upper lip or behind the dorsal fin. A variety of baitfish are used for still-fishing, including suckers, perch, chubs, shiners, ciscoes and whitefish. Whatever the species, the baitfish should measure 6 to 12 inches in length and be fresh and lively.

THE STRIKE of a large northern pike is often violent. The fish may yank the bobber so hard that it makes a splash as it is pulled under.

RELEASE line after the strike. A pike often grabs a minnow crosswise and runs with it. Then, it stops to swallow the bait headfirst.

SET the hook only after the pike has stopped. Reel in slack line until feeling the fish's weight. Then, snap the rod hard to sink the hook.

Speed Trolling for Northerns

Trolling at high speeds imparts a furious action to lures, triggering strikes from northerns that pass up slow-moving lures.

Speed trolling works best in summer, after pike have left the shallows and retreated to deeper weedbeds. Unlike most angling techniques, speed trolling seems to catch more pike during the hottest and brightest hours of the day.

Fishermen troll just off weedlines, usually in 10 to 20 feet of water, with wide-lipped, deep-diving plugs that track straight at high speeds. Most anglers use stiff trolling rods, heavy-duty level-wind reels and metered monofilament line, from 20- to 25-pound test. Metered line makes it easier to keep the lure at a consistent depth.

HIGH SPEEDS are essential to successful speed trolling. The lures should have a frenzied action, which is not possible at slower speeds. Most anglers are hesitant to troll fast enough to make the technique work.

172

Casting for Northerns

Casting enables the angler to fish water that is too weedy, shallow or snag-infested for trolling. It is most successful in spring and fall, when northerns spend much of their time in shallow water.

Tackle must be fairly heavy. Strong, short rods and 12- to 20-pound lines handle the stress from casting heavy lures. Northerns have extremely sharp teeth, so wire leaders should always be used.

Pike normally find food by sight, but also use their lateral line to sense the direction and speed of prey. As a result, lures with lively action work best. Metal spoons that wobble enticingly are all-time favorites. Bright colors, including red, yellow and silver, are most popular. Anglers vary the speed of the retrieve and occasionally pump the lure for extra action.

CASTING from a boat enables the fisherman to drop a lure in small pockets in weedbeds or to cast parallel to weedy edges, so the lure runs through prime territory over the length of the retrieve.

SHORE CASTING is effective in spring when large pike roam inshore waters. Shore fishermen catch northerns throughout the summer in lakes and rivers of the extreme northern United States and Canada.

LURES for northern pike include (1) Reaper, (2) Red Eye Wiggler, (3) Dardevle, (4) Pikie Minnow, (5) Fuzzy Grub, (6) Bomber, (7) Mepps spinner, (8) Rapala.

173

Muskellunge

Many fishermen regard the muskellunge as big game, a rare trophy that demands hours of patient searching and stalking. Even if the angler can get close to a muskie sunning in a quiet bay, he knows the fish is not likely to strike. A muskie routinely ignores lures passing within inches of its jaws. Or, it may follow a lure to the boat, give the fisherman a menacing glare, then slip back into the depths. But all the effort and frustration, all the hours of casting heavy lures and plugs, are suddenly forgotten once a big muskie is hooked.

Close relatives, muskies and northern pike are similar in appearance. Most muskies have dark bars or spots on a light body, although some are void of markings. Northern pike have light spots on a dark background. Northerns have scales on the lower half of their gills and cheeks; muskies do not. The two species have been successfully crossed to produce the *tiger muskie,* a hardy, fast-growing hybrid.

Northern pike and muskies share many of the same waters. However, pike almost always outnumber muskies, because their eggs hatch earlier and their offspring eat the smaller muskie fry. But given the chance to survive, a muskellunge will grow larger than a northern pike. Each year, anglers take many fish weighing over 35 pounds. The world record, 69 pounds, 15 ounces, was caught in the St. Lawrence River, New York in 1957.

Like northerns, muskies feed on a variety of fish, though almost anything that looks edible is fair

MUSKIE LURES are big, ranging in length from 8 to 14 inches. Popular types include bucktail spinners, jerk baits,

game. Muskies feed mainly at dawn and dusk, and occasionally at night. Most are caught during the hottest part of summer, but the largest fish are taken in fall. They bite best on overcast days.

Recent tagging studies have shown that muskies spend most of their time in deep water, often 30 feet or more. However, muskellunge are not active at these depths. Feeding muskies are generally found in large, weedy bays, around sunken islands topped with weeds or near flooded timber.

Muskie fishing requires heavy tackle. Because a muskie clamps down so hard on a lure, the angler must set the hook several times to break the fish's grip and to sink the barbs. Short, strong rods and heavy casting reels enable the fisherman to cast or troll over-sized lures. They also help turn a running muskie. Monofilament or braided dacron lines of

20- to 50-pound test are normally used. Steel leaders are necessary because of the muskie's sharp teeth.

Popular muskie lures feature flash, furious action or noise. Some lures, called *jerk baits*, have no built-in action. The fisherman simply jerks them through the water. Occasionally, a muskellunge will follow a lure to the boat several times, always turning away at the last moment. When this happens, the knowledgeable muskie fisherman plunges the rod tip into the water and quickly weaves the lure through a series of figure eights. Rather than scaring the fish, this last-ditch maneuver may trigger a strike.

Muskellunge Range

deep-running crankbaits and jointed plugs, such as this Pikie Minnow (shown actual size).

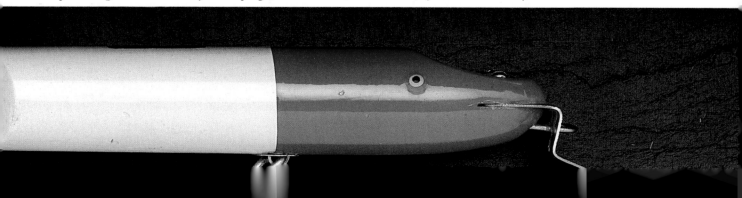

Stream Trout

Stream Trout Basics

When most fishermen think of stream trout, they picture a secluded, spring-fed brook. But in reality, stream trout can live in any cool, unpolluted water, including many natural lakes, reservoirs and ponds.

Fishermen pursue four major stream trout species in North America. Brook trout favor water of about 54°F, and are rarely found where the water temperature exceeds 65°F. As a result, they usually live in the upper reaches of streams or near the mouths of tributaries. Rainbows and cutthroats prefer water of about 55°F, but are found in waters up to 70°F. Brown trout favor water of about 65°F, but can tolerate temperatures as warm as 75°F. They some-times live in warmer, slower-moving streams unsuitable to other trout.

Stream-dwelling stream trout rely heavily on insects for food. Stream trout in lakes often feed on small fish, with insects of secondary importance. Small fish are also an important food in warmer, marginal-quality trout streams. These streams have fewer trout, but are more likely to produce a trophy.

In addition to man, many kinds of birds, mammals, crustaceans, fish and even insects prey upon trout. To survive, trout must be cautious. Their hideouts are overhanging vegetation, undercut banks, large rocks, fallen trees or deep pools. Large trout hooked in small streams are seldom landed. They are strong swimmers and once hooked, their first instinct is to dash for cover. A big trout may quickly wrap the line around a rock or other snag to break free.

Trout Combined Range

RAINBOW TROUT are named for the pinkish band along their sides. Black spots cover the tail and flanks. Rainbows prefer swift water, but will abandon home streams to live in downstream lakes. They usually leap when hooked and put up an unforgettable fight. The world-record rainbow, excluding steelhead (page 186), is 37 pounds and came from Lake Pend Oreille, Idaho in 1947.

BROWN TROUT, sometimes called *Loch Leven* trout, have backs and sides with black spots and sometimes a few orange spots with light halos. Tails may have a few scattered spots near the top, or none at all. Brown trout are the wariest and most difficult to catch. The world-record brown trout, 35 pounds, 15 ounces, was caught in Nahuel Huapi, Argentina in 1952.

BROOK TROUT, often called speckled trout, have light spots on their sides and pale, worm-like markings on their backs. Leading edges of the lower fins have white borders. Brook trout are considered the easiest trout to catch and the best to eat. The world-record brook trout, 14 pounds, 8 ounces, was caught in the Nipigon River, Ontario in 1916.

CUTTHROAT TROUT are named for the reddish-orange slashes on both sides of the lower jaw. Like rainbows, their tails and sides are covered with black spots, though background color is more yellowish. Cutthroats prefer habitat similar to that of rainbows, but are mainly found in the West. Pyramid Lake, Nevada, yielded the world-record cutthroat, 41 pounds, in 1925.

Approaching Stream Trout

Trout survive by being wary. Any sudden movement, shadow, noise or vibration will send them darting for cover. And once spooked, no amount of coaxing will get a trout to bite. If it is obvious that a trout has been disturbed, move on to another spot, because it may be awhile before the fish resumes feeding. Because trout are so skittish, the angler should take extra care when approaching a trout's lie and when presenting a lure.

WADING is the most common method of fishing trout in streams. Anglers should try to avoid scuffing the bottom, making large ripples and casting a shadow over the suspected lie of a trout.

ENEMIES of trout include fish-eating insects, such as this giant water beetle, plus otters, herons, kingfishers, loons and larger trout. Young trout must learn to be cautious or perish.

SNEAK up to the streambank and keep movement to a minimum. Study the water carefully to locate possible trout lies. Plan your fishing strategy before making the first cast.

WEAR drab colors, keep low and avoid open backgrounds. Because light rays bend at the water surface, trout can see all but the lowest objects along the streambank through a window in the water's surface.

When to Catch Stream Trout

Trout can be caught almost anytime of the day or night, although they normally feed when light is dim. And with good reason. Insect activity peaks during evening hours, leaving the stream teeming with prime trout food.

Water temperature also affects feeding activity. In spring, trout are most active in the afternoon when the water is warmest. Later in summer, they feed in the early morning when the water is coolest.

Insects emerge from the stream bottom in cycles. Trout may go on a feeding frenzy during a large insect hatch, and catching them can be fairly easy. Some stream anglers work their way downstream, thinking that mud and insects they stir up make trout more likely to bite. However, not all fishermen agree with this strategy.

The largest trout are usually caught during peak feeding times. They keep smaller ones away from the best feeding spots. Small trout feed only after the large fish have eaten their fill and departed.

Rising water may be a good indication that trout are feeding. Rains wash insects and other foods off streambanks and over-hanging trees. As the stream rises and the current grows stronger, insect larvae and other morsels are dislodged from bottom. Trout begin feeding when the swirling water carries food past their lies.

MORNING AND EVENING, when sunlight strikes the water at a low angle, are peak feeding times. Fishing is usually slowest on lakes and streams during mid-afternoon, though fish may feed on a cloudy day.

NIGHTTIME is best for catching large brown trout, one of the wariest gamefish. Under cover of darkness, the angler can get closer to fish and use heavier lines and lures.

INSECT HATCHES may cause trout to gorge themselves on any food or bait drifting in the water. Or, they may be quite choosy. Then, only an exact imitation of the hatching insect will entice them to bite.

179

Fishing for Stream Trout in Streams

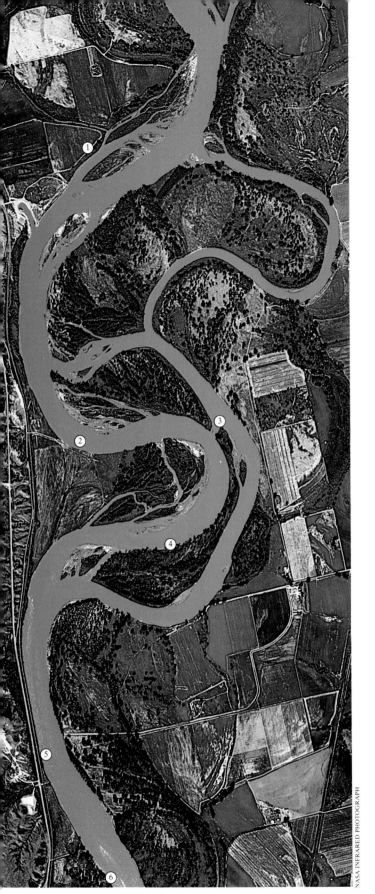

The number of trout living in a typical, coldwater stream would amaze most fishermen. Trout are seldom seen because they spend most of the day hiding. The only time they betray their presence is when they leave cover to find food.

Trout in streams depend on the current to carry food to them. So, the best feeding areas are those places where the natural flow of water gathers food. Examples are eddies, deep holes below rapids or waterfalls and shallow riffles. On warm, sunny days, trout may lie near shaded streambanks, eating food that falls or washes into the stream.

Trout seek shade and cover beneath undercut banks and logs, below large rocks, or in deep pools. They do not feed actively in these resting areas, but will dart from cover to grab food as it drifts by.

Trout location may change during the year, depending upon water temperature. A stream with springs scattered along its course stays cold enough for trout all summer. But if spring-flow is confined to one section, the remainder of the stream may become too warm, concentrating the trout in water cooled by the springs.

LARGE STREAMS provide a variety of trout habitat. Trout lies in this high-altitude, infrared photo include (1) area below a tributary stream, (2) deep hole along an outside bend, (3) cut between islands, (4) shaded streambank, (5) long riffle, (6) eddy below a boulder.

COLDWATER DRAWS pull water from the bottom of a reservoir rather than from the surface, creating streams cold enough for trout. In the south-central United States, trout exceeding 20 pounds are sometimes caught in streams of this type.

Fishing for Stream Trout in Lakes

Trout thrive in a wide variety of coldwater basins, from small lakes and ponds to huge Lake Superior, the largest body of fresh water in the world. In some lakes, trout populations are continually replenished by reproduction in tributary streams. However, most trout lakes and reservoirs must be stocked.

Much of the year, trout remain near shore, feeding on minnows, insects and crustaceans. They sometimes school around food-rich inlets or near rock bars, sunken islands and points extending from shore. Their location, however, depends more on water temperature than on structure or bottom type.

During summer, trout may be forced deeper as the lake warms. They often squeeze into the narrow band of the thermocline because water below this point has too little oxygen. Although the surface water is warm, trout rise to feed on insects in early morning and late evening.

Compared to most gamefish, lake-dwelling trout are easy to catch. As a result, their numbers can be quickly reduced if fishing pressure is heavy. Best angling is in lightly-fished waters where trout can grow for several years before they are caught.

RESERVOIRS, especially those at high altitudes in the West, grow huge trout. Shorelines usually drop off sharply, so trout are found close to shore. Many record-class brown trout are caught in western reservoirs.

PONDS need a permanent source of cold water to sustain trout. Often a large spring or artesian well is tapped to feed a series of man-made pools. Because water temperature in ponds is uniform, trout may be anywhere.

NATURAL LAKES in the northern United States and Canada or in mountainous regions sometimes have water cold enough to support trout. The fish normally cruise within casting distance of shore, although they may go deeper in summer.

GREAT LAKES trout, particularly rainbows and browns, concentrate near stream mouths, piers or discharges from power plants during spring and fall. In mid-summer, many trout are caught by trolling with downriggers in water 50 to 100 feet deep.

Bait Fishing for Stream Trout

Fishing with natural baits probably catches more trout than any other method. In spring and early summer when streams are high and clouded by runoff, it may be the only way to catch trout, especially if few insects are hatching.

A long rod, 7 to 9 feet, makes it easier to swing or drop the bait into hard-to-reach places. Choice of line depends on water clarity. Four-pound monofilament is best in clear water where trout spook easily. Eight-pound test can be used in muddy water. Most fishermen use #8 short-shank hooks.

Many anglers gather bait along the stream. Worms, minnows, grasshoppers and nymphs are the most popular. When using small and fragile baits, set the hook as soon as the fish bites. Wait longer with larger baits.

HOOK the bait so it moves naturally in the current. Hook worms through the collar, minnows in the head and nymphs and grasshoppers just behind the head. Be sure the bait is fresh and lively.

LOB the bait to avoid tearing it off the hook. Using an easy sidearm motion, angle the cast across current and upstream. Keep the line tight as the bait bounces along bottom. Set the hook when the bait stops drifting.

STREAM BOTTOMS produce most trout foods. Attach enough split-shot 8 to 10 inches above the hook to keep the bait near bottom. Too much weight keeps the bait from rolling with the current.

SPAWN works well in fall, winter and spring. Wrap it in a transparent nylon bag (page 202) or put a single egg on a hook. Trout instinctively respond to the color and smell of fresh spawn.

GROCERY BAITS, such as cheese, marshmallows and canned corn, are most effective on hatchery-reared trout. Wild trout prefer baits which more closely resemble natural foods.

Artificial Lures for Stream Trout

Most artificial lures resemble minnows and attract the larger, fish-eating trout. To imitate a swimming minnow, work the lure slowly along the bottom. A fast retrieve will sometimes provoke a reflex strike when a trout suddenly spots the flashing lure.

A delicate touch is not needed when fishing with artificials. Trout attack lures fiercely, usually hooking themselves. Some fishermen use lines as heavy as 12-pound monofilament to handle large fish and to retrieve snagged lures, but 8-pound test is usually strong enough.

An angler can cover a lot of water in a short time by casting an artificial lure. Trout that are feeding actively usually hit the lure immediately. If a few casts into a likely area fail to produce a strike, move on to another spot.

LURES for trout include (1) Panther Martin spinners, (2) Mepps spinners, (3) Wob-L-Rite spoon, (4) Super Duper, (5) Little Jewel spoon, (6) Countdown Rapala, (7) floating Rapala.

CAST the lure across current and upstream. Complete the retrieve before the line begins to bow downstream. Angle the cast farther upstream in faster current. This will eliminate downstream drag at the end of the retrieve.

FLIP the lure when casting into tight spots. Using a sharp, backhand motion, flick the lure under obstacles such as overhanging trees, bridges or logs across the stream. Try to keep the cast as low as possible.

RIFFLES hide actively-feeding fish. Cast the lure directly upstream and reel it back rapidly. Trout in the riffles often chase fast-moving foods.

SHORE CASTING with artificial lures in morning and evening catches trout cruising the shallows. Piers and stream mouths attract fish all day.

COWBELLS and other attractors draw trout to the bait or lure. They are especially effective when trolling for trout scattered in open water.

183

Fly-fishing for Stream Trout

Fly-fishing is not a mysterious art. The basic skills can be learned in a few hours. However, precision casting and a thorough knowledge of stream insect life take years of practice and study.

Artificial flies resemble specific items in a trout's diet, from tiny insect larvae to large minnows. Most flies fall into one of four basic categories:

DRY FLIES. Resembling newly-hatched insects, dry flies float lightly on the water surface. They have a fringe of delicate feathers or *hackle* near the head that keeps them afloat. They are tied with or without wings. Dry flies are rubbed with a waxy dressing or dipped in silicone to keep them buoyant.

WET FLIES. Tied with wings about the same length as the body, wet flies resemble a variety of trout foods, including immature aquatic insects, drowned land insects, crustaceans or minnows. They are retrieved below the surface. Hackles on wet flies are less prominent than on dry flies.

STREAMERS. Designed to imitate minnows, streamers are fished below the surface. The wings, made of feathers or hair, are longer than the body. Most streamers are brightly colored. Those made of hair are called *bucktails*.

NYMPHS. Although similar to wet flies, nymphs are tied without wings. They closely resemble many of the immature insects found in streams.

NYMPHS: (1) Light Hendrickson, (2) Emerging Caddis, (3) Bitch Creek, (4) Dark Hendrickson, (5) Caddis, (6) Light Cahill, (7) Wooly Worm, (8) Montana.
WET FLIES: (9) Black Gnat, (10) Ginger Quill, (11) Coachman, (12) Blue Dun, (13) Royal Coachman, (14) Dark Cahill.
DRY FLIES: (15) Pale Evening Dun, (16) Dark Cahill, (17) Gray Wulff, (18) Henryville Special, (19) Ginger

How to Fish a Dry Fly

CAST upstream, either straight or diagonally. Allow the fly to float naturally with the current. Strip in slack line, but take care not to drag the fly across the surface.

HACKLE keeps flies floating high on the water. It also creates a tiny depression which distorts the fly's image, so a trout is less likely to recognize it as a fake.

DRAG is the dry fly fisherman's biggest concern. If the fly floats faster or slower than the current, it leaves a wake that makes the fly appear unnatural to trout.

How to Fish Nymphs

CAST diagonally upstream, keeping the line tight as the nymph drifts along the bottom. Recognizing a strike can be difficult. Experts watch the fly line; then set the hook at the slightest twitch or hesitation.

NYMPHS imitate insect larvae that live on the lake or stream bottom. This multiple-exposure photograph shows a nymph being retrieved slowly along the bottom, as if it were rolling and drifting with the current.

Quill, (20) March Brown, (21) Adams, (22) Mosquito, (23) Royal Coachman, (24) Light Cahill, (25) Quill Gordon, (26) Ginger Bivisible, (27) Blue Dun.
STREAMERS: (28) Mickey Finn Mylar, (29) White-Orange Marion Marabou, (30) Muddler Minnow, (31) Royal Coachman, (32) Black Marabou Muddler, (33) Gray Ghost, (34) Supervisor, (35) Olive Matuka, (36) Integration Mylar.

How to Fish Wet Flies and Streamers

CAST across current when using a wet fly or streamer. For deeper water, angle the cast slightly upstream so the fly can sink longer before the current sweeps it downstream. More depth can be attained by using a sinking line, tiny split-shot or lead leader-wrap.

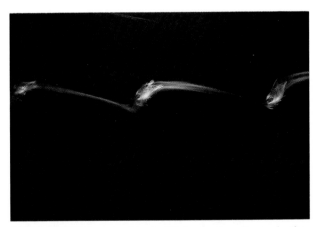

STREAMERS resemble baitfish darting through the water. Retrieve them in a jerky manner, as shown in this multiple-exposure photograph. Streamers are the largest of the artificial flies and they are normally used to catch larger trout.

Steelhead: The Sea-run Rainbow

The fighting ability of steelhead is legend. They have been clocked at 26.8 feet per second, fastest of any freshwater fish. A hooked steelhead will leap repeatedly, sometimes clearing the surface by 2 to 3 feet. Small wonder that even the best steelhead fishermen land few of the fish they hook.

Steelhead are rainbow trout that spend their adult lives at sea or in the open water of the Great Lakes. Each spring, they enter streams to spawn. Great Lakes tributaries have another, smaller run in fall, though no spawning takes place. Along the Pacific Coast, they may move into a stream in summer and remain until spawning time the following spring. Steelhead can be found somewhere along the Pacific Coast every month of the year.

Pacific Coast steelhead were introduced into the Great Lakes in the late 1800s. Runs have since developed in many streams, especially those with clean, cold water and gravel bottoms. Because non-migratory rainbows have also been stocked in the Great Lakes, fishermen sometimes mistake these deeper-bodied rainbows for steelhead.

Steelhead swim miles up tributary streams to find the right spawning area. They easily navigate raging cascades and most waterfalls. Only a dam or high waterfall blocks their progress. While in the stream, they bite reluctantly, ignoring baits drifted past them many times. When they suddenly decide to strike, they frequently catch the angler off-guard.

Steelhead generally grow larger than rainbows that live in streams. The average steelhead weighs 4 to 6 pounds, though some exceed 20 pounds. The world-record steelhead is 42 pounds, 2 ounces. It was caught at Bell Island, Alaska in 1970.

SPAWNING BEDS or redds may hold several steelhead. A female is sometimes accompanied by two or more smaller males.

WATERFALLS and dams block upstream migrations. Steelhead spawn in pools and runs from the stream mouth to the first impassable barrier.

STREAM MOUTHS are gathering spots for steelhead en route to upstream spawning grounds. The fish run when rain clouds the water.

How to Drift-fish for Steelhead

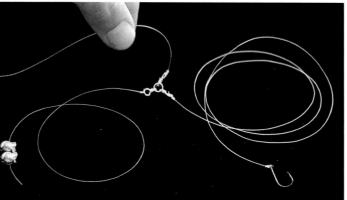

A DRIFT-FISHING RIG is made with a 3-way swivel. Tie an 8- to 10-pound dropper line to one eye and pinch on split-shot. Next, tie 20 to 30 inches of 12-pound line to another eye and attach a #4 or #6 hook.

SWING the bait upstream. Follow it with the rod tip as it drifts downstream. When it stops, set the hook. Good equipment for drift fishing is a 9-foot, heavy-action fly rod, a single-action reel and 12-pound monofilament.

THREE TYPES of rainbow trout are found in fresh water. Stream rainbows (top) have pronounced black spots on the back and sides with a distinct reddish band along the lateral line. Steelhead (middle) have sleek, silvery bodies with faint spots on the sides and back. As spawning time approaches, their bodies get darker and develop the characteristic red band. Lake rainbows (bottom) resemble steelhead, but have much deeper bodies.

BAITS AND LURES commonly used for drift-fishing include (1) spawn bags, (2) colored sponge balls, (3) Okie Drifter, (4) bulk yarn and finished yarn fly, (5) plastic salmon eggs. Spawn bags (page 202) probably take more steelhead than any other bait or artificial lure. Both trout and salmon spawn will attract steelhead. Yarn flies may be used alone or in combination with spawn bags or plastic salmon eggs.

Lake Trout

The prospect of battling a huge lake trout draws anglers to remote lakes as far north as the Arctic Circle. These waters yield many 30- to 40-pound lake trout each year. The sport fishing record, 65 pounds, was caught in Great Bear Lake, Northwest Territories in 1970. Even larger trout have been netted in Canadian waters, including a 102-pound giant caught in Saskatchewan's Lake Athabasca.

In parts of Canada and the western United States, lake trout are known as *Mackinaw* or *gray trout*, although the most popular nickname is *laker*. Lake trout resemble brook trout, except the tails of lakers are deeply forked, while those of brook trout are nearly square. Lake trout in the Great Lakes are silvery-gray with white spots. Elsewhere, they have light spots on a background that may vary from dark green to brown or black.

Lake trout prefer water from 48° to 52°F, colder than any other gamefish. They will die if unable to find water under 65°F. During summer, lakers might descend to 200 feet in search of cold water.

Many lakes have water cold enough for lake trout, but lack oxygen in their depths. As a result, lakers are restricted mainly to the cold, sterile lakes of the Canadian Shield, the Great Lakes and deep, mountain lakes of the West.

Lakers grow slowly in these frigid waters. In some lakes of northern Canada, a 10-pound laker might be 20 years or older. The age of a trophy lake trout may exceed 40 years. Because they grow so slowly, they can be easily over-harvested.

Unlike most other trout species, lakers spawn in lakes rather than rivers. Spawning occurs in fall over a bottom of baseball- to football-sized rocks. Water depth varies considerably, but is usually 5 to 20 feet.

Lake trout have excellent vision. However, because so little light reaches the depths, they rely heavily on their sense of smell and their lateral line to find food. In some waters, they feed exclusively on aquatic insects, worms and crustaceans. In other lakes, lake trout eat only fish, mainly ciscoes, whitefish, sculpins and smelt.

Lake Trout Range

A lake trout, brook trout hybrid, called *splake,* has been stocked in some northern lakes, including Lake Huron. Splake mature earlier than lake trout and grow faster than either parent, so they are less affected by fishing pressure.

WILDERNESS WATERS, particularly those in Canada's Northwest Territories, provide excellent lake trout fishing. The lakes and rivers are so cold that anglers can use light tackle to catch lakers in shallow water through-out summer. Many of these lakes are ice-free only two to three months and can be reached only by airplane. As a result, fishing pressure is light enough for these waters to produce many trophy lakers.

When and Where to Catch Lake Trout

EARLY SPRING, beginning shortly after ice-out, offers the fastest lake trout fishing of the year. Lakers crowd into warmer water near shore, usually remaining in water 30 feet or less.

Water temperature plays a major role in the lives of lake trout. Following ice-out, the upper layer of a lake warms faster than water in the depths. Lake trout move from deep water into the warmer shallows where they remain for two to three weeks or until the water becomes too warm.

In summer, trout go as deep as necessary to find water near 50°F. In the Great Lakes or in lakes of the southern Canadian Shield, lakers may plunge to 100 feet or more. In lakes of extreme northern Canada, the shallows are always cold enough for lakers, so they remain in water 20 feet or less throughout summer.

In many deep lakes, trout school near bottom where water is in the low 40s. However, these fish are virtually impossible to catch. The catchable trout are likely to suspend in water 50 to 70 feet deep, darting into shallower water to grab unsuspecting ciscoes or other baitfish. Novice anglers often make the mistake of fishing for the more numerous, bottom-hugging trout, while ignoring lakers that are more prone to bite.

Lake trout move into much shallower water just before the fall spawning period. They are easily

Using a Recording Depth Finder for Lake Trout

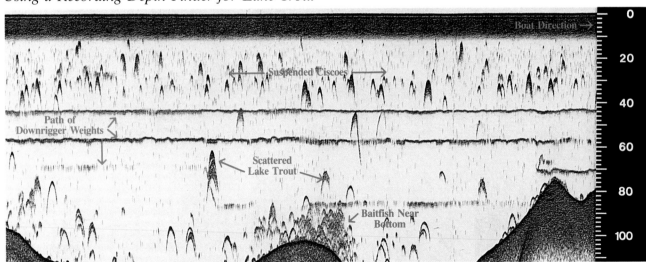

SUMMER finds lake trout in the depths. When trout are schooled in deep water, a recording depth finder is invaluable for locating the fish. This graph tape shows lake trout scattered from 40 feet to bottom. Above them, at 25 to 35 feet, is a dense band of ciscoes. Two lines are being trolled with downriggers through the shallower lake trout, the fish that are apt to bite. Another line is tracking through trout closer to the bottom.

caught on rocky reefs, sometimes in water only 5 feet deep. Because lake trout are so vulnerable, most states and provinces prohibit fishing during spawning time.

Regardless of the season, lake trout feed almost exclusively during the day, though shallow-water lakers feed when light is dim.

CANADIAN SHIELD lakes are ideally suited for lake trout. These coldwater, rocky basins are found mainly in the eastern half of Canada and the extreme northern United States, from Minnesota to Maine.

GREAT LAKES trout have made a remarkable comeback after they were nearly wiped out by the sea lamprey and commercial fishing. Lake trout populations have been rebuilt by lamprey control and restocking programs.

Springtime Lake Trout Spots

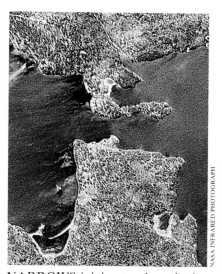

ROCKY POINTS often attract small lake trout to shallow water on top of the points, while larger fish remain in deeper water off the tips.

NARROWS joining two large basins may become crowded with lake trout searching for warmer water. Anglers catch lakers as they pass through.

RIVER MOUTHS bring in warm meltwater which attracts lake trout. They are also drawn to schools of baitfish that hang around the plume.

Shallow-water Lake Trout Techniques

When lakers move into shallow water in spring and fall, the best methods are casting with flashy spoons or still-fishing with natural bait. A moving boat may spook lake trout in shallow water, so trolling is often not as productive unless anglers use trolling boards (page 199) or very long lines.

Lake trout shy away from heavy line, so clear, low-diameter line from 8- to 12-pound test is recommended. In clear lakes, some anglers use line as light as 4-pound test. Most fishermen prefer medium-action spinning tackle.

CASTING with heavy gold or silver spoons is a proven technique when lakers are concentrated off points, in narrows, along islands or over spawning reefs. Cast from a long distance away to prevent spooking the trout.

STILL-FISHING takes advantage of the lake trout's habit of scavenging dead fish off bottom. Cast a whole or cut fish on a slip-sinker rig. Prop up the rod and open the bail so the rod cannot be pulled into the lake.

NATURAL BAITS include smelt and strips of sucker meat. Some anglers combine a chunk of sucker with a live sucker or chub hooked through the lips. Only one hook is needed, because lakers quickly swallow the bait.

Deep-water Lake Trout Techniques

In years past, wire-line trolling was the standard procedure for catching lake trout in the depths. New equipment and techniques, however, make it possible to fish deep with much lighter tackle. Downrigger trolling (page 198), used to catch salmon in the Great Lakes, works just as well for lakers.

Deep lake trout are frequently scattered and sluggish, so adding an attractor, such as a dodger or cowbells, can improve the troller's success. Another light-tackle technique, vertical jigging, is becoming popular on Canadian Shield lakes.

HEAVY SINKERS, some weighing 8 ounces or more, are used for trolling in deep lakes. A short, stiff rod is needed to handle the heavy weight.

WIRE-LINE trolling, though it takes away much of a fish's fight, is still an efficient way to catch lake trout in deep water.

DIVING PLANES pull the line downward, but flatten out when a trout strikes, enabling the angler to play a fish with less resistance.

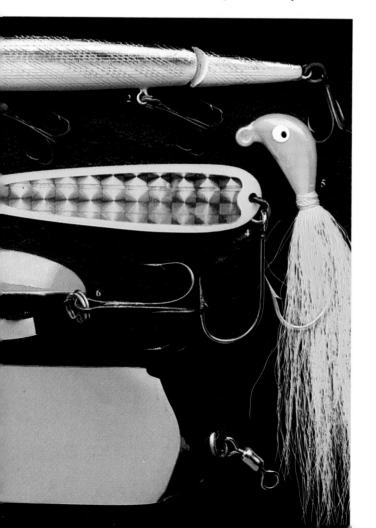

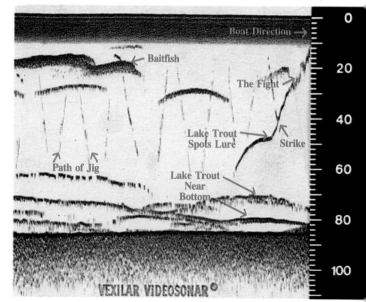

VERTICAL JIGGING works best with a lead-head jig or vibrating blade. Simply lower the lure to the bottom; then reel it back rapidly. This graph tape shows a laker striking a jig as it falls.

LAKE TROUT lures include (1) Sonar, (2) jointed Rebel, (3) Rapala, (4) Flutter Spoon, (5) bucktail, (6) Little Cleo spoon, (7) Dodger/fly combination.

193

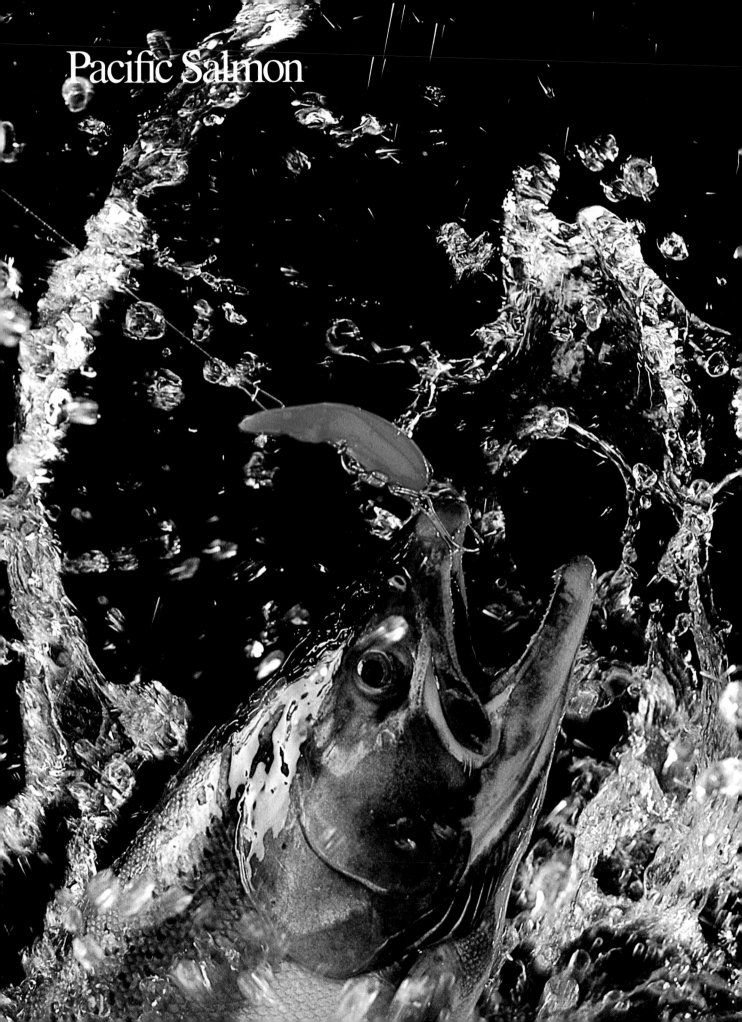

Pacific Salmon

Salmon Basics

For centuries, salmon have mystified man by their uncanny ability to cross thousands of miles of open sea, and return to spawn in the streams where their lives began. Because of their tremendous stamina and speed, salmon rank as the ultimate sport fishing prize among many fishermen.

Five species of salmon are native to the Pacific Coast of North America: chinook, coho, pink, sockeye and chum. Chinook and coho, largest of the Pacific salmon, are the favorites of fishermen.

For many years, fisheries agencies tried to stock salmon in freshwater lakes. Most of these efforts failed. Then, in 1966, coho salmon were introduced in Lake Michigan in an attempt to control the lake's huge population of alewives and to create a new sport fishery. The salmon thrived on the small baitfish. In 1967 and 1968, salmon weighing 7 to 17 pounds returned to the streams where they were stocked, signalling the beginning of a sport fishing bonanza. The project's success led to more coho stocking and later, to the introduction of chinooks. Today, Lakes Michigan and Huron support thriving salmon fisheries, while some fish are taken in Superior, Erie and Ontario.

In the Great Lakes, chinook and cohos feed on alewives, smelt and chubs. They also eat insects and crustaceans. The salmon grow at an astounding rate. Chinooks commonly reach 30 pounds over a normal 4-year life span. Sea-run salmon gain weight even faster, sometimes exceeding 50 pounds.

Salmon need cold water to survive, preferring temperatures about 55°F. They are seldom caught where the temperature is more than a few degrees from that mark. In the Great Lakes, winds and currents move huge masses of water, causing drastic temperature changes over short periods of time. Salmon detect these fluctuations and follow water of their preferred temperature. As a result, salmon may be near the shore one day and miles from shore the next. Or, they can be schooling on the surface at sunrise and lying in 100-foot depths in the afternoon.

Salmon are *anadromous* fish, which means they spend their adult lives in the sea, then return to freshwater streams to spawn. Barriers such as low dams and waterfalls cannot keep them from reaching their spawning grounds. They are powerful swimmers, capable of hurdling rapids and falls that would seem impossible to ascend.

Salmon in the Great Lakes spend their entire lives in fresh water. The vast open waters of the Great Lakes serve as their ocean and the tributary streams are their spawning grounds. Although some spawn successfully, not enough young are produced to maintain a quality fishery. So, state fisheries crews trap the returning salmon, remove their eggs and rear the fish in hatcheries. Then, the young salmon are released in streams. Unlike most fish, Pacific salmon have a set life span. Most individuals of the same species return to spawn at the same age, and then die.

Pacific Salmon
Combined Range

CHINOOK or king salmon are the largest of the Pacific salmon. Their life span is four years, though a few live five or six years. When hooked, a chinook may run 200 yards or more. Many a fisherman has watched awestruck and helpless as the line disappears from the reel. After the first run, a chinook usually fights deep and rarely jumps. The world-record chinook, 97 pounds, 4 ounces, was caught in the Kenai River, Alaska in 1985.

COHO, or silver salmon do not grow as large as chinooks, although many anglers regard cohos as the sportiest of the salmon. They jump repeatedly and change direction so quickly the angler mistakenly believes the fish has broken free. Cohos usually live only three years, gaining much of their weight in the last few months of life. The world-record coho, 31 pounds, was caught in Cowichan Bay, British Columbia in 1947.

How to Identify Chinook and Coho

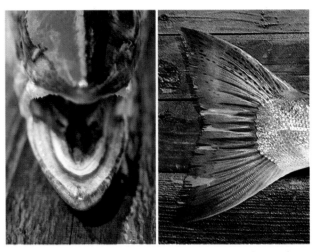

CHINOOKS have a lower jaw that comes to a sharp point. The inside of the mouth appears dusky gray or black and the teeth are set in black gums. The anal fin, the bottom fin closest to the tail, usually has 15 to 19 rays. The tail is broad and covered with spots.

COHOS have a lower jaw that appears more blunt than that of the chinook. The inside of the mouth is dusky gray or black, but the teeth are set in white gums. The anal fin is shorter, with only 12 to 15 rays. The tail may have no spots or just a few on the upper portion.

When and Where to Catch Salmon

Adult salmon rely on cover and structure less than other fish. They go where they must to find food and a comfortable water temperature.

In the Great Lakes, salmon schools are scattered during spring and early summer. Their search for 53° to 57°F temperatures may take them miles from shore or within casting distance of piers. Although fishing is excellent on some days, catching salmon consistently is difficult. But as spawning time nears, they gather near tributary streams where finding and catching them becomes easier.

OPEN-WATER fishing accounts for most salmon caught in the Great Lakes. Salmon have seasonal migration patterns in each lake, so anglers should check with local sources as to the location of fish as the season progresses.

STREAM FISHING for salmon in Great Lakes tributaries begins in September and continues into October. Along the Pacific Coast, some salmon enter streams in April, though most runs begin in September.

Factors Affecting Water Temperature

STREAM MOUTHS attract salmon, especially when surrounding water is too cold. Salmon move into the warm-water plume created by the stream to find suitable temperatures.

DISCHARGES from power plants draw in salmon when lakes are cold. Though the discharged water is too warm, it mixes with lake water, creating a zone of ideal temperature.

WINDS force salmon to move so they can stay at the right temperature. On-shore winds hold warm water along shore; offshore winds push it out and cold water wells up to replace it.

Trolling for Salmon

Trolling enables anglers to cover large areas in a short time, increasing their chances of finding salmon that are scattered in open water. Most trollers use several lines, so they can experiment with different lures and depths to find the combination that best fits the situation at hand.

Of course, it is possible to catch salmon simply by running a line behind the boat and trolling at random. But specialized equipment, such as a temperature gauge, recording sonar unit, downriggers and trolling boards, greatly improves the odds of finding and catching salmon.

A DOWNRIGGER consists of a large reel filled with steel cable, a crank and a brake to keep the reel from slipping. Some have a built-in rod holder and a counter to record the depth of the *cannonball*.

DOWNRIGGERS permit fishing in deep water with relatively light tackle. A 15- to 20-pound test line is attached to a release mechanism (inset) on the weight or cannonball, which is lowered on a cable to the desired depth. A striking salmon will jerk the line loose, so the angler can fight the fish on a free line. Two lines can be used with a *stacker*. This is a release device attached to the cable, rather than to the cannonball. Most salmon boats have at least two downriggers; many have four. Thus, as many as eight lines can be trolled at once.

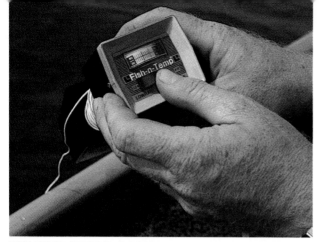

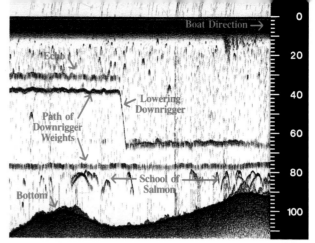

TEMPERATURE GAUGES help anglers find the best fishing depth. The probe is lowered until it reaches the salmon's preferred temperature range. Some trolling boats have built-in surface temperature gauges.

RECORDING SONAR units reveal both the salmon and the paths of downrigger weights. As salmon change depth, the location of the cannonball is adjusted so the lures run just above the fish.

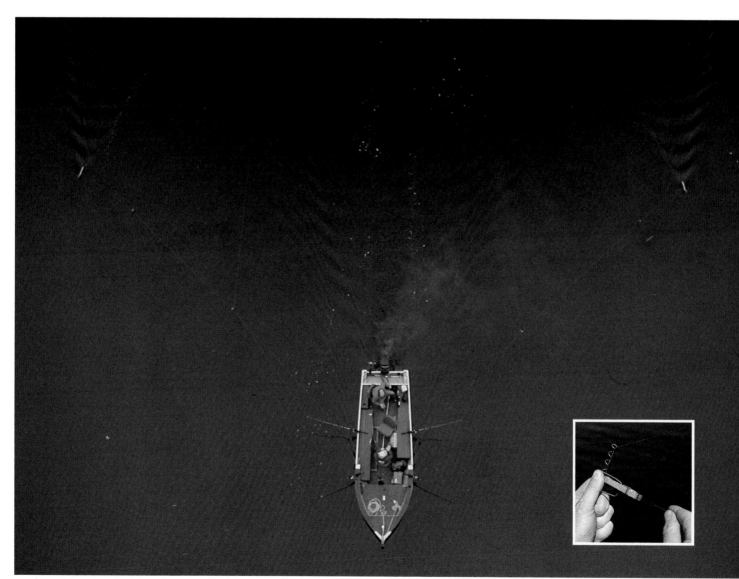

TROLLING BOARDS keep lines wide of the boat when fishing shallow water. Salmon are extremely boat-shy, so drawing the lines away from the wake reduces the chance of spooking fish near the surface. The boards are pulled by cords attached to a pole in the boat. They plane 50 to 75 feet to the side. Fishing lines are attached to release devices (inset) that slide down the cords toward the trolling boards. Two lines can be fished off each side of the boat. With lines spread 20 to 30 feet apart, the fisherman can cover a wide swath of water.

Shore Casting for Salmon

Shore fishermen begin catching salmon in early summer, months before the spawning run begins. Salmon stay in the vicinity of stream mouths, generally feeding just off shore for a few hours in early morning. During midday, they move miles from shore, but return again in evening.

Most fishermen cast with flashy spoons. Heavy lures are best, because they can be cast farther. Still-fishing with spawn bags and alewives also works well. A heavy-duty spinning rod and a large spinning reel with at least 250 yards of 20-pound test monofilament are ideal for shore casting.

ROCKY POINTS near stream mouths are schooling sites for salmon prior to spawning. They often porpoise on the surface in early morning and late afternoon, when they are caught by shore casters.

STREAM-MOUTH fishermen wear chest waders to reach salmon beyond casting distance from shore. To keep the surf from topping their waders, they wear raincoats with belts snug around the waist.

Pier Fishing for Salmon

Piers, especially those near stream mouths, attract salmon throughout the year. However, the best fishing is just before the spawning run or after the run has started. Piers are popular because they enable anglers to fish deep water that could not be reached from shore.

PIER fishermen use the same tackle and lures as shore casters. However, a long-handled landing net and a long stringer are helpful, because most piers stand high above the water surface.

Stream Fishing for Salmon

Even before salmon begin their upstream migrations, they begin changing from bright silver to dark brown and finally to black. Their digestive tracts shrink to almost nothing and they stop eating. As a result, salmon are reluctant to bite once they move into their home streams. Still, many are taken during the spawning run, probably because they strike out of instinct rather than hunger.

At the spawning sites, female salmon dig shallow nests or *redds* on the stream bottom. Once on their redds, salmon spook easily and are difficult to catch. Some anglers spend hours fishing the same redd.

DAMS AND WATERFALLS block or slow migrating salmon. Fish collect in downstream pools, where they are caught by casting spoons, spinners or jigs. Salmon in swifter current may be taken by drift-fishing (page 186).

DRIFT BOATS carry salmon fishermen down many Pacific Coast streams. The boat's swept-up ends make them safe in strong rapids. One person maneuvers the boat with oars, while another angler casts from the bow.

SPAWNING STREAMS become jammed with salmon during the run. As spawning time nears, male salmon develop a grotesque appearance. At right center in the photo is a hooked-jawed male; below it, a female.

201

Natural Bait for Salmon

Natural baits are used extensively by West Coast salmon fishermen and are becoming more popular on the Great Lakes. Favorite baits include alewives, smelt, herring and fresh spawn.

Trolling, still-fishing or *mooching* are common bait-fishing techniques. When mooching, the angler drops the bait to the bottom, then slowly raises and lowers the bait while the boat drifts. When fishing with fresh spawn, most anglers still-fish or drift-fish with a single egg, a gob of eggs or a spawn bag.

FRESH BAITFISH look more natural and stay on the hook better than frozen bait. Fishermen can catch their own bait around piers, harbors or warmwater discharges with umbrella nets (above), dip nets or cast nets.

LIVE FISH are rigged on a harness with a #4 single hook and a #6 treble hook as a trailer. Insert the first hook through the lips or nostrils and the trailer hook under the skin, just behind the dorsal fin.

How to Tie a Spawn Bag

A SPAWN BAG is made with a 2-inch square piece of nylon cut from a roll of mesh or a nylon stocking.

WRAP the eggs to form a bag about one-half inch in diameter. Tie it with thread and trim the excess material.

INSERT a #4 or #6 hook securely into the spawn bag. It should be well concealed in the bag.

Artificial Lures for Salmon

Salmon like colorful, flashy lures with a lot of action. Color of the lure depends on weather, location and season. In general, chartreuse, green, blue and silver lures work best. Red and orange lures often catch salmon just before spawning time.

Silvery colors are the best choice on sunny days; fluorescent or phosphorescent colors on cloudy days. Some fishermen flash their phosphorescent lures with a lantern or camera strobe to make them glow in the water.

DODGERS are large metal attractors that are attached ahead of a thin spoon, small plug or trolling fly. The added flash and action, as seen in this multiple-exposure photograph, entices salmon to strike.

LURES for chinook and coho salmon include (1) Tadpolly, (2) Krocodile, (3) Little Cleo spoon, (4) trolling squid, (5) trolling fly, (6) Fireplug, (7) Flatfish, (8) J-Plug, (9) Rebel, (10) Flutter Spoon.

Bluegills

Bluegills are the most widespread and abundant sunfish species. They were originally found only in the eastern half of the United States, but stocking has expanded their range to include every state except Alaska.

Clear waters with moderate weed growth support the best bluegill populations. But they can also be found in murky lakes. Like most sunfish, they prefer warm, quiet waters. Some bluegills live in slow-moving portions of streams, but they rarely inhabit areas with swift current. They can tolerate slightly brackish water in estuaries.

As their name implies, bluegills have a powder blue gill cover. Females have yellow breasts; males copper-orange. The ear flap is entirely black. The bluegill has a black blotch on the lower rear of the dorsal fin, a mark not found on other sunfish. Bluegills in Florida waters usually have dark, vertical bars on their sides.

Although they grow larger than most other sunfish, bluegills seldom exceed 10 inches or 1 pound in size. Anglers commonly catch 6- to 9-inch bluegills. The world record, caught in Ketona Lake, Alabama in 1950, weighed 4 pounds, 12 ounces.

Bluegills feed primarily on insects, crustaceans and small fish. If other foods become scarce, they will eat aquatic vegetation. During midday, they may suspend to feed on tiny aquatic organisms, called plankton.

In laboratory tests, bluegills fed most heavily in 81-degree water. They did not feed when the water was below 50°F or above 88°F.

Bluegill Range

Redear Sunfish

Known as the *shellcracker* to most southern fishermen, the redear sunfish grinds up snail shells with a special set of teeth in its throat.

Although snails make up a large part of its diet, the redear also eats insect larvae and other typical sunfish foods. Redears feed mostly on bottom, but occasionally grab food on the surface. They seldom feed in water colder than 45°F.

Like bluegills, redears prefer clear water with moderately dense weeds. Stumps, roots and logs are favorite hangouts. They prefer more shade and live in deeper water than most other sunfish, sometimes moving to depths of 25 to 35 feet during summer.

Native to the Southeast, redears have been stocked in a few southwestern and northwestern states. They favor large lakes and reservoirs, but can be found in smaller lakes, ponds and slow-moving streams. They can live in slightly brackish water.

Adult redears have a bright red or orange margin around the ear flap. The colored border is wider on males than it is on females. The back and sides are light olive-green to gold; the breast yellow to yellow-orange. Redears resemble pumpkinseeds, but they do not have wavy blue cheek lines.

Redears produce fewer young than other sunfish, so they are less likely to overpopulate a lake and become stunted. They grow more quickly and reach larger sizes than bluegills in the same body of water. Most redears are 7 to 10 inches long. The world record, 4 pounds, 13 ounces, was caught in Merritt's Mill Pond, Florida in 1986.

Redear Sunfish Range

Pumpkinseeds

Pumpkinseeds do not grow as large as bluegills or redears, but their stunning colors and willingness to bite make them a favorite among many anglers.

Originally a fish of the north central and eastern United States, pumpkinseeds have been stocked in many parts of the West. They prefer slightly cooler waters than other sunfish. Pumpkinseeds often thrive in small, shallow lakes, sheltered bays on larger lakes, or quiet areas of slow-moving streams. They seldom venture into expanses of open water. Pumpkinseeds inhabit shallower water and denser vegetation than bluegills and redears. They are not found in brackish water.

The sides of a pumpkinseed are mostly gold with green, orange and red flecks, and iridescent blue and emerald reflections. The underside is bronze to red-orange. Wavy blue lines mark the side of the head. The ear flap has a half-moon spot of bright red at the tip. Females have the same markings as males, but their colors are not quite as intense.

Insects make up the bulk of the pumpkinseed's diet, but it eats many other foods, including snails and small baitfish. Pumpkinseeds have smaller mouths than most other sunfish, which explains their habit of nibbling at baits.

Pumpkinseeds will take food on the surface or on bottom. They feed heavily during the spawning period and into early summer. Feeding slows in mid-summer, but picks up again in fall.

Often called *common sunfish*, pumpkinseeds usually reach 5 to 7 inches in length. An 8-inch or ½-pound fish is considered a good catch. The world-record pumpkinseed, 1 pound, 6 ounces, was caught in Oswego Pond, New York in 1985.

Pumpkinseed Range

Redbreast Sunfish

Redbreasts are at home in current or still water. Look for them in deep, slow stretches of clear, rocky streams, especially where there is vegetation. They will not hold in fast current. In lakes, they prefer deep, weedy areas with sand or mud bottoms. Like redears, redbreasts can live in slightly brackish water.

Native to the Atlantic Coast states and as far north as New Brunswick, redbreasts have been stocked in many southern states.

The redbreast, or *yellowbelly*, is named for its orange-red to yellow breast. Blue streaks and pale red spots mark its golden-brown sides. Its long, black ear flap does not have a light-colored margin.

The average size of an adult redbreast is only 6 inches or about 4 ounces. But they sometimes grow much larger. The world-record redbreast weighed 1 pound, 12 ounces. It was caught in the Suwannee River, Florida in 1984.

Redbreasts are more prone to feed at night than other sunfish. Primarily bottom feeders, they will also take food on the surface. Their diet is similar to that of other sunfish.

Although they form loose schools most of the year, redbreasts begin to congregate in dense schools in deep water once the temperature drops below 40°F. Fish in these schools seldom bite and almost seem to be hibernating.

Redbreast Sunfish Range

Warmouth

Swamps, sloughs, backwaters and weedy bays of lakes provide homes for warmouth. They can survive in water too stagnant for most other sunfish. Warmouth prefer warm, shallow areas with dense brush, logs, weeds or other thick cover. They can live in slightly brackish water, but cannot tolerate a salt content as high as redears or redbreasts.

Warmouth thrive in the southeastern United States. But their low reproductive rate prevents them from becoming as numerous as other sunfish. Their na-

tive range extends as far north as central Wisconsin and as far west as Texas. They have been stocked in waters west of the Rocky Mountains.

The warmouth is often confused with the rock bass. Both species have reddish eyes, large mouths and olive-brown sides with brown mottling. But the warmouth only has three spines in the anal fin compared to six on the rock bass. The warmouth also has several reddish-brown streaks that radiate from the eye and extend across the head.

During summer, warmouth feed heavily in early morning. Feeding slows by late afternoon. Adults prefer insects and small crayfish, although they eat many other sunfish foods.

Warmouth average 7 to 8 inches in length; a large one measures 10 inches. The world record, 2 pounds, 2 ounces, was caught in Douglas Swamp, South Carolina in 1973.

Warmouth Range

Green Sunfish

The green sunfish has a large mouth and a long body that closely resembles a bass. Its brown to olive-green sides are tinged with emerald green, and the undersides are white or yellow.

These hardy sunfish will tolerate conditions too harsh for most other sunfish. They can survive murky water, low oxygen levels and fluctuating temperatures and water levels. However, they are not found in brackish water. They prefer heavy cover such as large rocks, brush piles or dense weeds.

Green sunfish average only 5 to 6 inches, but two fish, each weighing 2 pounds, 2 ounces, have been recorded. One was caught in a Kansas strip mine in 1961; the other in Stockton Lake, Missouri in 1971. Because of its large mouth, the green sunfish can eat foods like crayfish, shad, young crappies and even small carp. Green sunfish feed most heavily at dawn and dusk.

Green Sunfish Range

Longear Sunfish

Longears are small but colorful, averaging only 4 to 5 inches in length. The largest longear on record, 1 pound, 12 ounces, was caught in Elephant Butte Lake, New Mexico in 1985.

Orange and turquoise mottle the longear's sides and wavy blue lines cross the cheeks. The back is olive-green to rust-brown, and the breast is pale red, orange or yellow. Like the green sunfish, the longear has a black ear flap with a red or yellow margin. But the longear's gill flap is much longer than that of the green sunfish.

Longears prefer slack-water areas of clear streams, but they also inhabit lakes, reservoirs, estuaries and ponds. They usually live in shallow, weedy areas, but do not require heavy cover. Because of their small size, longears eat tiny foods, particularly insects. They often take food on the surface, and may feed at night.

Longear Sunfish Range

How to Catch Sunfish

Catching small sunfish is easy. But taking big ones requires more know-how. Small sunfish form large, loose schools near the shelter of shallow weeds, docks, bridges or other cover in shallow water. Even inexperienced fishermen have little trouble finding them. In addition, small sunnies are curious, often swarming around any small object tossed into their midst.

Bigger sunfish tend to be loners, but occasionally collect in small groups. They stay in deeper water and are less inquisitive than small sunfish. They inspect baits carefully, backing off from anything that looks suspicious.

To present a bait or lure naturally, expert panfish anglers use light line and small hooks. Six-pound, clear monofilament works well in most situations. But some fishermen prefer 4-pound line in extremely clear water or when the fish seem reluctant to bite. In timber, brush or dense weeds, many use line as heavy as 20-pound test to free snagged hooks.

Most sunfish have tiny mouths, so #8 or #10 hooks are good choices. Some anglers use even smaller hooks when fishing with insect larvae. A #6 may work better for large sunfish or for species with large mouths, like warmouth and green sunfish.

Sunfish often swallow the bait. Some fishermen prefer long-shank hooks, so they can remove them quickly. But hooking fish is easier with a short-shank hook. You can remove the shorter hook with a disgorger or a longnose pliers.

A sunfish usually swims up to a bait, studies it for an instant, then inhales it by sucking in water which is expelled out the gills. But a sunfish may spit the bait just as quickly, especially if it feels the hook. To avoid this problem, some fishermen cover the point with bait. Normally, you should wait a few seconds before setting the hook. But when the fish are fussy, set the hook at the first sign of a bite.

When you hook a sunfish, it instinctively turns its body at a right angle to the pressure. Water resistance against the fish's broad, flat side makes it difficult to gain line. This trait makes sunfish one of the toughest fighting panfish.

You can catch sunfish with a wide variety of techniques. Most fishermen simply dangle live bait from a small bobber. But fly-fishing, casting small lures, and even slow-trolling or drifting in deep water often produce good catches.

If an area holds sunfish, they will usually bite within a few minutes after you begin fishing, or they will not bite at all. It seldom pays to wait them out. The best sunfish anglers spend only 5 to 10 minutes in a spot if they are not catching fish.

Many panfish anglers make the mistake of using heavy rods, big hooks or large floats. Some even attach thick steel leaders. Although sunfish are strong fighters, you do not need heavy-duty equipment to land them. Heavy tackle reduces the number of bites and detracts from the sport of fighting these scrappy fish.

Lures for Sunfish

Many sunfish anglers prefer artificial lures. Artificials eliminate the problems of buying and keeping live bait, especially when fishing in remote areas. And at certain times, lures are more productive.

Artificial lures work best in summer when the fish are most active. When you locate a concentration of active sunfish, artificials may outfish live bait because you do not waste time baiting the hook.

Many consider fly-fishing with surface lures to be the ultimate in panfish sport. Fly-fishing is most effective on warm summer evenings, at spawning time, or during an insect hatch. Surface-feeding sunfish will strike a popper, but may ignore live bait.

Sunfish prefer small lures. A big bluegill may strike a 6-inch plastic worm intended for bass, but an inch-long lure will catch sunfish more consistently. Always retrieve the lure slowly. Sunfish seldom strike fast-moving lures or those that produce too much noise or flash.

Anglers can make their own artificials or modify lures such as plastic worms and spinnerbaits to make them more effective.

LURES include: (1) popper, (2) Timberwolf, (3) Western Bee, (4) Emmy Jig with mealworm, (5) rubber spider, (6) Creme Angle Worm, (7) Beetle Spin™, (8) Devil Spinner, (9) Panther Martin, (10) Black Fury® Combo, (11) Hal-Fly®, (12) Road Runner®, (13) Sassy® Shad, (14) Jiggly.

Tips for Making Lures More Effective

SLICE a plastic worm into thin, 1- to 1½-inch strips. The small pieces can be easily inhaled by sunfish. Trim excess hair from a jig or popper to tempt more strikes and catch more fish.

CHANGE spinner blades or jig bodies on a spinnerbait to alter the color or action. Many anglers buy plain spinnerbait arms, then add blades and jig bodies to suit the conditions.

Natural Bait for Sunfish

Sunfish rely heavily on scent to find food, so it is not surprising that the vast majority of sunfish are caught on natural bait.

Natural bait works best early and late in the year when the water is too cold for sunfish to chase artificial lures. It is also the best choice for fishing deep or murky water. When a cold front slows fishing, sunfish may refuse artificials but continue to bite on natural bait.

Small baits like waxworms, red wigglers and mayfly nymphs usually work best in spring and fall. Larger baits like grasshoppers, crickets, catalpa worms, nightcrawlers and cockroaches may work better during summer when sunfish feed more actively.

Sunfish prefer a bait that squirms enticingly on the hook. When using worms, for example, let the ends dangle. To keep your bait alive as long as possible, use light-wire hooks because they do the least damage to the bait.

Some anglers chum with worms or bits of fish, clams or shrimp to draw sunfish into an area. Check local regulations before using this technique.

BAITS include: (1) cricket, (2) grasshopper, (3) piece of nightcrawler, (4) garden worm, (5) red wiggler, (6) small leech, (7) minnow, (8) grass shrimp, (9) clam meat, (10) waxworm, (11) mealworm. Hook sizes range from a #10 with a cricket to a #6 with a garden worm.

Tips for Using Natural Bait

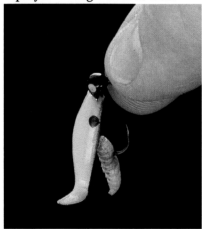

ADD natural bait to an artificial to make the lure more appealing. Sunfish will hold the lure an instant longer before spitting it.

ATTACH a trailer hook with live bait behind an artificial lure, such as a small spinnerbait. The lure attracts sunfish to the bait.

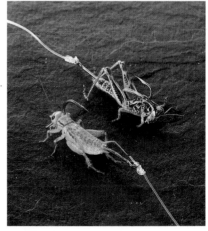

THREAD crickets and grasshoppers on long-shank, light-wire hooks. The point should protrude between the collar and head, or pierce the collar.

Fishing for Spawning Sunfish

Spawning time offers the fastest sunfish action of the year. The fish concentrate in shallow areas where fishermen can easily find them. Nest-guarding males attack baits or lures that come too close, and females feed through the spawning period.

Your chances of finding heavy concentrations of fish are best early in the spawning season. Sometimes individual fish will nest several times over the course of the summer. Many experts believe that sunfish spawn only within a few days of a full or new moon.

In murky waters, sunfish may nest as shallow as 6 inches. But in clear lakes, anglers sometimes catch spawning sunfish in water 15 feet deep. Big sunfish usually nest deeper than small ones.

Sunfish often return to the same spawning grounds year after year. The same fish may spawn several times over the course of the season. Once you find a spawning area, carefully note its location so you can find it again. Many southern fishermen claim they can locate spawning sunfish by smell. The fish, especially bluegills and redears, emit a musky, fish-like odor.

You can prolong your fishing by moving to new waters as the spawning season progresses. Sunfish nest earliest in shallow, murky lakes because they warm the fastest. When they complete spawning in these waters, others are just beginning in deep, clear lakes. Sunfish spawn earlier in the South than in the North. In Florida, bluegills begin spawning in February compared to May and June in Wisconsin.

Avoid spooking fish when you approach beds in shallow water. Move slowly, keep a low profile and do not make unnecessary noise. Cast beyond, then retrieve your lure or bait into the nest area.

Some anglers motor slowly through likely spawning areas, then mark the nests by poking sticks into the bottom or tossing out small styrofoam markers. The activity may spook the fish, but they usually return within 15 minutes. Fishermen then sneak back to work the nests.

When fishing for spawners, set the hook the instant you feel a bite. Males instinctively grab any object that invades the nest, then carry it away. If you wait for the fish to swallow the bait, it may be too late.

Where to Find Spawning Sunfish

STUMP FIELDS in shallow water provide extra cover. A stump protects one side of the nest, making it easier for the male to guard the young.

OVERHANGING COVER, like willow branches, offers protection from birds and other predators. But sunfish will not nest in heavy shade.

EMERGENT PLANTS provide prime spawning cover. Look for fish in pockets or along the edges of bulrushes, buttonbush and cattails.

Tips for Finding Spawning Sunfish

POLE slowly through a likely spawning area or use an electric trolling motor. Look for round, light-colored depressions on bottom.

LOOK for ripples, wakes or other surface disturbances that reveal the location of spawners. Keep the sun at your back for best visibility.

MOVE SLOWLY along the edge of emergent weeds, while casting toward the vegetation. Or fan-cast a potential spawning area to locate fish.

217

How to Use a Bobber Rig for Spawning Sunfish

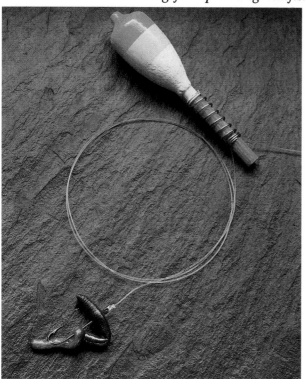

ATTACH a small float to 6-pound monofilament and tie on a #8 light-wire hook. Do not use a sinker. Bait with a small worm or cricket.

LOB the rig beyond the spawning bed to prevent spooking the fish. Reel slowly, then stop when the float is directly above the nest.

How to Fly-cast for Spawning Sunfish

FLY LURES include: (1) Black Gnat, (2) rubber spider, (3) Wooly Worm, (4) Royal Coachman, (5) Miller, (6) popper, (7) McGinty, (8) Mosquito, (9) Light Cahill.

MULTIPLE EXPOSURE PHOTOGRAPH

PAUSE a few seconds while your bug or fly sinks. Twitch the line, then pause again. To detect a strike, watch for a slight tug where the line enters the water.

KEEP the bait 6 to 12 inches off bottom. Twitch the bobber periodically so the bait rises a few inches, then settles toward bottom. If this technique fails to catch fish, remove the bobber, attach a small split-shot, and drag the bait slowly along bottom. Sunfish will attack any bait that comes too close to the nest.

TWITCH a surface lure gently, then wait for the ripples to die. Avoid twitching it too hard because the sudden motion may spook the fish.

SET the hook immediately when a sunfish strikes. Sometimes a fish will make a swirl or splash as it grabs the lure. Or it may suck in the lure with barely a ripple.

STUMPS, especially large ones, provide excellent cover. Wave action washes soil away from the roots, creating open spaces where sunfish can hide.

Fishing for Sunfish in Trees and Brush

Submerged trees or brush provide prime sunfish habitat in almost every type of fresh water. In spring, sunfish spawn in or near timber and brush in shallow water. Later in the year, they find cover and food around trees and brush in deeper water.

All types of sunfish relate to timber and brush, but these cover types are especially attractive to bluegills, redears and warmouth.

Any woody cover will hold sunfish. But some trees hold more fish than others. Cedars and oaks, for example, offer excellent cover. They have a dense network of branches and they rot more slowly than most other trees.

When scouting for sunfish, look for trees that indicate bottom type. Pine trees, for instance, grow mainly on sandy soil, so they may reveal the locations of spawning areas.

Trees and brush near some type of structure generally hold more sunfish than a flat expanse with similar cover. For example, a fallen tree on a point will usually attract more sunfish than a fallen tree along a straight shoreline with uniform depth. A change in the height of trees often provides a clue to bottom structure. A stand of trees growing higher than the surrounding timber may pinpoint the location of a drop-off.

Snags pose a constant problem when fishing in timber and brush. To offset this problem, try the following strategies. Rig your rod and reel with 12- to 15-pound line and a heavy sinker. The extra weight enables you to bounce the sinker to free a snagged lure. Or use 4-pound mono and a tiny lure like a 1/32-ounce jig. Cast over submerged brush or tree limbs, then retrieve slowly, allowing the jig to occasionally bump the branches. If you snag a branch, do not shake it violently while trying to free the lure. This will scare the fish away. Instead, break the line, tie on a new hook and resume fishing.

FLOODED TIMBER near the banks of shallow coves often holds sunfish in spring. In summer, look for trees along a creek channel or near the entrance to a cove.

FALLEN TREES near deep water usually hold sunfish, especially if they have a lot of branches. Some anglers cut down trees to make hiding spots for sunfish.

OVERHANGING LIMBS offer shade and a source of food. Insects collect on the limbs and fall into the water, where they are eaten by sunfish.

SHALLOW BRUSH provides cover in early season and during periods of high water. Sunfish use deeper brush patches in summer.

How to Fish Submerged Limbs

REACH into openings with a long pole. A heavy sinker supported by a large bobber helps avoid snags.

SLIDE a clip-on sinker down the line if you become snagged. The impact will usually free the hook.

USE a light-wire hook and strong line in thick brush. If you snag a limb, pull hard to straighten the hook.

How to Fish Standing Timber

CAST beyond a large submerged tree, then let the line flow from the spool as the lure or bait sinks to bottom. Retrieve as close to the tree as possible.

DROP your bait or lure straight down alongside a tree. If the tree has branches protruding at different depths, cover them all thoroughly.

How to Fish a Stump

MOVE your rod tip to the side as you retrieve so the bait hits a stump. Sunfish usually ignore a bait more than a foot away from their hiding place.

COVER the edge of a stump by circling it with a long pole. Sunfish hide among the roots, so you must place your bait close to the stump.

How to Fish a Fallen Tree

CLIMB out onto the trunk of a fallen tree. Or tie your boat to a limb, or anchor off to one side and cast toward the tree. In early season, concentrate on shallow water near shore. When the water warms, fish the submerged branches in deeper water. If fishing a stream, work the slack water downstream of the tree.

How to Fish Overhanging Limbs

POSITION your boat to the side of overhanging limbs and fly-cast a surface lure under the branches. Fly-casting works well in this situation, because sunfish are accustomed to feeding on insects that drop into the water. Or you can flip a bait into the opening with a flippin' rod or any type of long pole.

How to Fish Shoreline Brush

MOVE along shore, dropping your bait into openings in the brush. Sunfish often hang in pockets on the inshore side of brushy cover.

POKE your bait under shoreline brush by using a long pole with only 6 to 12 inches of line at the tip. Keep the bait as close to the bank as possible.

MATTED WEEDS, or *slop,* block out sunlight. Sunfish find shade and cooler temperatures below the dense layer of vegetation. Slop usually consists of lily pads mixed with coontail or milfoil, and some type of filamentous algae. In the South, water hyacinth forms dense mats that cover entire lakes.

Fishing for Sunfish in Weeds

Weeds are prime sunfish habitat. Small sunfish hide among the leaves to escape predators. Larger fish seek the shade of overhead vegetation. Sunfish also feed on aquatic insects attracted to the weeds.

The best sunfish waters have light to moderate weed growth. If a lake has dense weeds throughout, too many sunfish survive so they become stunted.

Aquatic plants with large, wide leaves offer better cover than weeds with sparse, thin leaves. Look for sunfish in shallow weedbeds in spring. Small fish often remain in weedy shallows all summer, but larger fish prefer weeds close to deep water.

The biggest sunfish usually hang along the edges of weedbeds. Weedlines form where the water becomes too deep for plants to get enough sunlight, or where the bottom changes to a different material.

Like trees, aquatic weeds provide a clue to sunfish location by indicating the bottom type. Bulrushes, for example, grow mainly on sandy bottoms, while lily pads grow in mud. A fisherman searching for spawning sunfish would have better luck near a bulrush bed, because most species of sunfish prefer to nest on a hard bottom.

To catch sunfish in weeds, most fishermen use a light rod, a small bobber and live bait. Some prefer a long pole to reach small pockets and to lift fish straight up before they can tangle the line around plant stems. Accomplished fly-fishermen can place a popper or bug in a tiny opening by casting from a distance.

EMERGENT WEEDS like bulrushes, pickerelweed and maidencane provide spawning habitat. Some fish continue to use deep emergent weeds during summer.

FLOATING-LEAVED WEEDS such as lily pads offer early season cover as the leaves grow toward the surface. In summer, look for sunfish in lily pads near drop-offs.

SUBMERGED WEEDS, especially large-leaved pondweed, or *cabbage,* provide good summer habitat. Look for tiny flowering spikes protruding above the surface.

SAND GRASSES often form low-growing mats on large shallow flats. Look for sunfish in open holes, especially in fall. Many sand grasses have a musky odor.

IRREGULARITIES along beds of emergent weeds usually hold the most sunfish. Look for points and notches. Then cast your lure or bait close to the weeds, let it sink straight down and retrieve slowly. Sunfish hang near the base of the weeds and refuse to chase the bait or lure into open water.

STRAIGHT EDGES usually have some sunfish, but they may be scattered. To cover the edge most efficiently, stay close to the weeds and cast parallel to them.

INSIDE EDGES sometimes hold more sunfish than outside margins because they are sheltered from the wind. Look for deep areas along the inside of the weeds.

BOAT LANES cleared through emergent vegetation provide access to lakeshore cabins. Sunfish concentrate along edges of the boat lanes. Work each edge by casting parallel.

POCKETS in emergent vegetation are prime sunfish spots. In summer, look for pockets in deep water. To avoid snagging the surrounding weeds, drop the bait into the exact spot.

How to Fish Floating-leaved Weeds

LOOK for shaking lily pads to locate sunfish. The fish bump the stems and pads to dislodge insects. Or listen for the sound of sunfish slurping bugs off the surface.

KEEP your rod tip high to slide sunfish over the pads. If the fish swims below the surface, it will wrap your line around the tough stems.

How to Fish Matted Vegetation

RIP a hole in matted vegetation with an L-shaped rod made from ¾-inch, aluminum electrical conduit. Use a cane or extension pole to drop your bait into the opening.

RUN your boat into the vegetation to spread the weeds and dislodge insects. Back out, wait several minutes for the fish to return, then drop your bait into the opening.

How to Fish Submerged Weeds

RETRIEVE a plastic bubble rig so the bait just brushes the weedtops. A filled bubble will sink at about 1 foot per second. Count down to the desired depth, then reel just fast enough to keep the bait at the right level.

REEL a small spinnerbait over the weeds. A slow retrieve works best. If the lure begins to touch the weeds, raise your rod tip and reel faster. The sudden change of action may trigger a strike.

Fishing for Sunfish on Structure

SHORELINE BREAKS hold sunfish throughout the year. Look for points and inside turns along the breakline. Large sunfish sometimes spawn along shallow breaklines at depths of 5 to 8 feet.

Sunfish experts know that the biggest fish are usually found where the depth drops rapidly or the bottom type suddenly changes.

Any type of structure may hold sunfish, but the best structure has ample cover like brush, trees or weeds.

In early morning and late afternoon, sunfish feed in shallows adjacent to shoreline breaks and creek channels, or on the tops of points and humps. In midday, they retreat to deeper water. During summer, bluegills may go as deep as 25 feet and redears to 35 feet. Other sunfish species seldom go deeper than 15 feet.

When you locate sunfish on structure, carefully note the depth. Chances are, others will be at the same depth. Sunfish on structure rarely hang more than a foot or two off bottom. But they sometimes move away from structure and suspend in open water.

To catch sunfish on structure, most fishermen use live bait. Crickets, grasshoppers, small nightcrawlers, leeches, and insect larvae are among the favorites. Attach split-shot about a foot above the bait, and fish it on a $\frac{1}{8}$- or $\frac{1}{4}$-ounce slip-sinker rig. Or suspend the bait a few inches off bottom with a bobber. Some anglers tip a $\frac{1}{16}$- or $\frac{1}{32}$-ounce jig with live bait. You can add split-shot just ahead of the jig so it sinks faster.

HUMPS that peak from 10 to 15 feet below the surface are good summertime spots. This graph tape shows sunfish at 11 to 15 feet alongside a hump.

POINTS attract sunfish year-round. The fish usually hold near the tip of a point or around fingers projecting off the side.

DEPRESSIONS, such as a hole in a shallow flat, draw sunfish in spring and early fall. These areas become too warm in summer.

TROLL slowly along a breakline. Zig-zag into deeper and shallower water to locate fish. Some fishermen back-troll to reduce the boat's speed. Point the stern into the wind and run the motor in reverse.

WORK the edge of a creek channel by motoring slowly within easy casting distance of the timber. Cast into the shallows, then retrieve the bait or lure down the slope, keeping it close to bottom.

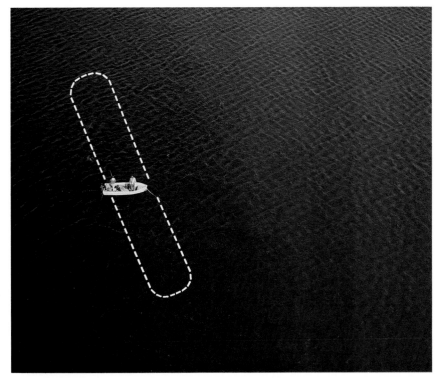

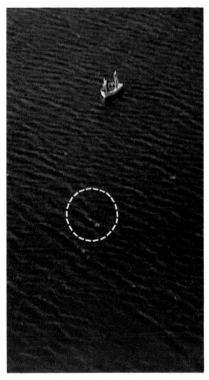

ANCHOR the boat when you locate sunfish. To work a drop-off efficiently, place one anchor in the shallows and another in deep water. Then cast parallel to the breakline at the depth you found fish. From this position, you can cover all the area within the dotted lines.

AVOID anchoring in deep water, then casting into the shallows. Your lure or bait will pass through the strike zone (circle) for only an instant.

ANCHORED BOATS, rafts and other floating objects may provide the only shade in areas that have flat, barren bottoms. Sunfish will form loose schools just below a boat that has been moored for several days.

Fishing for Sunfish Around Man-made Features

In lakes that lack natural cover and structure, man-made features are excellent sunfish spots. Docks, piers, boat houses, duck blinds and swimming platforms offer shade and overhead cover. Other features like bridges, submerged roadbeds, riprap banks and even anchored boats hold fish. Where there is an abundance of natural sunfish habitat, man-made features attract fewer fish.

Many anglers place brush piles or other homemade attractors near docks or favorite fishing spots. An attractor can make a good spot even better.

Man-made features in the shallows draw large sunfish in spring and fall, especially if deep water is nearby. But only small fish remain when the water warms. Man-made objects in 10 to 15 feet of water will hold big fish during the summer months.

Most anglers suspend their bait near submerged man-made objects. But you need special techniques to reach sunfish under platform-like features. If the water is calm, try skipping a lure under a dock, much like you would skip a rock across the water. Or use a long pole to poke your bait under a swimming platform.

Where to Find Sunfish Around Man-made Features

BANK PROTECTORS, especially those made of corrugated metal, offer hiding spots for sunfish. The fish hold in the indentations.

FISH ATTRACTORS vary from crib shelters to bundles of brush. These crib shelters will be hauled to a desired location, then sunk with blocks.

DOCKS in water 10 to 15 feet deep with some weeds or brush nearby may draw large sunfish. But docks in shallow water attract only small fish.

How to Fish Docks and Swimming Platforms

FLICK your lure or bait under a dock with an underhand motion. Or cast sidearm so your lure hits the water in front of the dock and skips under it.

PUSH your bobber under a swimming platform, then bring your pole back out. This technique places your bait near fish in the shade of the platform.

Tips for Catching Sunfish Around Fish Attractors

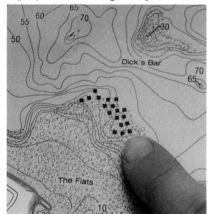

PINPOINT the location of fish attractors by referring to a lake map. Attractors (squares) placed by resource agencies are usually marked on maps.

SUSPEND your bait so it hangs just above a stakebed or other type of attractor. Some anglers prefer bobbers; others fish vertically without floats.

LINE UP two distant objects so you can find the attractor on future trips. These anglers have lined up the edge of a house with a water tower.

Tips for Fishing Other Man-made Features

WALK along the top of a bank protector. Drop your bait next to the wall, because sunfish usually hug the wall tightly. Or pull your boat close to the wall and cast parallel to it.

FLY-CAST around lighted fishing piers just after dark. Use a dry fly or tiny popper to catch sunfish rising to feed on insects attracted by the lights. Listen for slurping sounds to determine if the fish are feeding.

Ice Fishing for Sunfish

Ice fishermen catch more sunfish than any other type of panfish. Anglers have little trouble finding sunfish; the challenge is locating the keepers.

Big sunfish bite best in early winter when the ice is only 2 to 3 inches thick and again just before ice-out.

Sunfish school by size. Large fish generally stay within a foot of bottom, while small sunfish may suspend several feet. If you begin catching small fish, try a different depth or move to another area. Once you find a good spot, look for landmarks to pinpoint the location. Chances are, it will produce fish next season.

Just after freeze-up, look for sunfish in weedy areas less than 8 feet deep. Holes in weedy bays are prime early season locations. Later in the winter, sunfish move to deeper water along drop-offs, but seldom stray far from cover. If the water has enough oxygen, the fish may be as deep as 25 feet. Most species of sunfish require higher oxygen levels than crappies or yellow perch.

Tips for Finding Sunfish

EARLY MORNING and late afternoon offer the best angling, although sunfish bite throughout the day. They seldom bite after dark.

LATE SEASON anglers enjoy fast action. Use a ladder or plank to cross unsafe ice near shore. Check ice thickness before walking to your spot.

LOOK for tips of emergent weeds, such as bulrushes, projecting above the ice. Sunfish often hold near the weedline early and late in the season. They move deeper in mid-winter.

COVER your head with a coat or blanket, then peer down the hole to check for weed growth. Sunfish usually hang in open areas in the weeds. In clear water, you may be able to spot fish.

Ice-fishing Techniques for Sunfish

Sunfish generally inspect baits or lures closely, ignoring anything of the wrong size or color. For greatest consistency, use light line, small baits and delicate bobbers. Four-pound monofilament will handle any sunfish. Heavier line usually results in fewer bites.

Most ice fishermen prefer insect larvae for sunfish. Thread them on a #8 or #10 hook, or on a small jig, spoon or teardrop. Favorite lure colors include orange, yellow and chartreuse. When hooking insect larvae, tear the skin slightly so the juices ooze into the water. The scent attracts sunfish.

Spring-bobbers work better than standard floats for signalling sunfish bites, which may be very subtle. A sunfish sometimes grabs the bait without moving the wire. But when you lift the rod, the wire bends from the weight of the fish. Other times, fish will push the bait upward, relieving tension on the wire. Another advantage of a spring-bobber: you can easily change depth without stopping to adjust a float.

How to Customize a Sunfish Rod

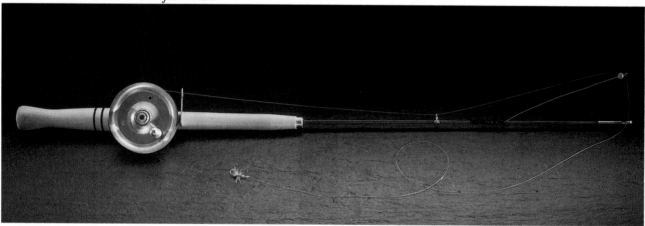

ICE-FISHING RODS for sunfish should be moderately stiff. Bend the end guide so it lies flat. Then, attach a spring-bobber so the eye on the spring lines up with the end guide. Tape on a small metal or plastic reel, or a spin-cast reel to store line and provide a drag. Thread 4-pound mono through the spring-bobber and then through the end guide. Tie on a small lure. Do not add split-shot unless necessary to reach bottom.

How to Detect a Bite With a Spring-bobber

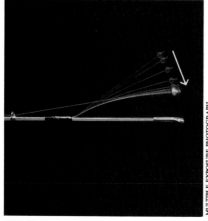

JIGGLE the lure, then stop for a few seconds. Watch the spring-bobber closely. Even a subtle bite will pull the wire downward.

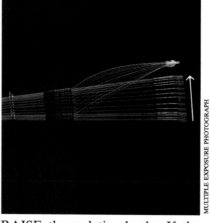

RAISE the rod tip slowly. If the spring-bobber does not move upward at the same rate as the rod tip, a sunfish has taken the lure.

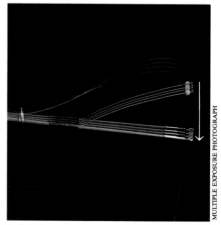

LOWER the lure toward bottom. If the line goes slack when you drop the rod tip, chances are a fish has grabbed the sinking lure.

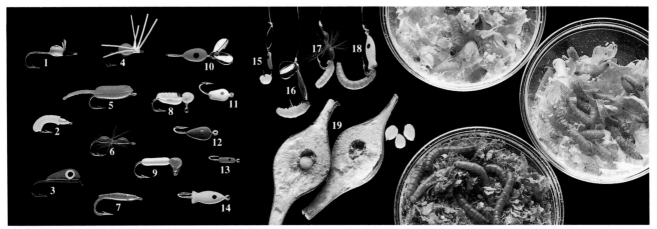

LURES AND BAITS include: (1) Jig-A-Spider, (2) Purist, (3) Chippy, (4) Skin-Yas, (5) Flavored Mouse, (6) Panti® Ant, (7) Moon Glitter, (8) Hott Head, (9) Rat Finky, (10) Fairy, (11) Nubbin, (12) Tear Dot, (13) Speck, (14) Chubby, (15) goldenrod grub, (16) waxworm, (17) silver wiggler, (18) mealworm, (19) goldenrod gall.

Tips for Catching Sunfish

LOOK for patches of snow when the ice is clear. The patches provide shade and reduce spooking. Some anglers spread black plastic on the ice.

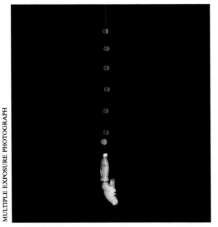

ATTACH your lure with a loop knot. This allows the lure to swing freely, providing extra action when you jiggle the rod.

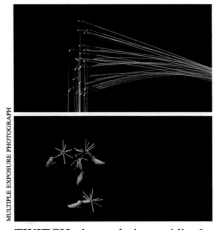

TWITCH the rod tip rapidly for several seconds. The action attracts sunfish. The fish almost always strike when the lure stops moving.

OPEN a hole in weeds by swinging a heavy weight in a circle. Sunfish move in and feed on organisms churned up by the disturbance.

THREAD a colored bead on your line. A sharp twitch moves the bead up the line, then it slides down slowly, attracting sunfish.

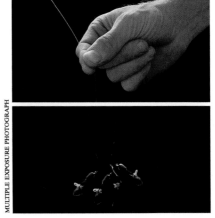

ROLL the line between your fingers to make the lure spin rapidly. When sunfish are fussy, this technique may work better than vertical jigging.

Crappies

Crappie Basics

Crappies rank near the top with panfish anglers because they are easy to catch and live in a wide variety of waters.

There are two species of crappies: black and white. Depending on the region, fishermen refer to both types as *specks, papermouths, bachelor perch, white perch, calico bass* and many other colorful names.

Crappies belong to the sunfish family. They have flat, silvery bodies with black to dark green markings that vary in intensity, depending on time of year and type of water. During the spawning period, a male black crappie may be jet black over much of its body. Markings on male white crappies darken around the head, breast and back. Crappies from clear waters usually have bolder patterns than fish from murky waters.

Although black and white crappies share many of the same waters, black crappies are most abundant in cool, northern lakes with gravel or sand bottoms. They are almost always found around vegetation.

Both species live in rivers and streams, but black crappies prefer quieter waters. They can tolerate a higher salt content, which explains why they are more common than white crappies in estuaries along the East and Gulf coasts.

White crappies are most common in reservoirs, lakes, rivers and bayous of the South, but they are not found as far south as the black crappie. They can tolerate murkier water than black crappies and can thrive in basins with either soft or hard bottoms. They usually live near some type of cover.

The two species vary somewhat in their behavior. White crappies do not school as tightly as blacks. In waters where both kinds are found, white crappies normally spawn slightly deeper.

Although they differ slightly in appearance, habitat and behavior, black and white crappies have many common characteristics. Both have a large number of gill rakers, which they use to strain plankton from the water. Crappies also eat small fish, insects, mollusks and crustaceans. In

Black Crappie Range

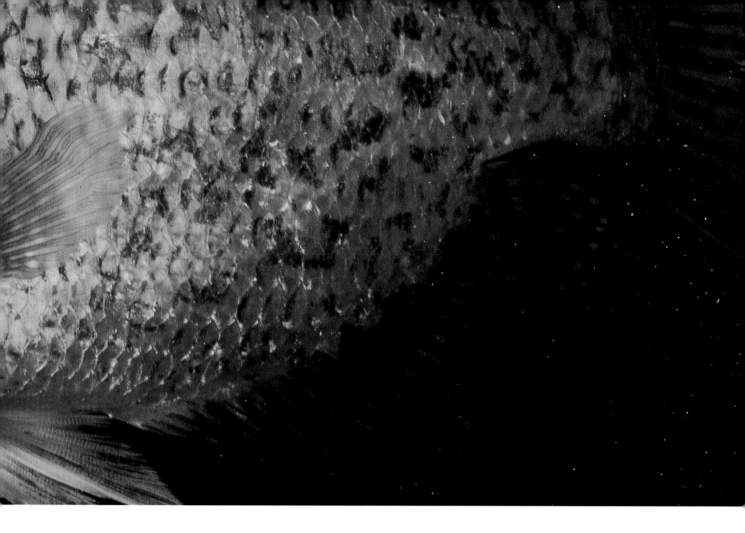

many southern reservoirs, they feed heavily on gizzard and threadfin shad.

More sensitive to light than sunfish, crappies feed most heavily at dawn, dusk or at night. They bite throughout the year, but feed less often once the water drops below 50°F.

Crappies spawn earlier than any other member of the sunfish family. They usually nest when the water temperature reaches 62° to 65°F, which can be as early as January in the Deep South or as late as June in the North.

Spawning crappies prefer gravel bottoms, but will nest on sand or mud if gravel is not available. They also spawn on boulders, dense mats of plant roots and shell beds. Most nest in weeds or brush, or near logs and other large objects. In streams, they often spawn beneath overhanging banks.

White Crappie Range

Males are the first to arrive on the spawning grounds and the last to leave. They establish and defend a territory, then build a nest by fanning away debris. After the female deposits her eggs, the male stays to protect the nest. The eggs hatch in three to five days, depending on water temperature.

Most crappies spawn in water 2 to 10 feet deep. But nesting fish have been seen in water from several inches to 20 feet deep. Usually, the larger the fish, the deeper it spawns. Spotting crappie nests can be difficult, because their beds are not as distinct as those of sunfish.

Crappie populations fluctuate widely in most waters. About once every three to five years, an unusually large percentage of young crappies survive. They grow slowly because so many fish compete for a limited food supply. As a result, anglers catch only small fish for two or three years. But once predation, angling pressure and natural mortality reduce the population, fishermen will enjoy a year or two of good fishing for large crappies.

In most waters, a good-sized crappie is ½ to 1 pound. Crappies seldom live longer than five years. The world-record white crappie weighed 5 pounds, 3 ounces. It was taken from Enid Dam, Mississippi in 1957. The world-record black crappie came from Kerr Lake, Virginia in 1981. It weighed 4 pounds, 8 ounces.

237

BLACK CRAPPIES have irregular, dark blotches or speckles on their sides and seven or eight dorsal fin spines. The distance from the eye to the dorsal fin is equal to the length of the dorsal fin base.

WHITE CRAPPIES have five to ten vertical bands. Most have five or six dorsal fin spines; a few have seven. The distance from the eye to the dorsal fin is greater than the length of the dorsal fin base.

Fishing for Crappies

Catching crappies can be ridiculously easy; or it can be next to impossible. In spring, when crappies school in shallow bays, youngsters with cane poles take home heavy stringers. But when the fish suspend in open water, even expert anglers have trouble catching them.

Unlike sunfish which are naturally curious, crappies shy away from any unusual disturbance, especially in clear water. Even experienced scuba divers can seldom approach crappies. This fact has a bearing on your angling techniques. Keep your distance, avoid unnecessary movements or noise, and use the lightest line possible for the conditions.

The standard crappie rig consists of a small float, split-shot, and a plain hook baited with a minnow. Most fishermen in the North use #4 or #6 hooks. But southern anglers often use much larger hooks.

Many southern fishermen *tightline* for crappies. They lower the bait to bottom on a tandem hook rig tied with 2/0 to 4/0 light-wire hooks and a 1-ounce sinker. With the line nearly vertical, they bounce the sinker off stumps, logs or other snaggy cover. The heavy weight allows them to feel the cover without snagging the hooks. If a hook should become snagged, a strong pull will bend the light wire enough to free the hook.

When tightlining, most anglers use bait-casting gear or medium power spinning tackle. You can get by with ultralight spinning gear and 4-pound line in snag-free water. Veteran anglers prefer cane or extension poles with 15- to 20-pound line for fishing tight spots.

Fly-fishing for crappies has not gained widespread popularity, but it can be extremely effective, particularly at spawning time. Subsurface flies take more fish than poppers or floating bugs.

Crappies strike less aggressively than most other panfish. At times, they barely move the bobber. Or the float may start to move against the wind. With an artificial lure, the only sign of a strike may be a slight sideways movement of the line.

A slow retrieve will usually catch the most crappies. They seldom strike a fast-moving lure. Keep your line tight after setting the hook. A crappie's soft mouth tears easily, so the hook can fall out if the line goes slack.

Lures and Baits for Crappies

Minnows account for the vast majority of crappies in most waters. They are so popular that bait dealers refer to any small baitfish as a crappie minnow.

Crappies prefer 1½- to 2-inch minnows, but 3-inch baitfish sometimes work better for large crappies. Fathead minnows, called *tuffies* or *mudminnows,* are a good choice because they stay alive in the bait bucket and on the hook. Shiners are difficult to keep alive, but many fishermen consider them the best crappie bait.

Because crappies frequently suspend off bottom, many anglers use tandem hook rigs (page 246) to present minnows at different depths.

When fishing is slow, smaller baits often work better than minnows. Small jigs or teardrops tipped with insect larvae have long been popular for ice fishing. But the combination works equally well for crappies in open water.

Crappies will strike almost any small lure, but tiny jigs and spinnerbaits catch the most fish. In southern crappie tournaments, more fish are taken on jigs and jig-minnow combinations than on minnows alone. Plain jigs work well in murky waters. But when fishing clear waters, most anglers tip their jigs with minnows.

HOOK a minnow through (1) the back or (2) tail when still-fishing for crappies. When casting or trolling, hook the minnow through the (3) lips or (4) eye sockets so it swims naturally.

OTHER LIVE BAITS for crappies include: (1) crappie meat, (2) gob of garden worms, (3) piece of nightcrawler, (4) leech, (5) grasshopper, (6) cricket, (7) mayfly nymph, (8) grass shrimp.

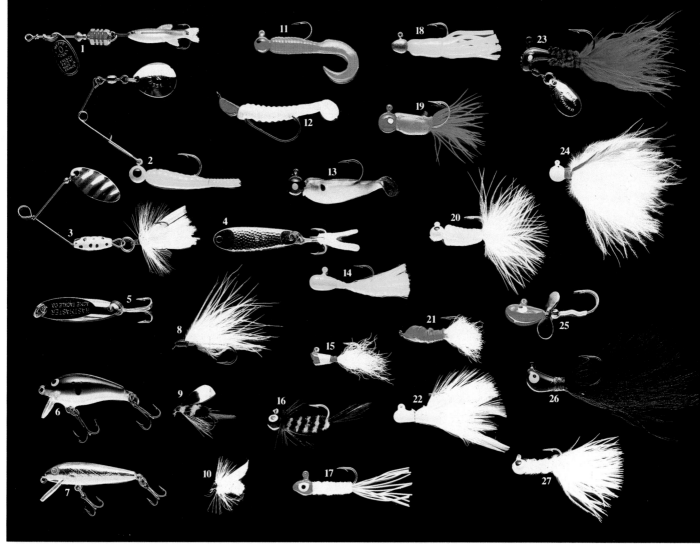

LURES for crappies include: (1) Comet®-Mino, (2) Beetle Spin™, (3) Super Shyster®, (4) Hopkins Shorty® with pork rind, (5) Kastmaster, (6) Fat Rap®, (7) Minnow/ Floater, (8) streamer, (9) McGinty, (10) White Miller, (11) Twister® Teeny, (12) Crappie Slider, (13) Sassy® Shad, (14) Quiver® Jig, (15) Dart, (16) Bumblebee Jig, (17) Lightnin'™ Bug, (18) Tiny Tube™, (19) Hal-Fly®, (20) Fuzz-E-Grub®, (21) Crappie Killer, (22) No-Alibi, (23) Road Runner®, (24) Maribou Jig, (25) Whistler®, (26) bucktail jig, (27) Crappie Jig™.

Tips for Using Live Bait

ADD a stress-reducing chemical to the water to keep shiners and other sensitive baitfish alive. This works especially well during warm weather.

CUT a thin, tapered strip of meat from the belly or side of a small crappie. Tip a spinner or jig with the strip. Or you can add a piece of pork rind.

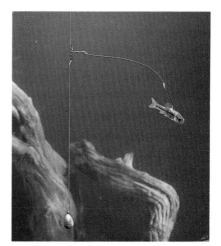

USE a tandem hook rig tied with wire spreader arms. A spreader prevents the leader from tangling with the main line or the other leader.

Fishing for Spawning Crappies

BULRUSHES offer prime spawning cover, especially in northern waters. Early in the spawning period, look for crappies along the deep edges. Later, they move into shallower parts of bulrush beds.

A stealthy approach is the key to catching spawning crappies. Even the slightest disturbance will scatter the fish off their beds. Many fishermen make the mistake of anchoring their boats in spawning areas.

To catch spawning crappies, you must place your bait near the fish, sometimes within inches. Crappies seldom leave their beds to chase food. Instead, they hover motionless near cover, waiting for baitfish to swim past. Fishermen who toss out a minnow, then wait for crappies to come to them, have little chance of success.

The depth of your bait or lure can be critical. Spawning crappies rarely feed on bottom, nor will they swim upward more than a few inches. Experiment with different depths to find the exact level.

In clear lakes, look for crappies by poling or drifting through a spawning area on a calm day. You may scare off the fish by approaching too closely, but if you mark the spot and return a few minutes later, the fish will be there.

Use light spinning gear and small minnows for spawning crappies. Suspend the baitfish below a small float, then cast beyond the spawning area and inch the bait toward the fish. Or simply dangle the minnow in front of a crappie with only a split-shot for weight.

A long pole works better than any other gear when you can see crappies. It enables you to place the bait in exactly the right spot without disturbing the fish. In southern reservoirs, fishermen use long poles to work brushy shorelines of coves. The brush is often too thick to work with standard gear, but with a long pole, you can drop your bait into small openings without getting snagged.

Fly-fishing works well for crappies spawning in light cover. Cast a minnow-like streamer beyond the fish, allow it to sink a few seconds, then retrieve slowly. Experiment to determine the right depth and whether a steady or erratic retrieve works best.

Where to Find Spawning Crappies

FLOODED BRUSH provides spawning cover in many reservoirs. Crappies also spawn in seasonally flooded brush in river backwaters.

MAIDENCANE draws spawners in waters of the Deep South. Sparse beds are the best. If fishing a thick bed, work the openings or edges.

STUMPS AND LOGS attract spawning crappies. Look for the largest stumps and those with root systems that have been washed free of soil.

How to Use a Long Pole for Spawning Crappies

MOVE quietly along the edge of a spawning area while your companion looks for crappies. Use a 12- to 14-foot extension pole with 4 to 6 feet of line at the end. Tip a jig with a small minnow hooked through the lips.

DANGLE the jig and minnow in front of the darker crappies. During the spawning period, males turn blacker than females and strike more aggressively, so your chances of catching them are greater.

How to Swim a Jig for Spawning Crappies

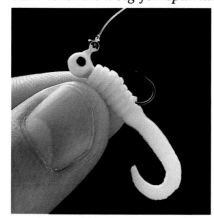

SELECT a 1/32- or 1/64-ounce jig with a small, soft plastic tail. Some crappie fishermen attach a tiny float to keep the jig off bottom.

CAST the jig beyond the spawning area, then retrieve it slowly. Without moving the boat, fan-cast to cover the area thoroughly.

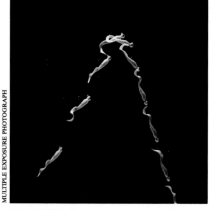

MULTIPLE EXPOSURE PHOTOGRAPH

TWITCH the jig as you retrieve it over the spawning bed. As the jig slowly sinks, the curly plastic tail will wiggle enticingly.

FLOODED BRUSH draws crappies, especially in spring. Rising water floods scrub vegetation in reservoirs, along stream banks and in river backwaters. Deep brush piles hold crappies in summer.

Fishing for Crappies in Timber and Brush

Reservoir fishermen catch the vast majority of their crappies around various types of woody cover. Natural lakes generally have less timber and brush than reservoirs. But where anglers find such cover, they usually catch fish.

Baitfish move into timber and brush to find cover and to pick tiny organisms off the branches. Schools of crappies then move in to feed on the minnows. The cover also offers the crappies shade and protection from predators.

Shallow timber and brush provide excellent spring-time cover. You can generally find crappies in water less than 6 feet deep. The wood absorbs heat from the sun and transfers it into the water, drawing fish from the surrounding area. Crappies also use this cover in fall.

During summer, crappies use woody cover in deeper water, usually 10 to 20 feet. In winter, open-water anglers catch crappies in stands of flooded timber, often as deep as 35 feet.

Most crappie fishermen use 12- to 20-pound monofilament and light-wire hooks when fishing in dense brush. Some use line as heavy as 30-pound test. Crappies do not notice the line because the branches break up its outline.

Many anglers prefer a tiny jig and a float when fishing in brushy cover where snags pose a constant problem. Adjust the float to keep the jig just above the branches, then retrieve with short twitches. The dancing jig will lure crappies out of cover.

Short casts work best in timber and brush. They enable you to place your bait or artificial lure accurately, and to control the path of your retrieve to avoid snags.

244

FALLEN TREES, particularly those that have toppled into deep water, are excellent spots. During midday, the fish hide among the dense branches. They may move a short distance away in morning and evening.

STUMP FIELDS attract crappies, especially if the treetops were cut off and left in the water. Stump fields near deep water hold more crappies than those on a large, shallow flat.

ROOT SYSTEMS of large trees have many crevices that offer ideal cover. Some trees have extensive lateral root systems that provide cover several feet to the side of the trunk.

STANDING TIMBER offers good crappie habitat. Crappies find cover in the treetops, among limbs and branches along the trunk and in exposed roots. Trees with bare trunks seldom hold crappies.

How to Fish Stumps and Trees

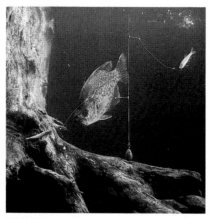

ADJUST your float so the bait rides just above an underwater stump field. Retrieve slowly or let the float drift over the stumps.

BUMP a tandem hook rig around the base of flooded trees or stumps. The heavy weight makes it easier to feel the woody cover.

JIG vertically along the shady side of a stump or standing tree. Work different depths with a lead-head jig or small jigging spoon.

How to Fish Submerged Brush

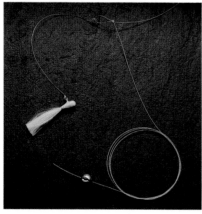

MAKE a loop in 12-pound mono 2 feet from the end. Tie on a 4-inch, 6-pound dropper and a 1/32-ounce jig. Add a split-shot heavier than the jig.

RETRIEVE so the split-shot just touches the brushtops. The shot signals contact with the brush, so you can keep the rig from constantly snagging.

PULL on the line to free the rig if you become snagged. The split-shot will slide off or the light dropper will break, leaving the rest of the rig intact.

How to Fish a Brushy Shoreline

LOOK for brush patches, standing timber, fallen trees, stumps or any other type of woody cover along a shoreline. Fish one piece of cover for a few minutes, then move on to the next. You will usually catch more crappies by covering a large area than by staying in one spot.

HOLD your boat in position with a brush clamp. This way, you do not have to drop anchor near the cover and risk spooking the fish.

DROP your bait into openings between the roots of a tree. A crappie will often hold tight in a small crevice and refuse to bite unless you dangle the bait directly in front of its nose.

WORK the stump thoroughly. Circle the entire perimeter with a long pole, but concentrate on the shady side. If the stump is hollow, try dropping your bait or lure into the center.

How to Tie a Brushguard Jig

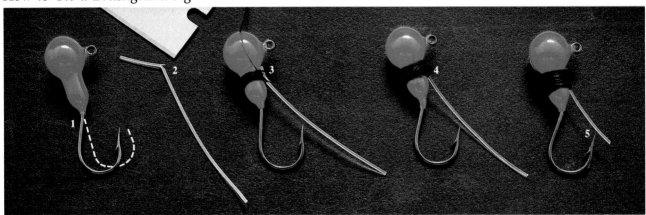

MAKE a brushguard jig by (1) bending down the shank of a small jig just behind the lead head. The dotted line shows the hook's original position. (2) With a razor blade, cut a slit in stiff, 40-pound mono. (3) Wrap winding thread around the collar several times, secure the thread in the slit, then continue wrapping. (4) Make 20 wraps, then tie off the thread with several half-hitches. (5) Trim the mono so it extends just beyond the point.

How to Free Snagged Lures

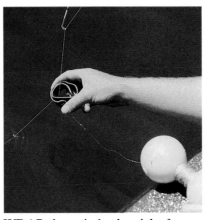

REEL in line until your rod tip touches the lure. Then push the rod to exert backward force on the lure and free the hook.

WRAP the strip-lead weight from a marker buoy around your line. With the marker cord attached, lower the weight to knock the lure free.

SLIDE a lure retriever down your line. The impact may free the lure or the chains may catch the hooks so you can pull them loose.

WEEDLINES offer excellent crappie fishing, especially at twilight or on overcast days when crappies cruise the edge of the weeds in search of food. In bright sunlight, they seek shade and cover in the weeds, but usually no more than a few feet from the edge. Weedlines provide protection from large predators as well as ambush sites where crappies can lie motionless, then dart out to grab passing baitfish.

Fishing for Crappies in Weeds

Anglers who fish natural lakes know that if they find the right kinds of weeds, they will probably find crappies. Weeds are not as important in most reservoirs, but coontail and milfoil provide good crappie cover in some man-made lakes.

In spring, crappies generally seek out some type of emergent or floating-leaved vegetation. But in summer and fall, they prefer submerged weeds. Wide-leaved varieties usually hold more crappies than narrow-leaved types. The fish prefer cabbage, but they will use narrow-leaved plants when other types are not available.

When weeds begin to die back in fall, look for crappies around plants that are still green. This vegetation offers better cover than weeds that have deteriorated. In clear lakes, you may be able to see the tops of green weeds. But in murky or deep water, you will have to snag the plants with your rod and reel.

Unlike most other panfish, crappies seldom use dense weedbeds. They prefer sparser vegetation. This allows you to use light tackle, and to retrieve jigs and other open-hooked lures without constantly snagging weeds.

WEEDTOPS often hold crappies in morning and evening, especially if there is at least 6 feet of water above the weeds. Crappies cruise through the weedtops in search of baitfish and other foods.

CLEARINGS or deep pockets in submerged weeds offer crappies an edge to which they can relate. Clearings often appear as light areas in the weeds; deep pockets look darker than the surrounding vegetation.

How to Fish a Weedline

TROLL into the wind using a jig or jig-minnow combination. When you catch a fish, mark the spot. Then work the area thoroughly, using an electric trolling motor to hold your position.

DRIFT back along the weedline, using your trolling motor to adjust the boat's direction. With the speed control set properly, the boat will drift parallel to the weedline even if the wind is blowing at an angle.

How to Fish Weedtops

SET a slip-float so your bait rides just above the weeds. Let the float drift. A strong wind will lift the bait too far above the weeds, so you must use more weight or lower the bait by readjusting the bobber stop.

RETRIEVE a slow-sinking lure such as a spinnerbait just above the weedtops. The slower you reel, the deeper the lure will run. A ¹⁄₁₆- or ¹⁄₈-ounce spinnerbait works best in weeds less than 10 feet below the surface.

CAST a ¹⁄₁₆- or ⅛-ounce jig (1) parallel to the weedline, let it sink to bottom, then retrieve it along the edge of the weeds. Work the edge thoroughly, then (2) make a few casts into deeper water several feet out from the weeds. If these tactics fail to produce crappies, tie on a weedless lure like a Crappie Slider or a small spinnerbait. (3) Cast the lure several feet into the weeds and retrieve it slowly through the vegetation.

How to Fish in Pockets

WORK the weedtops with a plastic bubble-minnow rig. Fill the bubble with enough water so it barely sinks. Reel slowly over the weeds until you reach a deep pocket, then let the bubble and minnow settle into the hole.

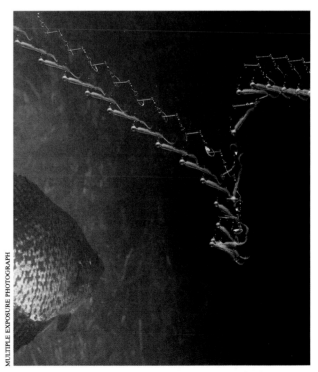

MULTIPLE EXPOSURE PHOTOGRAPH

REEL a ¹⁄₁₆-ounce spinnerbait into a pocket in the weeds, then pause as the lure settles. The helicopter action of the blade makes the lure sink slowly, so crappies have plenty of time to grab it.

251

Fishing for Crappies on Structure

ROCK PILES that top off at 12 to 20 feet hold crappies in summer. Algae on the rocks harbors tiny insect larvae that attract baitfish, which then draw crappies.

Crappies roam widely throughout most waters, using structure as underwater navigation routes. In reservoirs, for instance, crappies follow creek channels from deep water to shallow feeding areas.

Veteran crappie fishermen know which structure to fish at different times of the day and year. The upstream end of a creek channel holds few fish in midday, but often teems with crappies in the evening. A deep hump that comes alive with crappies in summer will be devoid of fish in early spring.

Many fishermen make the mistake of anchoring near structure and waiting for crappies to come to them. If they wait long enough, they may catch some fish. But you can greatly improve your odds by moving along structure until you find crappies.

Trolling with jigs works well for finding crappies on structure. Work the breakline slowly with a ⅛- or ¼-ounce jig, or use a jig-minnow combination. Lift the jig about a foot off bottom, let it sink, then repeat. Crappies usually lie in a narrow band along the breakline, so once you find the fish, you must keep the boat at the exact depth.

When you locate a school, hover over the area with an electric trolling motor. If you throw an anchor near the school, crappies will scatter.

INSIDE TURNS along a breakline hold more crappies than straight edges. Wind concentrates food in pockets formed by inside turns.

HUMPS with moderately dense weed growth on top are good summertime crappie spots. Bald humps seldom hold crappies.

POINTS with large underwater shelves protruding from the end hold more crappies than points that plunge sharply from shore.

How to Find Crappies on a Breakline

LOCATE crappies along structure with a depth finder. Crappies are easier to find than most other panfish because they usually hang farther off bottom. You can easily distinguish between the fish and the bottom signal.

PINPOINT the fish by tossing out a marker near the edge of the school. Do not throw the marker into the school. It might spook the fish and it will prevent you from working the area properly.

How to Find and Fish a Rock Pile

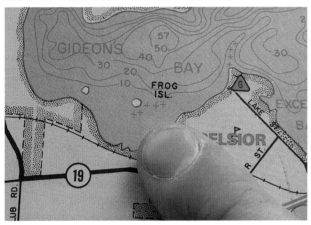

LOOK for rocky areas on your lake map. Some maps label rock reefs or indicate them by groups of closely-spaced Xs.

WATCH your depth finder for signs of a hard bottom. Rocks will return a strong signal, usually with a double or triple echo.

USE a nail instead of a sinker when snags are a problem. Tie the end of a 4-pound mono dropper around the head of a nail.

PINCH hollow, lead wire on a dropper when fishing over rocks. When snagged, the lead pulls loose so you can save the rest of the rig.

TIE on a floating jig-head to keep your bait above the rocks. The slower you retrieve, the higher the bait will ride above bottom.

Fishing for Crappies on Man-made Features

Crappies use man-made features more than any other panfish. Features like fish attractors, bridges and docks are especially important in waters that lack natural cover. In studies on two Tennessee Valley Authority reservoirs, an acre of water with artificial brush piles attracted 4.8 times more crappies than areas without the brush. And crappies in the brushy areas were substantially larger.

Features near deep water attract the most crappies. A fish attractor in water shallower than 10 feet may draw crappies in morning and evening, but seldom holds fish at midday.

Fishermen catch crappies around a variety of man-made objects. Bridges, piers, docks and submerged features like roadbeds, building foundations and fencelines will hold fish at some time of the year.

Fish attractors, especially brush piles, produce crappies more consistently than other man-made features. Fisheries agencies often place brush piles in reservoirs where trees and other cover were removed before the lake was formed. Many fishermen make their own brush piles, then sink them off the end of a dock or along a drop-off. Other attractors include hay bales, tires, stakebeds and crib shelters.

Because of the crappie's roving nature, attractors that hold fish one day may be worthless the next. In lakes with many submerged brush piles, fishermen often establish *milk runs,* moving from one pile to the next until they find fish.

Most anglers use a bobber and minnow when fishing a brush pile. The fish generally hold in a small area, so still-fishing produces more fish than casting or trolling. But the angler who can work a small jig over the brushtops without snagging will usually catch more crappies than the still-fisherman.

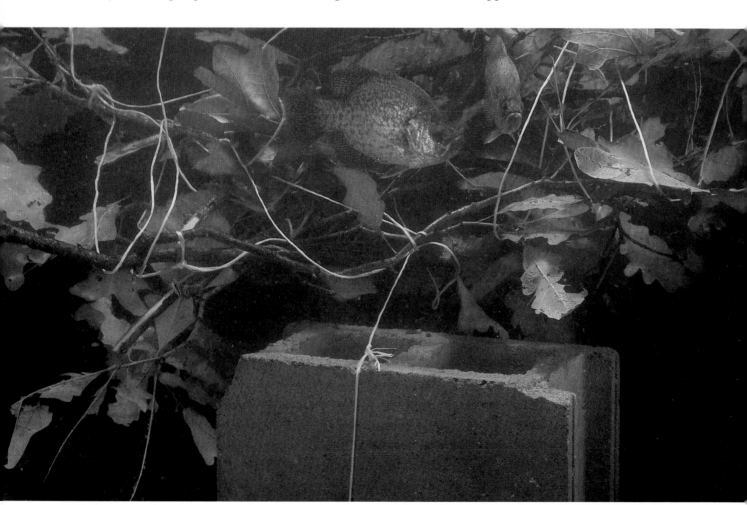

BRUSH PILES are excellent crappie producers, especially if they stand several feet above bottom and have many openings between the branches. Look for brush piles on bald humps or along drop-offs with little cover. Fish attractors placed in areas with abundant cover seldom draw large numbers of crappies.

RIPRAP often holds crappies in spring. The rocks absorb sunlight and warm the surrounding water, attracting baitfish and other crappie foods.

BOAT HARBORS, channels and canals also warm quickly in spring. Look for crappies along sunny shorelines protected from the wind.

BOATHOUSES, docks and swimming platforms attract crappies. During summer, the most productive structures are in water at least 10 feet deep.

BRIDGE PILINGS provide shade for crappies, especially if they have numerous cross-members. Algae growth on wooden pilings draws insects that attract baitfish.

FISHING LOUNGES offer good crappie action because operators often drop chum into the area. Most lounges have covered tops and are heated during cold weather.

How to Fish Bridges

CAST beyond a piling, then retrieve the lure or bait as close to the piling as possible. Or bump the piling to create an erratic action that may trigger a strike.

DROP a ⅛- or ¼-ounce jigging spoon into the shade next to a piling. Jig vertically at different depths to find fish. Work the lure alongside any cross-members.

How to Fish a Floating Dock

CAST a small jig off one side of a floating dock. Strip off line as the lure sinks to bottom.

HOLD your rod tip under the surface, then swing it around the end of the dock. Walk to the opposite side.

RETRIEVE the jig so it passes below the dock. This may be the only way to reach fish hiding underneath.

How to Fish Docks With Posts

BOUNCE a small jig off bottom while walking slowly along the dock. Keep the lure close to the edge and work each post thoroughly.

LOWER a bobber and minnow off the upwind side of a dock. Allow the wind to push the float under the dock to reach crappies in the shade.

How to Fish a Brush Pile

ANCHOR your boat within casting distance on the downwind side of a brush pile. If your anchor pulls loose, the boat will not drift over the brush and spook the fish.

CAST a minnow and small float beyond the brush pile. Let the wind drift the bait over and alongside the brush. Land fish quickly so they will not tangle in the branches.

How to Make a Brush Pile

BUNDLE fresh branches with plastic bailing twine or copper wire. Tie on a cement block. Do not pack the branches too tightly; crappies prefer large openings.

SINK a discarded Christmas tree by wedging the trunk into the hole of a heavy cement block. Lash the tree in place, then drop it into the water.

How to Make Other Fish Attractors

BUILD a stakebed with a 4×8-foot frame made of 2×4s. Use 1×2 uprights that are 4 to 7 feet long. Place two, 40-pound blocks over the stakes in each corner.

TIE three tires together with nylon rope. Drill holes in the tops of the tires so air can escape. Wedge a cement block into each tire.

Fishing for Suspended Crappies

Crappies have a greater tendency to suspend than any other panfish. Fishermen commonly find the fish hanging in mid-water, sometimes far from structure or cover. They will suspend in any season but mainly during summer.

Schools of crappies suspend to feed on plankton or on small baitfish that gather to eat the minute organisms. Most types of plankton are sensitive to light. They move shallower in the evening and deeper at midday.

When crappies are hanging over open water, you may waste a lot of time searching for them. A depth finder will improve your odds dramatically. Many fishermen troll or drift along a breakline, periodically changing depths until they find the fish.

How Crappies Suspend

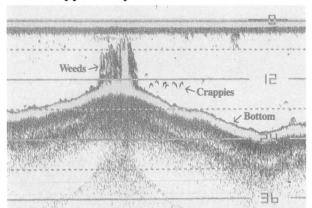

HORIZONTAL layering usually takes place just off a weedline at the same depth as the base of the weeds. Crappies may move away from the weeds and form a horizontal layer in open water.

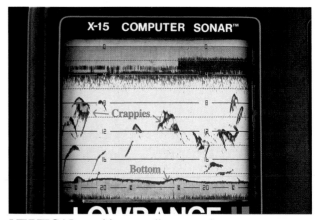

VERTICAL stacking usually occurs in open water, not far from some type of structure. This graph tape shows crappies suspended from just above bottom to within 7 feet of the surface.

The Yo-Yo Technique

TIE on a jig with a marabou or soft plastic tail below a slip-bobber. Adjust the bobber stop so the jig hangs at the depth of the fish.

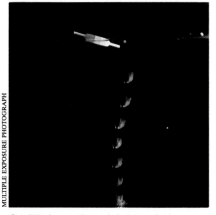

CAST into the vicinity of the suspended crappies. Strip line from your reel so the jig can slide freely through the slip-bobber.

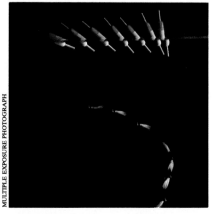

RETRIEVE slowly with jerks and pauses. With each jerk, the line slides up through the float. Crappies strike when the jig sinks.

How to Troll for Suspended Crappies

PLACE several long poles in rod holders so the tips ride 1 to 2 feet above the water. Many fishermen use 12-foot extension poles with jig-minnow combinations or tandem hook rigs baited with minnows.

TROLL slowly along a drop-off with each bait running at a different depth. If one of the rods produces more crappies than the others, set the other rods to fish the same depth.

The Countdown Method for Suspended Crappies

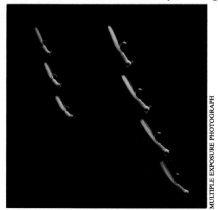

CAST a jig, then count as it sinks. With 6-pound line, a 1/32-ounce marabou jig (left) drops about 1 foot in one second; a 1/8-ounce jig (right) about 2 feet.

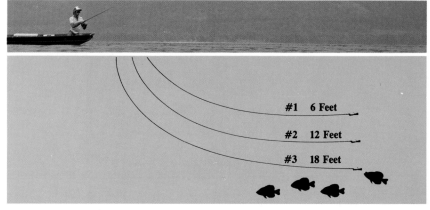

BEGIN your retrieve at different counts until you find crappies. With a 1/8-ounce jig, retrieve #1 (started at 3 seconds) and retrieve #2 (6 seconds) pass too far above the fish. But retrieve #3 (9 seconds) draws a strike. If you know where fish are located, count down to 1 to 2 feet above that depth.

Night Fishing for Crappies

On warm summer evenings, fishermen crowd the docks of many southern reservoirs. Night fishing is popular because anglers can escape the sweltering daytime heat and enjoy fast crappie action. In a study on a California reservoir, summertime anglers caught crappies 16 times faster at night than they did during the day.

Fishermen use lights to attract minnows, which in turn draw crappies. Most bring their own lanterns or floating lights, but some fish at docks with permanently-mounted floodlights.

Night fishing is best during the dark of the moon. Lights draw fewer fish on moonlit nights. Crappies generally begin to bite just after dark. Good fishing usually lasts one to two hours, although the fish may continue to bite through the night. Night-fishing success tapers off in fall.

Most night fishing takes place around docks, piers, bridges and other easy-to-reach places. But some veteran anglers prefer tree lines or creek channel edges that can be reached only by boat. Almost all night fishermen use live minnows on bobber rigs.

Lights for Night Fishing

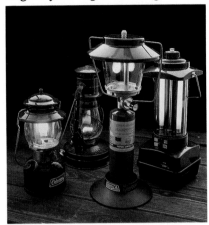

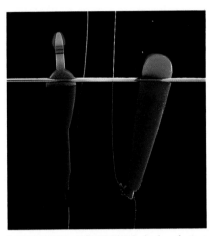

GAS LANTERNS and battery-powered fluorescent lamps provide enough light to draw minnows. But they also attract swarms of insects.

FLOATING LIGHTS draw minnows, but not pesky insects. This model is supported by a styrofoam ring and powered by a car battery.

LIGHTED BOBBERS help detect bites if you do not have a lantern. Tiny lithium batteries provide power. Some can be rigged as slip-floats.

How to Rig and Use a Lantern

SUSPEND a lantern on a board or pole so it hangs just above the water. Some anglers use commercial lantern hangers which clamp onto the side of the boat. Fish around the edge of the lighted area, because crappies will not feed in intense light. Experiment with different depths to find the fish.

TIE your lantern to a limb along a steep bank. Anchor away from the light and use a long fishing pole. This prevents you from spooking the fish and enables you to stay away from insects that swarm around the light.

DIRECT the light downward by making a lantern shield from a circle of tinfoil. Cut out the center and a wedge from one side. Wrap the foil around the lantern just under the vents, then crimp the edge at the seam.

Ice Fishing for Crappies

Crappies inhabit deeper water than most other pan-fish. In mid-winter, they may be found at depths of 30 feet or more. They usually hang near structure, but may suspend just off structure or in open water. Crappies suspend farther off bottom than other pan-fish, sometimes rising 15 to 20 feet.

Early and late winter offer the best crappie action. Look for the fish around their usual springtime haunts in water 15 feet or shallower. They prefer a weedy area near the top of a drop-off. Just after freeze-up, fishermen catch crappies in water as shallow as 3 feet.

Crappies are more sensitive to light than other pan-fish, so cloudy weather usually means better fishing.

They often go on a feeding binge one to two hours before a snowstorm. But the clear, bright skies following a cold front usually slow fishing. Crappies form dense, suspended schools in deeper water and refuse to bite.

Many crappie experts use portable depth finders to locate likely spots. The units save time because you can sound through the ice rather than drill holes to check the depth. You can also spot suspended crappies by sounding through the ice.

If you do not have a depth finder, continually adjust the depth of your bait until you find fish. At times, crappies pack into extremely tight schools. To catch these fish, you must find the exact spot.

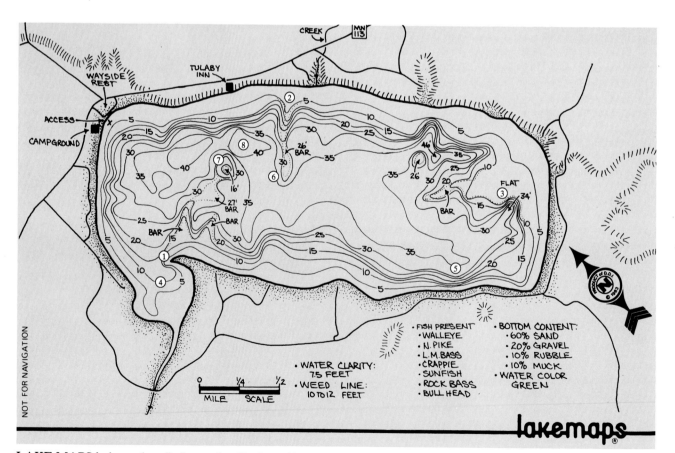

LAKE MAPS help anglers find crappies. Early and late winter spots include: (1) shallow shoreline points, (2) shallow submerged points, (3) edges of flats near deep water, (4) shallow bays. Mid-winter spots include: (5) sharp shoreline breaks, (6) deep extensions of submerged points, (7) mid-lake humps, (8) suspended over deep hole.

NIGHTTIME is often best for crappie fishing, especially in clear lakes. To attract crappies, set a lantern on the ice. The light should not beam down the hole, because it may spook the fish. Crappie fishing usually peaks during the two-hour period after dusk. The fish start to bite again an hour or two before dawn.

Ice-fishing Techniques for Crappies

A small minnow dangled below a tiny bobber undoubtedly accounts for more wintertime crappies than any other technique. An active, 1½- to 2-inch minnow usually works best. When fishing is slow, some anglers switch to larval baits like waxworms, goldenrod grubs, maggots and mayfly nymphs, often sold as mayfly *wigglers*.

Most fishermen use larvae to tip small jigs or teardrops. Crappies do not rely on scent as much as sunfish, but the larvae often seem to help. Jigs with soft plastic molded around the hook also work well. Crappies evidently mistake the plastic for real food.

Fishermen sometimes have trouble hooking crappies because the fish mouth the bait before they swallow it. When your bobber goes under, wait a few seconds to set the hook. If you miss the fish, wait longer the next time. If you still cannot hook the fish, switch to a small bait or try a jigging lure.

When fishing is fast, a minnow-like jigging lure or a small spoon may catch several fish in the time it takes to catch one on live bait.

Popular Crappie Rigs

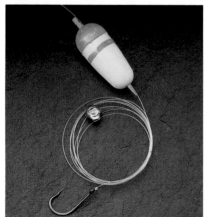

STANDARD RIGS include a peg bobber, enough split-shot for balance and a #4 or #6 short-shank hook. Most anglers use 4- or 6-pound line.

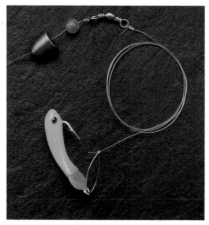

SWIVEL RIGS prevent line twist when jigging. Splice a swivel into the line about 8 inches above the hook; add a small bead and slip-sinker.

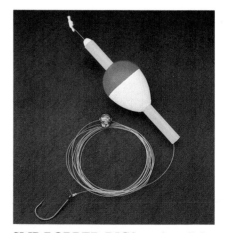

SLIP-BOBBER RIGS work well for deep water, but only when temperatures are above freezing. With ice on the line, the bobber cannot slide.

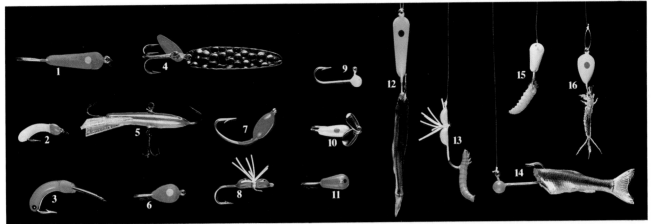

LURES AND BAITS for crappies include: (1) Crappie Rocket, (2) Purist, (3) Rembrant, (4) Swedish Pimple®, (5) Rapala® Jigging Lure, (6) 3-D, (7) Carlson, (8) Ant, (9) Balls-O-Fire, (10) Moxy, (11) Jig-A-Bitzi, (12) minnow, (13) mealworm, (14) rear portion of minnow, (15) waxworm, (16) mayfly nymph.

How to Jig for Crappies

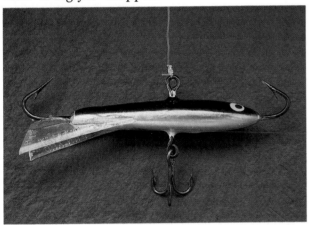

TIE a Jigging Rapala® directly to your line. Most fishermen use 8-pound monofilament. Lighter line may snap when you set the hook. Lower the lure to about 1 foot off the bottom.

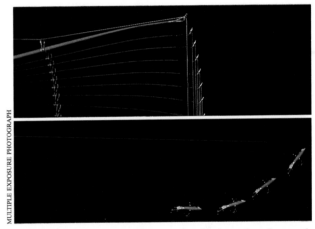

TWITCH the rod sharply to make the lure dart forward. Wait until the lure settles to rest, pause several seconds, then twitch again. Crappies generally strike during the pause. Set the hook immediately.

Tips for Catching Crappies

STORE leftover minnows in a perforated can. Attach a rope, sink the can and let the rope freeze in. The bait will be fresh when you return.

FIX the depth when you locate fish by placing a tab-type rubber band around the spool. Then you can easily return your bait to the right depth.

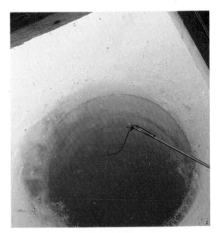

WATCH your line when a fish bites. If the line consistently moves off to the same side, it may indicate the whereabouts of the school.

Yellow Perch

YELLOW PERCH, sometimes called *raccoon* or *ringed perch*, are strikingly marked with six to nine greenish-black or olive vertical bars on each side. The back may be black or dark olive-green, while the belly varies from pale yellow to white. The perch has two separate dorsal fins and its tail fin is distinctly forked.

Yellow Perch Basics

Fillets of yellow perch command a high price at the market. If you have ever tasted them, you know why. But once you have seen a swarm of tiny yellow perch following your bait, you can also understand why some fishermen consider them to be bait-stealing pests.

The yellow perch is a mid-sized member of the perch family. Most fish caught by anglers are 6 to 9 inches long. Any perch larger than 9 inches or ½ pound is considered a *jumbo*. Of the 100 other species in the perch family, most are darters that seldom grow longer than 3 inches. At the other extreme is the walleye, which can exceed 15 pounds.

Perch were originally found in the north central and northeastern states and in all of the Canadian provinces with the exception of British Columbia. Widespread stocking has expanded their range as far south as New Mexico and Texas. Yellow perch continue to spread naturally into many new waters.

Good-sized yellow perch abound in relatively clear, cool lakes and reservoirs with sand, gravel or rock bottoms and moderate vegetation. Weedy, mud-bottomed lakes sometimes have large populations, but smaller fish. The dense weeds provide cover where young perch can escape predators. Too many perch survive, resulting in stunted fish that rarely grow larger than a few ounces.

Yellow perch thrive in the Great Lakes, with the exception of Lake Superior. They are also found in the brackish waters of Atlantic Coast estuaries, in large rivers, and occasionally in deep ponds.

Unlike crappies, perch are comfortable in bright light. In fact, they cannot see well in dim light, which explains why they are easy prey for night-feeding predators such as the walleye. Anglers rarely catch yellow perch after dark.

Most yellow perch spawn at night or early in the morning, normally in water 43° to 48°F. Several males will flank a female, then release their milt as she deposits her eggs. The eggs are clustered within jelly-like bands, called *egg strands*, that cling to weeds, brush and debris.

The eggs hatch in 10 to 14 days. The newly-hatched fry move to open water where they remain for several weeks. Then, they return to the shallows, forming huge schools that provide a lush food supply for predator fish. As the perch grow, they begin spending more time in deeper areas of the lake.

The diet of perch changes as they grow larger. Young fish feed on zooplankton and the larvae of aquatic insects. Adult perch eat small minnows and crustaceans, snails, leeches and other invertebrates.

Yellow perch in northern waters grow more slowly but live longer than perch in the southern parts of their range. Few yellow perch live longer than 9 or 10 years. The world record, 4 pounds, 3 ounces, was caught in 1865 from the Delaware River in New Jersey.

Yellow Perch Range

Fishing for Yellow Perch

Luckily for fishermen, large perch are seldom found in the same areas as the tiny bait-stealers. The bigger fish generally prefer deeper water and almost always stay within inches of bottom. If you start catching small perch, move to another spot.

When you locate a school, fishing may be slow at first. But once you begin catching fish, the commotion will often draw more perch into the area and start a feeding frenzy. If this happens, land your fish quickly and get your line back into the water, because another perch will bite immediately.

Many perch fishermen prefer multiple-hook rigs. When a fish bites, set the hook, then leave the rig in the water. The struggling perch attracts other fish, which grab the remaining baits.

The yellow perch has a small mouth compared to the size of its body, so small hooks and baits work best. Most fishermen prefer #4 or #6 short-shank hooks. Some choose long-shank hooks because they are easier to remove from the fish.

Ice-fishing baits and lures work equally well during the open-water season. Small insect larvae, ice flies and tiny jigging lures often catch perch that only nibble at larger offerings.

Lively baits work best when perch are not actively feeding. You can also entice perch to strike by adding attractors such as spinners or colored beads. When feeding actively, the fish will readily strike small pieces of minnow. If you run out of bait, use the eye from a freshly-caught perch.

Perch sometimes grab the end of the bait, then swim off rapidly. When you set the hook, you retrieve only half a worm or a chewed-up minnow. If this happens continuously, try gently pulling the bait away from the fish. When the perch feels its meal trying to escape, it will swallow the bait.

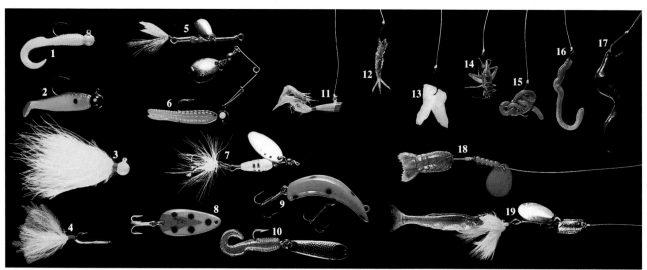

LURES AND BAITS for yellow perch include: (1) Twister® Teeny, (2) Sassy® Shad, (3) Maribou Jig, (4) no name spoon, (5) spinner/fly combo, (6) Beetle Spin™, (7) Toni™, (8) Dardevle®, (9) Lazy Ike, (10) Hopkins® ST, (11) Shad Dart with grass shrimp, (12) mayfly nymph, (13) perch meat, (14) cricket, (15) garden worm, (16) piece of nightcrawler, (17) leech, (18) snelled spinner with crayfish tail, (19) Paul Bunyan's® "66" with minnow.

Tips for Catching Perch

MAKE a spinner rig by first threading a spinner blade and clevis onto your line. The dished side of the blade should face the hook. Add several colorful, plastic beads and a #6 hook. Bait with a worm or minnow.

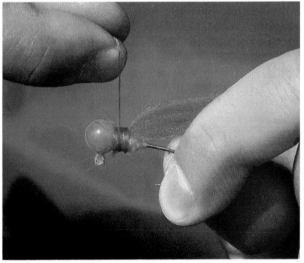

ADD several strands of bright red yarn to the shank of a plain hook or small jig. Wrap the yarn with winding thread to hold it in place. The bright color has special appeal to perch, especially during a feeding frenzy.

WEEDS and submerged branches along protected shorelines provide ideal spawning habitat, especially in natural lakes. Perch mill around these areas before spawning, then drape their eggs over the vegetation.

Fishing for Spawning Yellow Perch

When huge schools of spawning perch invade the shallows, even novice anglers fill their stringers quickly. Despite frigid water temperatures, perch bite eagerly at spawning time.

Firm, sand-gravel bottoms generally hold more spawners than soft, mucky areas. Once spawning begins, you can find the fish by looking for egg strands on shallow weeds or brush.

Most anglers use a small bobber, split-shot and a plain hook baited with a tiny minnow. Small baits and lures work best, because the fish are feeding on aquatic insects. Many fishermen prefer ice flies baited with insect larvae or bits of worm.

Fishermen on the Great Lakes use floating dropper rigs to catch perch off piers and breakwaters. These rigs can be easily adjusted so the bait is at the level of the perch. Some pier fishermen prefer spreader rigs.

In rivers and streams flowing into East Coast estuaries, anglers catch spawning perch on small, flat-headed jigs called *shad darts*. Many fishermen bait the darts with grass shrimp and suspend them from a bobber. Others combine shad darts with small spoons for extra attraction.

The techniques used to catch spawning perch also work in fall when the fish return to the shallows.

PIERS AND BREAKWALLS extending into water 20 feet or deeper attract Great Lakes perch in spring and fall. The fish move out of deep water to spawn among rocks on the inshore end of a pier.

SMALL STREAMS flowing into Atlantic Coast estuaries draw spawning perch. Look for fish in slack-water pockets or below dams. Perch move upstream on an incoming tide, downstream on an ebbing tide.

How to Make and Fish a Floating Dropper Rig

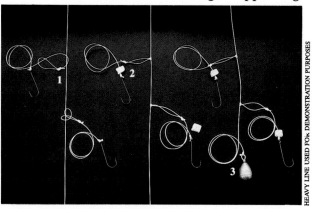

TIE two, 6-inch monofilament leaders, each with a #6 hook on one end and a loop on the other. (1) Wrap each leader around the main line and pull the hook through the loop. (2) Thread bits of styrofoam over the hooks. (3) Add a ½-ounce bell sinker.

SPREAD the droppers 1 to 2 feet apart and bait with minnows. Cast from a pier, then tighten the line; or lower the rig over the side of the pier. The styrofoam will raise the baits slightly. If nothing bites after several minutes, slide the droppers farther up the line.

How to Make and Fish a Shad Dart Rig

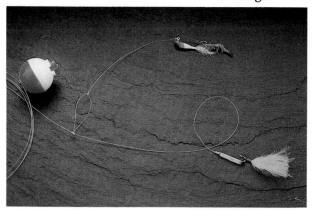

MAKE a loop 8 inches from the end of your line. Tie a 4-inch dropper to the loop and attach a ⅟₁₆-ounce shad dart. Add a no name spoon, then clip on a small float. Bait the dart with a grass shrimp.

ADJUST the float so the spoon rides about 2 inches off bottom. Cast, let the rig settle, then reel back slowly with occasional twitches followed by pauses. The fluttering spoon will draw fish to the dart.

Other Popular Rigs for Perch

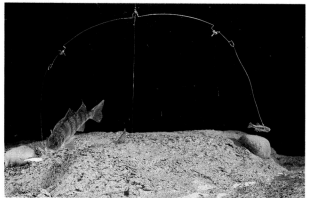

WIRE SPREADERS work well for vertical fishing because the wire keeps the baits apart. Many spreaders have spinners on the ends. Suspend a bell sinker from a piece of mono to keep the hooks above bottom.

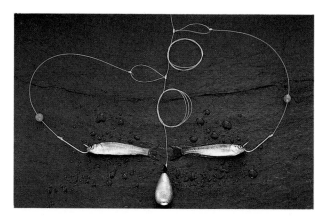

COLORED BEAD RIGS work best when jigged. The beads will slide up the leaders, then fall back down. The extra color and action may attract yellow perch when other techniques fail.

YELLOW PERCH are drawn to bright colors. Lake Erie fishermen attach flags to their anchor ropes.

Fishing for Yellow Perch in Open Water

After spawning, large yellow perch abandon shallow cover and head for open water. They school around rock or sand-gravel reefs and sparse weedbeds. At times, they can be caught over soft, mucky bottoms, especially when mayflies or other aquatic insects are emerging from the mud.

Perch in open water normally stay near bottom at depths of 20 to 35 feet, but they may feed on reefs that top out at 10 to 15 feet. In some lakes, they suspend while feeding on plankton or schools of small baitfish.

To locate open-water perch, drift or troll slowly using a fluorescent spinner baited with a worm, minnow or strip of perch belly meat. The spinner will often catch fish that ignore other offerings. Troll just fast enough to make the blade turn.

When you find perch, a slip-bobber rig, tandem hook rig or other still-fishing technique may work better. Many fishermen prefer small jigs.

Anglers have devised some novel methods to concentrate perch. Some tie colored plastic flags to the anchor rope. Others lower pieces of metal on a rope, so they clang on the rocks. Chumming with small pieces of baitfish will attract perch and may excite them enough to trigger a feeding burst. A jigging lure spliced into the line just above the hook will also draw perch toward the bait.

How to Make a Trolling Rig for Perch

TIE on a barrel swivel, then add 2 feet of 6-pound mono. Attach a #4 or #6 hook and pinch on split-shot above the swivel. Bait with a plain or peeled crayfish tail or a minnow. The swivel prevents line twist.

MAKE a line release for each rod when trolling with several lines. Open the bail, then slide a loop of line under a rubber band. When a perch strikes, it pulls the line free and can mouth the bait without feeling tension.

How to Attract Perch With a Jigging Spoon

REMOVE the hook from a jigging lure, then tie the lure to your line. Add 12 inches of 6-pound mono to the split-ring at the bottom of the lure. Attach a #4 or #6 hook and a minnow hooked through the lips.

LOWER the jigging spoon until it touches bottom, then reel up several inches. Jig the lure up and down to attract yellow perch to the minnow. Set the hook immediately when you feel a bite.

Other Tips for Attracting Perch

TWIST a 4- to 5-inch strip of aluminum foil around your line to attract yellow perch in open water. Some fishermen wad the foil to create rough edges that reflect light in all directions.

ATTACH a cement block to a rope, then lower it to bottom from an anchored boat. Tie the rope to the bow, leaving no slack. Wave action will raise and lower the block, or *mudder,* stirring up silt and attracting perch.

Ice Fishing for Yellow Perch

Ice fishing for yellow perch peaks just before ice-out when they cruise shallow flats and rock piles. In early winter, anglers on natural lakes catch many perch in the back ends of bays or off shoreline points in water only 4 to 8 feet deep. By mid-winter, most perch have moved to deep water, generally from 20 to 40 feet. They gather along breaklines just off sand or mud flats, often near the base of a drop-off.

Mid-morning to mid-afternoon offers the fastest action. Changing weather conditions have little effect on perch fishing.

Most perch fishermen rate minnows as the best bait. Using a #6 hook, pierce the minnow's back just below the dorsal fin. Use a bobber to suspend the baitfish about 6 inches off bottom. Some anglers prefer to drop a dead minnow to bottom. Perch fishermen often tip artificials with larval baits, worms, marshmallows or perch eyes. Favorite lure colors include silver, red, yellow and chartreuse.

Veteran perch anglers use a unique piece of equipment called a *tube rig*. Attach a short leader to a piece of metal tubing, bait with a minnow or perch eye, and drop the rig to bottom in deep water. The heavy tube stirs up the sediment, attracting perch. Let the rig rest on bottom and lift periodically to see if a perch has taken the bait.

SAND-GRAVEL FLATS in water from 10 to 15 feet deep are prime late winter habitat. Yellow perch prefer a clean bottom that is devoid of weeds, brush, trees or other vegetation.

HONEYCOMBED ICE means good perch fishing. But late winter fishing demands extreme caution. Although the ice may still be over 1 foot thick, there may be scattered weak spots.

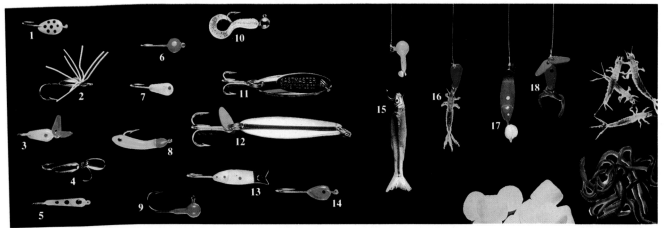

LURES AND BAITS include: (1) Speck'l, (2) Chrome Spider, (3) Jig-A-Flipper, (4) Diamond Back, (5) Slim-Fin, (6) Falcon, (7) Jig-A-Bitzi, (8) Purist, (9) Panfish Assassin, (10) Jiggly, (11) Kastmaster, (12) Swedish Pimple®, (13) Jig-A-Spoon, (14) Darby, (15) minnow, (16) mayfly nymph, (17) piece of marshmallow, (18) red wiggler.

How to Jig With a Swedish Pimple®

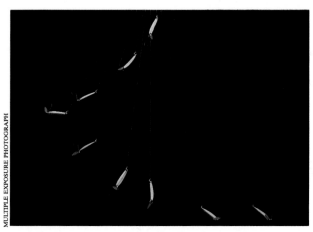

RAISE a Swedish Pimple® 2 to 3 feet off bottom, then quickly drop the rod tip. Allow the lure to fall to within 6 inches of bottom. Some anglers tip the lure with a wax-worm or small piece of minnow.

HOLD the rod still as the lure flutters downward. It will flare to one side and then the other before settling to rest. Perch strike after the lure stops moving. Set the hook at the slightest tug.

Tips for Catching Yellow Perch

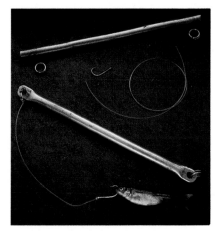

SCATTER *tip-ups* over a large area to locate perch. When a flag signals a bite, drill a hole nearby and try jigging or bobber-fishing.

LEAVE a hooked perch on the line. The hooked fish may attract other perch and start a feeding frenzy. Fish in a nearby hole.

MAKE a tube rig from a 10-inch piece of copper tubing. Drill holes in the flattened ends, then attach split-rings, a leader and a #6 hook.

275

Fishing for White Bass

White bass feed in packs, pushing baitfish to the surface or into confined areas, then slashing into their prey. Anglers who work these rampaging schools often catch fish on every cast.

But fishing for white bass is not always easy. They can be extremely selective about the size of lure they strike. And whites spook more easily than other panfish. When you find a school, you must keep your distance or the fish will quickly disappear.

White bass put up a strong fight when hooked on light tackle. Six- to eight-pound line works well in most situations, but you should check the line frequently for cuts. Their razor sharp gill covers may nick the line, causing it to snap at the slightest tug.

Weather has little effect on white bass fishing, although surface-feeding may last longer on overcast days. White bass usually continue to feed despite cold front conditions.

FAST RETRIEVES generally work best for white bass, because the fish are accustomed to chasing fast-moving

WHITE BASS school according to size. If you locate a school and begin catching small fish, chances are you will continue to catch only small fish. Instead, try to find another school.

WATCH for swirls, slurps or splashes, signs that white bass are feeding on the surface. Fishermen routinely look for circling gulls to find schools of bass surface-feeding on shad.

prey in open water. Quite often, an angler will draw his lure slowly through a school, then begin reeling quickly as he nears the end of his retrieve. White bass strike just before he pulls the lure from the water.

APPROACH white bass quietly. They will move away from the sound of an outboard or the clanking of gear on the bottom of the boat. Use an electric trolling motor or drift along the edge of the school.

AVOID grabbing a white bass across the gill plates. Each plate has a needle-sharp spine (arrow) that can inflict a painful wound. Instead, hold the fish by the lower lip or grip it firmly across the back.

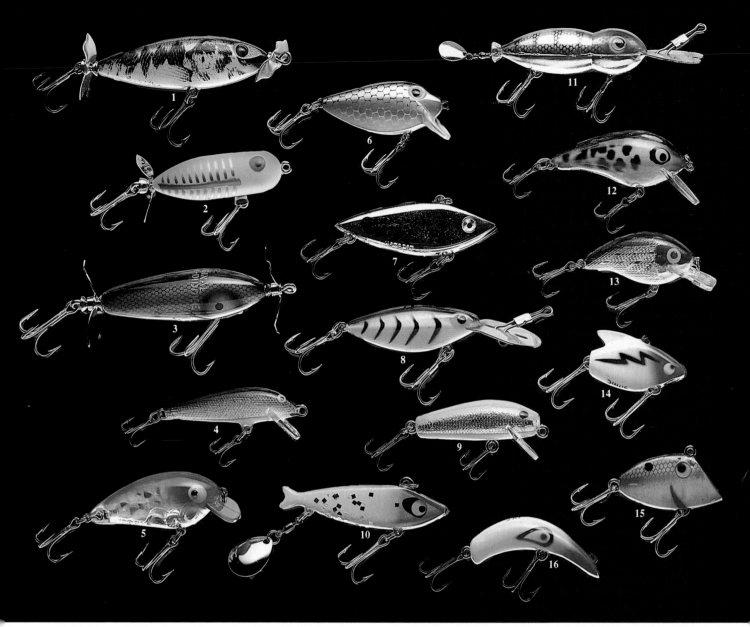

LURES for white bass include: (1) Crazy Shad®, (2) Tiny Torpedo®, (3) Spin-I-Diddee®, (4) Floating Rapala®, (5) Big Jim™, (6) Thin Fin® XT™, (7) Th' Spot®, (8) Hot 'N Tot®, (9) A.C. Shiner, (10) Tail Gater, (11) Hellbender, (12) Bo-Jack, (13) Teeny-R®, (14) Sonic®, (15) Bayou Boogie, (16) Lazy Ike, (17) Aglia®, (18) Shyster®, (19)

Lures for White Bass

White bass will strike almost any kind of lure, provided it is similar in size to their food.

Shad, an important food item, usually hatch in late spring or early summer and grow rapidly through fall. But some shad continue to hatch throughout summer. This complicates lure selection, because the size of shad eaten by white bass may change from day to day. Injured shad on the surface or regurgitated shad in a live well may provide a clue to lure size.

Asked to choose an all-around white bass lure, most veteran fishermen would name the jig. You can bump a jig along bottom for deep-running whites, or crank it across the surface when the fish are breaking water. And you can remove a jig hook from a fish's mouth in seconds and get your line back into the water.

In many southern reservoirs, tailspins rival jigs in popularity. Like jigs, tailspins can be fished shallow or deep, but the spinner blade provides flash that jigs lack.

The tailspin is an excellent choice for vertical jigging, because the spinner helicopters as the lure

Cottontail®, (20) Little Suzy™, (21) Little George, (22) Sonar™, (23) Slab Spoon®, (24) Gay Blade®, (25) Krocodile®, (26) Hopkins Shorty®, (27) Mepps® Spoon, (28) Little Cleo®, (29) Dardevle Imp Klicker®, (30) Twister® Meeny, (31) Fuzz-E-Grub®, (32) Whistler®, (33) Road Runner®, (34) Maribou Jig.

drops. This slows the lure's descent, giving the fish more time to strike. Anglers also use vibrating blades and jigging spoons for vertical jigging.

Crankbaits work well when white bass are scattered because they enable you to cover a lot of water. Any crankbait will work, but many fishermen prefer models with tight, vibrating actions and rattle chambers. The vibration and noise may coax white bass to strike.

Some anglers cast small, thick-bodied spoons. These artificial lures can be tossed long distances, enabling fishermen to avoid spooking surface-feeding bass.

White bass will also strike fly lures, especially streamers that resemble minnows. Fishermen sometimes jerk poppers violently across the surface to incite a feeding frenzy.

During a mayfly hatch, white bass feed heavily on emerging nymphs. Anglers often have trouble catching fish when a hatch is in progress. But bass will strike a fly that imitates the emerging insect. When fly-fishing, a sinking line usually works better than a floating one.

Some anglers attach a popping plug just ahead of the lure. The plug adds weight for casting and keeps the lure near the surface. The popping sounds help to attract fish.

A few anglers prefer minnows for white bass. But live bait takes longer to rig, costing you valuable time when fish are biting.

DAMS halt the progress of white bass moving upstream to spawn. The fish deposit their eggs at night, usually in the main current. During the day, they hang in eddies just to the side of fast-moving water.

Fishing for Spawning White Bass

Spawning time offers the easiest white bass fishing of the year. Tailraces come alive with fish and the angler has only to look or listen for swirling bass, then toss a lure somewhere near. It is not uncommon for a fisherman to catch 50 to 100 whites a day at the peak of the spawning run.

But fishing for spawning whites can be frustrating. Even when bass are churning the water, they may ignore your lure. You can often entice these fish to strike by switching to a very small lure, like a ¹⁄₁₆-ounce jig.

Fishermen begin catching white bass several weeks before spawning time. The fish start moving upstream when the water reaches the low 50s. As white bass migrate, they gather in eddies, isolated bays, and other slow-current areas just off the main channel. They usually hold at depths of 5 to 15 feet during the pre-spawn period, but may move into holes as deep as 25 feet during cold snaps.

White bass gather in their spawning areas when water temperatures reach the upper 50s. Look for fish in eddies closer to the dam, often in water only 1 to 3 feet deep.

Most fish spawn at night or during evening hours. When ready to spawn, a female swims toward the surface, attracting several males. During the spawning act, the fish thrash and roll on the water. Nighttime anglers listen for the spawning fish, then cast toward the sound.

Not all white bass swim upstream to spawn. In reservoirs, some fish spawn on sand or gravel shoals near the upper end of the main lake. These areas hold many spawners in low-water years when the streams do not have enough current to attract fish. In Lake Erie, most fish spawn in the major tributaries, but some deposit their eggs on large, off-shore reefs that top off at 5 to 10 feet.

Where to Find White Bass During the Spawning Period

FLOODED WILLOWS attract white bass moving upstream. The fish hold at the base of the willows in water 5 feet or less.

LOG JAMS, fallen trees and other obstructions break the current. White bass congregate in slack-water holding areas just downstream.

SMALL CREEKS flowing into the upper end of a reservoir or a spawning stream will draw bass, especially if they have clear water.

How to Fish an Eddy

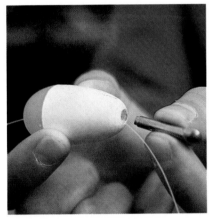

ATTACH a casting bobber 2 feet ahead of a small jig. The bobber adds casting weight and attracts bass as you jerk it across the surface.

CAST the bobber rig into the area where white bass are working. Some anglers use a two-handed cast to reach fish far from shore.

ALLOW the current to sweep your rig in a large circle around the eddy. Twitch the rod frequently to give the jig more action.

How to Drift for Spawning White Bass

DRIFT with the current while one person bumps a jig along bottom and the other casts toward shore. Keep moving until you find the fish.

HOLD the boat in position when you locate white bass. Point the bow upstream and adjust your throttle to counteract the current.

Jump-fishing for White Bass

For fast action, nothing rivals jump-fishing for white bass. Huge schools of bass herd baitfish, especially shad, to the surface. Attracted by the commotion, gulls swoop down to grab baitfish injured by the feeding bass.

Jump-fishing refers to the technique for catching white bass when they attack, or *jump,* baitfish on the surface. Anglers look for circling gulls or signs of feeding white bass. Once they spot a school, they quickly motor toward it. Most fishermen cast shallow-running lures into the fish. When the school sounds, they begin vertical jigging with heavy spoons or jigs.

Fishing the jumps generally peaks in fall, when shad form dense schools that feed on plankton near the surface. But in some waters, jump-fishing begins in early summer, when white bass feed on hatching mayflies or small minnows. Anglers often find surface-feeding whites on sand or gravel flats less than 10 feet deep.

In clear weather, jump-fishing is best early and late in the day. Whites may feed all day under cloudy skies. Windy conditions make it difficult to spot fish that are feeding on the surface.

White bass spook easily when surface-feeding. Move in quietly and do not anchor. A heavy lure enables you to cast farther, so you can stay away from the school.

WATCH for gulls swooping down to catch injured shad,

How to Fish the Jumps

Wind Direction →

MOTOR quickly to the feeding area when you spot a flock of circling and diving gulls. A school may feed for only a few minutes. If you hesitate, the fish may be gone when you arrive.

STOP short of the school to avoid spooking the fish. Cut the motor on the upwind side and let the boat glide into position. Be ready to cast as soon as you reach the school; the first few casts are the most productive.

or look for white bass breaking the surface. Many jump-fishermen use binoculars to spot the action from a distance.

DRIFT along the edge of the feeding area while casting into the school. Use an electric trolling motor or oars to control the path of the drift. Try to keep the boat just within casting distance.

START the engine when the boat drifts too far from the school. Swing away from the feeding area, then head upwind and drift back again. Never run the motor through a school of feeding bass.

How to Get the Most Fish Out of a School

When a school of white bass breaks water, be ready to take advantage of the situation because the fish can disappear quickly. The following techniques will improve your jump-fishing success.

How to Rig and Use a Double Jig

TIE a three-way swivel to your line. Attach 6- and 10-inch droppers of 12-pound mono to the swivel, then tie a ¼-ounce jig on each dropper.

RETRIEVE the jig through a school. When a fish grabs one jig, the commotion attracts other fish which strike the trailing jig.

SWING the fish into the boat with a smooth motion. If you net them, you may tangle the lines and lose valuable fishing time.

How to Fish a School After it Sounds

LOOK for gulls resting on the surface, then work the area thoroughly. The birds will usually remain after the school sounds.

TROLL along the edge of a flat where white bass were surfacing. The fish often remain in the vicinity, but drop into deeper water after they feed. Bounce a lead-head jig or tailspin slowly along the drop-off while watching for fish on your depth finder.

Tips for Jump-fishing

FLATTEN your barbs with a pliers. This enables you to unhook white bass quickly and catch more before the school disappears.

REPLACE trebles with single hooks or clip off two of the hooks with a wire cutter. These techniques also let you unhook white bass faster.

How to Fish by the Buddy System

HOOK a white bass, then let it fight while you keep a tight line. Because of their competitive nature, other bass swarm toward the hooked fish. Sometimes several fish follow within inches in an attempt to steal the lure.

WAIT a few seconds before reeling to give your partner time to cast toward your hooked bass. When he hooks a fish, quickly land your fish and cast toward his. Continue this tactic as long as white bass remain in the area.

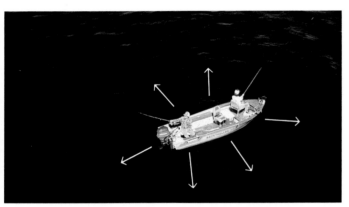

FAN-CAST with a crankbait while drifting over the area where bass were feeding. If nothing bites, try a drift off to each side. If fish are still in the area, a fast-moving lure will usually trigger a strike.

DRAW white bass back to the surface with a noisy top-water lure. A small jig trailing 1 to 2 feet behind the lure will catch fish attracted by the commotion. Sometimes the entire school will resume surface-feeding.

CARRY several rods rigged with your favorite lures for jump-fishing. If you snap your line or switch to a different presentation, you will not have to waste time retying.

TOSS white bass into a cooler partially filled with ice. They die quickly on a stringer. A cooler keeps them fresh and saves time that would be wasted stringing fish.

Night Fishing for White Bass

During the heat of summer, you can often improve your white bass success by fishing after dark. Night fishing also works well at spawning time, but most anglers catch all the fish they want during the day.

Night fishing for white bass and crappies has many similarities. It is not unusual for fishermen to catch a mixed bag. During summer, anglers use lights to concentrate fish. Dark nights are best; the lights may not attract fish during a full moon. Minnows work well for both species, but white bass will also strike jigs.

The bridges, piers and lighted docks that produce crappies at night may also yield white bass. Other good locations include the edges of creek and river channels, drop-offs adjacent to sand flats and the mouths of creek arms.

White bass may feed at any time during the night. Most fishermen anchor in a spot that has produced in the past and wait for the fish to move in. The bass generally arrive at the same location at the same hour several nights in succession. If the fish do not show up, try locating them with a graph recorder or a flasher.

Some night fishermen use a handline baited with a minnow. A handline enables you to detect bites easily, even in darkness.

How to Make a Lighted Slip-bobber

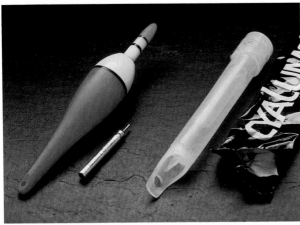

BUY a lighted slip-bobber (left) powered by a lithium battery or make your own float with a 4-inch Cyalume® light stick (right). The stick will protrude just above the surface and will glow from 8 to 12 hours.

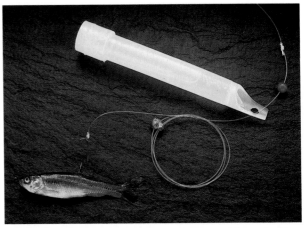

TIE a lighted slip-bobber rig by first attaching a bobber stop. Thread on a small bead so the knot cannot slip through the hole in the bobber. Add a #4 hook and enough split-shot to balance the bobber.

How to Make and Use a Handline

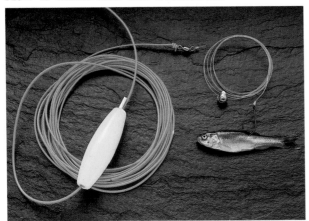

THREAD a small peg bobber on No. 5 or No. 6 sinking fly line. Tie the line to one end of a barrel swivel and 4 feet of 6-pound mono to the other end. Pinch on a split-shot, then add a #4 hook and a minnow.

DRAPE the line over the side so the bobber hangs along the inside of the boat. Watch the bobber closely for any movement. The fly line will slide easily up the side when a white bass strikes.

LIGHTS play an important role in night fishing for white bass. Baitfish drawn to the light will eventually attract bass. Most fishermen use gas lanterns. Others prefer floating crappie lights (page 261) or submerged lights be-cause they draw fewer insects and add more illumination to the water. In murky water, white bass will move into the beam of light. In clear water, they generally remain around the dimly-lit perimeter.

Tips for Night Fishing

SET the depth with a bobberless rig by counting the number of times you turn the reel handle to reach the proper depth. Then you can return your lure or bait to the same depth after you catch a fish.

SINK a headlight in a wire cage to attract bass. Grease the headlight contacts to prevent electrolytic corrosion, then run wires to a car battery. Add enough lead weight to sink the light, then lower it about 4 to 6 feet.

Fishing for White Bass in Warmwater Discharges

Warmwater discharges from power plants offer excellent, but often overlooked fishing opportunities. The plants draw water from rivers or lakes to cool their turbines, then return the heated water. White bass begin congregating around discharge areas in late fall, when the water temperature of rivers and lakes drops below 50°F. The fish remain until spring.

Heated discharges also attract shad and other bass foods. White bass feed actively through the winter, because the warm water keeps their metabolism at a high level.

Because the fish are active, anglers should use a moderately fast retrieve. The fish usually ignore slow-moving lures. The best lures include small crankbaits, spoons and jigs.

Most power plants allow fishing in the discharge areas. Some even provide parking areas, launching ramps and other facilities for the angler's convenience. To find out about warmwater discharges in your area, call the public relations office of your local power company.

DISCHARGE CANALS carry water as much as 40 degrees warmer than the river or lake. Most anglers fish from shore, but some use small boats.

EDDIES near the upstream end of the canal usually harbor the most white bass. Fishermen also catch bass in slow-moving water farther downstream.

Fishing for White Bass in Deep Water

White bass move to the depths in summer to escape warm surface waters. It is not unusual to find schools of bass in water as deep as 30 feet. But in late fall and winter, the depths become slightly warmer than water at the surface. White bass are drawn to the warmer water, sometimes to depths of 50 feet or more.

When white bass move to deep water, most fishermen give up and concentrate on other types of fish. But you can still catch white bass, and often in good numbers, if you use the proper techniques.

In summer, white bass seldom stay in one spot for long. They follow schools of shad, so you must cover a lot of water to find the fish. Most anglers troll with deep-running lures, always watching their depth finders for schools.

In late fall and winter, white bass form tighter schools and stay in one area for long periods. They feed very little and seldom chase fast-moving lures. Anglers mark the schools carefully, then catch the fish by vertical jigging.

DEEP-DIVING LURES, when trolled at high speed, catch white bass in summer. Some fishermen attach trailing jigs or spinners to tempt more strikes.

VERTICAL JIGGING may be the only way to catch white bass in late fall and winter. Jig at or slightly above the level of the fish, as shown on this graph tape.

METERED LEAD-CORE LINE enables you to troll in deep water. When you hook a fish, note the color of the line so you can return to the same depth.

291

Catfish

Anyone who has battled a monstrous catfish or dined on fresh catfish fillets, knows why these be-whiskered fish have such a loyal following.

Flathead and blue catfish often exceed 50 pounds and many topping 100 pounds have been recorded, but not officially documented. Channel catfish weighing more than 20 pounds are seldom caught, though some big rivers produce much larger fish.

Channels and flatheads are the most common catfish species. Blue catfish populations are declining in many areas, but huge blues are caught in some parts of the central and southern United States. The smaller white catfish are confined mainly to the East and West Coasts. Other members of the catfish family include several types of bullheads and mad-toms. Also called *willow cats,* some madtom species are popular bait for walleyes and smallmouth bass.

Although catfish prefer warm water, some cool northern rivers have large populations. Catfish can tolerate extremely muddy water and even moderately high levels of pollution. However, unlike bullheads, catfish cannot live in waters prone to winterkill.

Catfish
Combined Range

Catfish spawn in late spring when the water reaches about 70°F. They have a curious habit of spawning in enclosed areas such as muskrat runs and other holes in riverbanks, sunken barrels or hollow logs.

CHANNEL CATFISH (above) and blue catfish have forked tails. Blues have 30 to 35 anal fin rays, and channels 24 to 29. The world-record blue, 97 pounds, was caught in the Missouri River, South Dakota in 1959. The record channel cat, 58 pounds, was taken in Santee-Cooper Reservoir, South Carolina in 1964.

FLATHEAD CATFISH, also called mud or yellow cats, have flat heads, protruding lower jaws, mottled brownish sides and rounded tails that are usually slightly notched. The anal fin has about 16 rays. The world-record flathead, 91 pounds, 4 ounces, was caught in Lake Lewisville, Texas in 1982.

Bullheads

Bullheads are popular simply because they are abundant and easy to catch. An old lawn chair, a cane pole and a can of angleworms are all a fisherman needs to fill a gunnysack with bullheads.

Three species of bullheads, black, brown and yellow, are caught by fishermen. Black bullheads seldom grow larger than 1 pound, yet this species boasts the largest world record bullhead, an 8-pounder caught in Lake Waccabuc, New York in 1951. Yellow bullheads frequently grow larger than blacks, although the world record is smaller, only 4 pounds, 4 ounces. It was caught in Mormon Lake, Arizona in 1984. The world-record brown bullhead, 5 pounds, 8 ounces, was taken from Veal Pond, Georgia in 1975.

Prime time for bullhead fishing is late spring and summer, after the water temperature has warmed above 60°F. Bullheads may feed anytime during the day, but become more active toward evening when they cruise the shallows for insect larvae, snails, worms, fish eggs and small fish. Bullheads also eat a variety of aquatic plants.

Warm waters of shallow lakes, rivers, marshes and ponds may become over-crowded with stunted bullheads. In winterkill lakes, bullheads often outlast other fish species, because they require only minute amounts of oxygen. Bullheads have been known to survive in lakes that freeze almost to the bottom by simply burrowing several inches into the soft ooze.

Bullheads are delicious to eat if caught during spring and early summer, but as the water warms, their flesh softens and may develop a muddy taste. Fishermen should be extremely careful when handling or cleaning bullheads, because their venom-coated spines can inflict a painful wound.

Bullhead Combined Range

MUDDY WATERS of slow-moving rivers, shallow lakes or ponds are favorite bullhead spots. Black bullheads tolerate the muddiest water; browns and yellows prefer clearer water with more weeds.

LATE EVENING or nighttime is best for bullhead fishing. Like catfish, bullheads have little trouble finding food in the dark. They rely on an acute sense of smell, plus taste buds in their barbels.

BAITS for bullheads are similar to those used for catfish. Included are (1) doughballs concocted from flour, Parmesan cheese and water, (2) chicken liver, (3) soft plastic worm smeared with stinkbait and threaded with a line and small treble hook, (4) gob of worms on a long-shanked hook, (5) cotton ball soaked with blood, (6) cheese ball. Other proven baits are nightcrawlers, live or dead minnows and chunks of laundry soap.

How to Handle Bullheads

GRIP a bullhead firmly, because its skin is slippery. Carefully position the fingers and thumb to avoid the sharp dorsal and pectoral spines (arrows).

UNHOOK a bullhead using a hook disgorger (above) or longnose pliers. Bullheads have powerful jaws, so anglers should not attempt to remove hooks with their fingers.

Cleaning Your Catch

Field Dressing Fish

For top quality and flavor, fish should be field dressed as quickly as possible by removing the gills, guts and kidney, all of which spoil fast in a dead fish.

Field dress fish that are to be cooked whole or steaked. It is not necessary to field dress fish if they are to be filleted within an hour or two. Scale fish that are to be cooked with their skin on, but only if they have large scales. These fish include bluegills, perch, crappies, black bass, striped bass, walleyes, northern pike and large salmon.

When field dressing and scaling at home, place your catch on several layers of newspaper to ease cleanup. Before field dressing, wipe the fish with paper towels to remove slime. This makes it easier to hold the fish firmly. If you puncture the guts, wash the body cavity with cold water. Use water sparingly, because it softens the flesh.

The head can be removed after scaling. Paper towels are excellent for wiping off scales and blood spots, and for drying fish.

Field dressing is easier if you have the right tools, and if you clean the fish in a convenient location. Practice the different cleaning techniques until you can clean fish quickly and with little waste.

How to Field Dress Other Fish

REMOVE gills by cutting the throat connection, then along both sides of the arch so the gills pull out easily.

INSERT the knife in the vent. Run the blade tip to the gills. Pull the guts and gills out of the cavity.

CUT the membrane along the backbone. Scrape out the kidney or bloodline underneath the membrane.

Basic Filleting Technique

Fishermen use a variety of filleting techniques. The method shown below is the easiest and quickest for most anglers. Fillets can be stripped from the backbone in 30 seconds with a very sharp knife. Removing the rib bones takes a few additional seconds. Other methods are described on following pages.

If your fillet board does not have a clip, you can use a fork to pin the head of a small fish. A fork or pliers can also be useful during skinning. Salt on the hands helps hold a slippery fish.

The skin can be removed or left on. Fish such as largemouth bass have strong-tasting skin, so many anglers remove it. However, the skin on small trout and panfish is tasty. Panfish have large scales which must be removed if the skin is retained.

How to Fillet and Skin a Fish

LIFT the pectoral fin. Angle the knife towards the back of the head and cut to the backbone.

TURN the blade parallel to the backbone. Cut towards tail with a sawing motion. Cut fillet off.

REMOVE the rib bones by sliding the blade along the ribs. Turn fish over and remove second fillet.

Keep the skin on fillets that will be charcoal grilled. This helps prevent the flesh from falling apart, sticking to the grill and overcooking. Cut long fillets into serving-size pieces before they are cooked or stored. Thick fillets can be divided into two thin fillets for easier cooking.

Remove the thin strip of fatty belly flesh on oily fish such as salmon and large trout. Any contaminants will settle into this fatty tissue. To clean fillets, wipe with paper towels or rinse quickly under cold running water. Dry thoroughly with paper towels.

After filleting, rinse hands with clear water before using soap. Rub hands with vinegar and salt, lemon juice or toothpaste to remove the fishy smell.

Some fishermen save the bones and head after filleting. These pieces can be used for stock, chowder, fish cakes or other dishes.

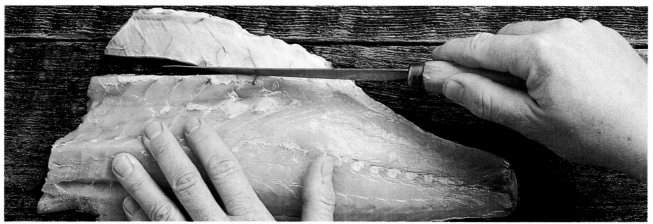

CUT off the strip of fatty belly flesh. Discard guts and belly. Save bones and head for stock.

SKIN the fillet, if desired, by cutting into the tail flesh to the skin. Turn the blade parallel to the skin.

PULL the skin firmly while moving the knife in a sawing action between the skin and the flesh.

Canadian Filleting Technique

Some fishermen find this technique easier than the basic method (page 300), especially when used on fish with a heavy rib structure such as white bass and large black bass. The Canadian technique takes a little longer and leaves more flesh on the bones. But many anglers are comfortable with this method,

How to Fillet Using the Canadian Technique

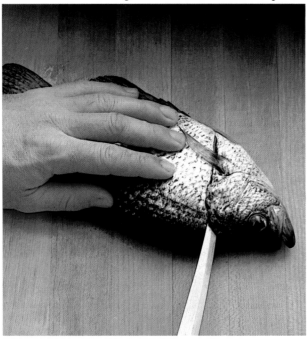

CUT behind the pectoral fin straight down to the backbone. Angle the cut towards the top of the head.

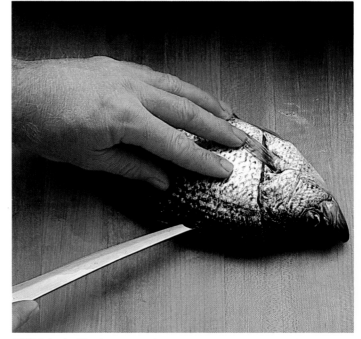

RUN the knife along one side of the backbone. The knife should scrape the rib bones without cutting them.

REMOVE the first boneless fillet by cutting through the skin of the stomach area.

TURN the fish over. Remove the second fillet using the same filleting technique.

because it eliminates the extra step of cutting the rib bones from the fillet. As a bonus, your knife stays sharp longer, because the boneless fillet is removed without cutting through the rib bones. Be careful when cutting the belly, so the knife does not penetrate the guts.

PUSH the knife through the flesh near the vent just behind the rib bones. Cut the fillet free at the tail.

CUT the flesh carefully away from the rib cage. To save flesh, the blade should graze the bones.

RINSE fillets quickly with cold water or wipe with paper towels. If desired, save head and skeleton for stock.

SKIN fillets. Hold the tail with your fingertips and cut between flesh and skin with a sawing motion.

Filleting With an Electric Knife

An electric knife is particularly useful for filleting panfish, catfish or any large fish that has heavy rib bones. Scale fish before filleting if the skin will be retained for cooking. Skin is usually removed from largemouth bass, striped bass, and other fish which have strong-tasting skin.

How to Fillet With an Electric Knife

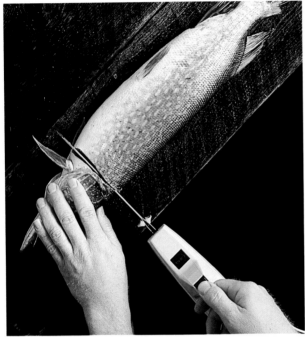

CUT behind the pectoral fin straight down to the backbone, holding the fish at the edge of the counter.

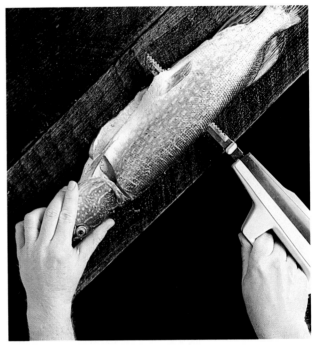

TURN the knife parallel to the backbone and cut toward the tail, firmly grasping the head.

AVOID cutting the fillet from the tail if skin is to be removed. Turn fillet over, hold the tail and begin the cut.

GUIDE the knife between skin and flesh. Remove rib bones with small knife. Turn fish; fillet other side.

Pan Dressing Fish

Panfish, including bluegills, crappies and yellow perch, are often too small for filleting. They are usually pan dressed instead. Scales, fins, guts and head are always removed. The tail is quite tasty and can be left on. Most of the tiny fin bones in a fish are removed by pan dressing.

How to Pan Dress Whole Fish

SLICE along the dorsal fin of the scaled panfish. Make the same cut on the other side, then pull out the fin.

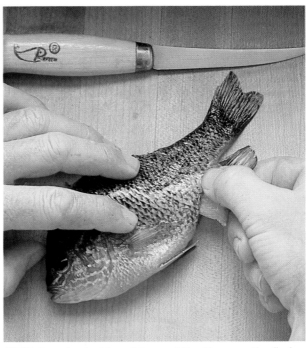

CUT along both sides of the anal fin. Remove the fin by pulling it towards the tail.

REMOVE the head. Angle the blade over the top of the head to save as much flesh as possible.

SLIT the belly and pull out the guts. Cut off tail, if desired. Rinse fish quickly; dry with paper towels.

Y Bones

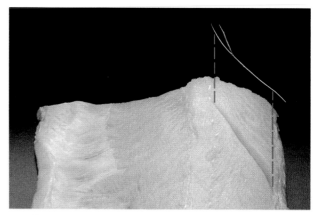

Northern pike, muskellunge and pickerel have a row of Y-shaped bones that float just above the ribs. The Y bones run lengthwise along the fillet, ending above the vent.

Many anglers remove Y bones before cooking, even though some flesh is lost when they are cut out. The alternative is to pull out the Y bones after cooking.

Y BONES lie within a narrow strip of flesh just above the rib cage.

How to Remove Y Bones

SLICE through the flesh along the edge of the Y bones (arrows). The fillet at left will be boneless.

CUT the flesh from the Y bones by guiding the knife blade along the bones (arrow), scraping lightly.

REMOVE the triangular strip of bones and flesh; save them for stock. Two long boneless fillets remain.

The Lateral Line

Some gamefish such as largemouth bass, striped bass, northern pike and white bass have a lateral line of strong-tasting flesh.

For cleaning and cooking purposes, the lateral line is defined as the band of dark-colored flesh along the side of a fish. It covers the entire side of some fish. This flesh spoils easily and develops an odor when the fish has been frozen too long.

In some species, such as trout and salmon, the lateral line does not have a strong flavor and may be retained. Many people enjoy the "fishy" taste of the lateral line. It is particularly flavorful when the fish is smoked or cooked and served cold.

Many anglers remove the lateral line if the fish are taken from waters of marginal quality. Contaminants tend to concentrate in the lateral line flesh.

How to Remove the Lateral Line

SKIN the fillet to expose the lateral line. In most species, it is an oily layer of reddish or brownish flesh.

CUT away the shallow band of dark flesh, using an extremely sharp fillet knife. Remove the lateral line; discard.

ANOTHER method is to tip the blade up while skinning so the lateral line is removed with the skin.

307

Cleaning Catfish & Bullheads

Catfish and bullheads are skinned regardless of size, which ranges from pan-size to over 70 pounds. The skin is thin and slippery, which demands a special skinning technique.

Cleaning and skinning requires a wide-jawed pliers, a sharp knife, and sometimes, a board with a nail to hold the head in place. Many anglers improvise. Fish can be hand-held instead of impaled on a nail. Fishermen's or regular pliers can be used.

The technique for skinning small catfish and bullheads is a little different from that used for larger catfish. Two popular methods are described below and on the next page.

Catfish or bullheads smaller than 10 inches long are cooked whole after skinning. Larger fish are filleted, steaked or chunked. Thick fillets from extremely large catfish can be sliced into thinner fillets that can be cooked easily.

How to Clean Bullheads and Small Catfish

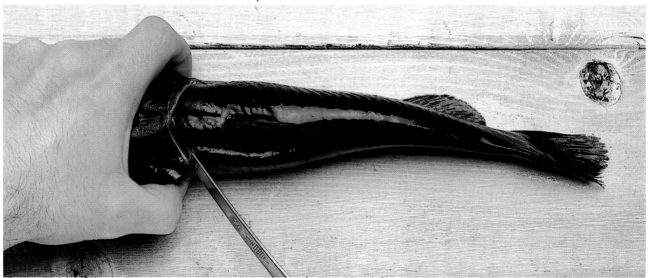

GRIP the head tightly, taking care to avoid the *horns* or pectoral spines. Cut just behind the head.

SLICE the skin cleanly along the backbone to a point just behind the dorsal fin. The fish is now ready for skinning.

GRASP the skin with the pliers and pull it all the way to the tail. Repeat the process on the other side.

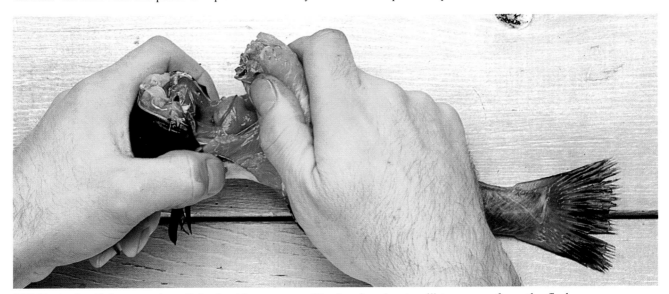

BEND the head downward until the backbone snaps. The head and guts will tear away from the flesh.

CUT along both sides of the dorsal and anal fins. Pull out both fins with the pliers. Slice off the tail.

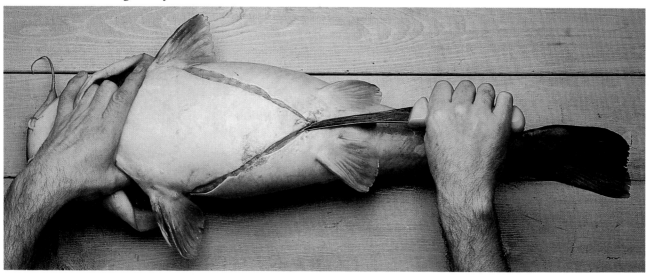

CUT a diamond-shaped pattern on the belly. The cut should slice the skin from the pectoral spines to the pelvic fins.

TURN the fish onto its belly. Cut behind the head, extending down the sides to the diamond cut behind the pectoral spines.

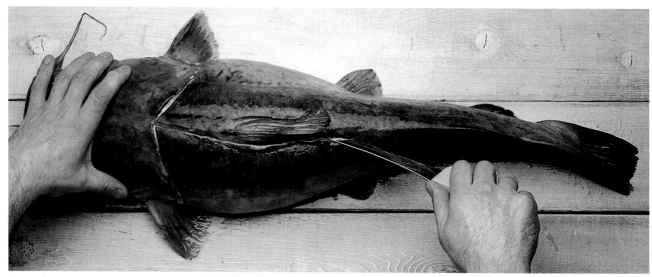

SLICE the skin, beginning at the cut behind the head and continuing to a point just behind the dorsal fin.

GRASP the skin with the pliers. Pull with a sharp jerk. Remove one side at a time. Grasp the skin again if it tears.

FLOP the fish. Grasp the skin at the back of the diamond-shaped cut. Yank the belly skin toward the head.

SEVER the backbone with a heavy knife or cleaver and a hammer. Remove the fins (page 309) and guts.

Steaking Large Fish

Gamefish of 6 pounds or more *can* be steaked. Fish over 15 pounds *should* be steaked or chunked, so they are easier to cook. Before steaking, scale fish that have large scales. Then, remove the guts, kidney (bloodline) and dorsal fin. Rinse in cold running water and wipe with paper towels.

Partially frozen fish are easier to cut into steaks. Firm up the flesh by placing them in a freezer until they begin to stiffen.

Lay the fish on its side. Use a sharp knife to cut even, ¾- to 1-inch thick steaks from the fish. Cut through the backbone with a sturdy knife, electric knife, kitchen saw or frozen-food knife. After steaking, trim fatty belly flesh from oily fish such as salmon, trout or striped bass.

The tail sections of large gamefish can be left whole, filleted or cut into 1½- to 2-inch chunks for baking or smoking. You can save the head to make stock.

Tips for Steaking Fish

TRIM and throw away pieces of fatty belly flesh from the ends of the steaks.

FILLET the tail section by sliding a sharp knife along the backbone in a sawing motion.

Freezing & Thawing Fish

Freezing is a convenient way to preserve the quality of fish. Freeze them immediately after cleaning unless they will be eaten within 24 hours.

Proper packaging shields the fish from air, which causes freezer burn. Air cannot penetrate ice, so fish frozen in a solid block of ice or with a glaze are well-protected. A double wrap of aluminum foil or plastic wrap and freezer paper is added insurance against air penetration.

Cut fillets into serving-size pieces before freezing. Fish that are being frozen in a block of ice often float to the top before the water freezes. If this happens, add a little ice water and freeze again before double-wrapping. Glazed fish should be checked periodically and the glaze renewed, if necessary.

Store fish in a 0° freezer. If ice cream remains firm, the freezer should be adequate. A frost-free freezer is not recommended, because the fan pulls moisture

How to Freeze Fish in a Block of Ice

SELECT plastic containers, thoroughly washed milk cartons, or small cake or bread pans to freeze whole fish, fillets or steaks.

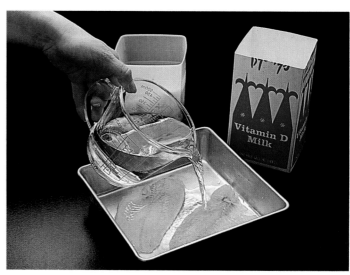

PACK fish for one meal in a container, leaving 1½ inches of airspace; or, layer fish on bottom of pan. Cover fish with very cold water. Freeze the fish in the pan.

Alternate Freezing Techniques

DOUBLE-WRAP whole fish, steaks or fillets that are frozen without a protective block of ice. Separate the fillets or steaks with waxed paper to make thawing easier. This method saves freezer space.

GLAZE whole fish by first freezing without wrapping. Dip frozen fish in very cold water; freeze again. Repeat three to five times, until ⅛ inch of ice builds up. Double-wrap in airtight package, handling fish carefully.

314

from wrapped fish and quickly causes freezer burn. The chart (right) shows storage times. For top quality, cook within the suggested time.

Fish fillets and steaks may be treated to extend their freezer life by 3 months. Mix 2 tablespoons of ascorbic acid (available in drugstores) and 1 quart water. Place fish in the mixture for 20 seconds. Double-wrap and freeze immediately.

Never thaw fish at room temperature. Bacteria flourishes in warm temperatures. Use the thawing methods described below.

Freezer Storage Chart

TYPE	WHOLE	STEAKS	FILLETS
Large Oily	2 months	1½ months	1 month
Small Oily	1½ months	1 month	1 month
Large Lean	6 months	4 months	3½ months
Small Lean	4 months	3 months	2½ months

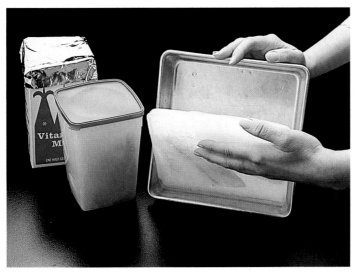

COVER milk carton with aluminum foil. Place lid on plastic container. Freeze. Pop out block of frozen fish from the pan by running cold water on the bottom.

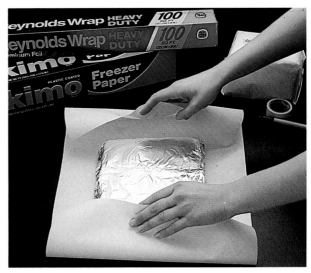

WRAP the solid block of fish in plastic wrap or aluminum foil. Overwrap with freezer paper, sealing tightly. Label package; include species, date and number of servings.

How to Thaw Fish

MELT the block of ice under cold, running water. When fish are free from ice, place them on a plate lined with paper towels. Cover the fish with plastic wrap and thaw in the refrigerator.

THAW ice-free fish by refrigerating them for 24 hours. To speed the process, place the fish in a heavy, *waterproof* plastic bag. Seal the bag, put it in a bowl of cold water and refrigerate. Or, thaw the fish in a microwave.

Index